KILLER Instinct

KILLER Instinct

How Two Young Producers Took On Hollywood and Made the Most Controversial Film of the Decade

Jane Hamsher

Broadway Books New York

BROADWAY

Broadway Books titles may be purchased for business or promotional use or for special sales. For information, please write to: Special Markets Department, Bantam Doubleday Dell Publishing Group, Inc., 1540 Broadway, New York, NY 10036.

BROADWAY BOOKS and its logo, a letter B bisected on the diagonal, are trademarks of Broadway Books, a division of Bantam Doubleday Dell Publishing Group, Inc.

All photos in center spread copyright Jane and Don Productions, Inc.

Library of Congress Cataloging-in-Publication Data

Hamsher, Jane.
  Killer instinct : how two young producers took on Hollywood and made the most controversial film of the decade / Jane Hamsher. — 1st ed.
    p. cm
  ISBN 0-7679-0074-X
  1. Natural born killers (Motion picture) 2. Hamsher, Jane. 3. Murphy, Don, 1962– . I. Title.
PN1997.N335H36 1997
791.43′72—dc21   97-1072
                                                                   CIP

FIRST EDITION

Designed by Bonni Leon-Berman

97 98 99 00 01 10 9 8 7 6 5 4 3 2 1

For my dad, Russell Charles Murphy

Acknowledgments

Writing a book is one of the most terrible and terrifying things I've ever done in my life. I had no idea what I was getting into when I committed to do this in the first place, and I can only express my most heartfelt gratitude to the people who were supportive throughout the entire process: my very best friend and partner in crime, Don Murphy, who came up with the brainstorm that our experiences in Hollywood might make an interesting book, and then held down the business for a year while I tore my hair out trying to write it; my agent, Amanda Urban, the first person to see the book outline in its nascent stages, decided that it didn't deserve to be strangled in its crib; my editors at Broadway Books, John Sterling and Suzanne Oaks, who could always be counted upon for intelligent feedback and occasional psychotherapy; Bill Shinker, Lauren Marino, Trigg Robinson, Kathy Spinelli, and Elizabeth McNamara, also of Broadway, who should have thrown up their hands in frustration a long time ago, but for no discernible reason were unflaggingly supportive; Oliver Jones, upon whom the thankless task of fact-checking this uncontrollable screed fell; and my amazing friends and critics—Dave Veloz, David Jenison, Blair Tefkin, Neil Gaiman, and Kendall Hoffman—who read the manuscript repeatedly during the writing process and cared enough to honestly (and diplomatically) tell me when they thought I was churning out crap.

And then, of course, there are the people without whose support there would be no story to tell. Our agent, Joe Rosenberg, who has kept us out of trouble more times than we probably deserve. Karl Austen, who stuck his neck out for us when he didn't have to, just because it was the right thing to do. "Godfather" Thom Mount, Craig Emmanuel, Peter Rice, Julia Ross, Jorge Saralegui, Donald DeLine, Michael Lynton, Michael Costigan, Amy Pascal, Barry Josephson, Lucy Fisher, Dan Field, Robert Newman, David Simone, Danny Benair, Howard Paar, Roger Avary, Cathryn Jaymes, Craig Hamman, Rick Benattar, Jefery Levy, Pam Skaist, Linda Meltzer, J. D. Zeik, Alan Moore, Terry Hayes, Lindsay Wineberg, Basil Iwanyk, Nicholee Miller, the late and dearly missed Taizan Maezumi

Roshi, Dr. Armando Giuliano, Azita Zendel, Ian Calip, Scott Mabbutt, Richard Baltin, Colin Malone, Eddie Perez, Michael Zoumas, Dean Paras, Michael Sanville, Trevor Dolby, Charles McDonald, James Harding, Sloan Harris, and of course our families—my mother, Greta, my sister Pam, and the entire Murphy clan—without whose love and support none of this madness would have been possible.

And it goes without saying, to Oliver Stone. Whose two-year, private film school was the best education we ever got. We feel privileged beyond belief to have had the opportunity to attend, and lucky as hell to have survived.

Jane Hamsher
April 1997

Contents

Contents

KILLER
Instinct

Chapter 1

In the Beginning, There Was the Spooge

I awoke on Tuesday morning with a world-class hangover on top of a bad case of the flu that had finally been coaxed into fruition by wanton disregard for my own health the night before. On such mornings, it's great to be your own boss; reporting to no one, you can simply decide to stay home from the office and nurse your self-induced ailments. Which is exactly what I did. Unfortunately, this sort of power does you flat fucking no good when your office is in the dining room of your apartment. And I knew, even as I shut off my alarm clock and stuffed my head under my pillow, that nothing I could do or say, no act of man or God could impede the impending horror that would walk through my front door come 10:00 A.M., stoked on caffeinated diet Coke and Froot Loops, loaded down with magazines and comic books, action toys and pretzels and Pez, ready to tear the head off Hollywood.

My business partner, Don Murphy.

And he would have no sympathy for my predicament. In fact, I could roll around on the floor in misery, coughing and wailing at his feet, and he probably wouldn't notice anything was wrong until I did something which affected him directly. Which I was going to have to do, if I was going to fulfill my urgent desire to lie indolently in bed and feel sorry for myself. I couldn't quite recollect what bit of business Don had cooked up for us that day, but I was pretty sure it would require me to stand erect and pretend that I hadn't been stoned out of my box the night before. But as I wasn't up to being the charm princess at that particular moment, it seemed the lesser of two evils to invite his wrath at the cancellation than to suffer through a meeting with the uncontrollable urge to vomit on his shoes.

The sound of "Hey, Partner!" came booming up my stairs predictably at

10:00, and into my apartment bounded all 6'2", 220 pounds of Irish-American twenty-something film-student-turned-wannabe-producer.

"How you doing this morning?" he said, throwing down (as he did every morning) heaps of crap, or "spooge" as we commonly referred to it, which he seemed to have a strong affection for depositing on my floor, despite the fact that he will probably have no use for it during the day.

I crawled into the dining room in my robe and slippers in that "please notice I'm ill" kind of way.

"Hey, (cough cough), good morning (sniff sniff)." I threw in a hacking death rattle for good measure.

"So, I got a call from this guy named Kevin Michaels, who says he's just finished a script that everyone is dying for," he began, jabbering at a breakneck speed that made my head hurt. "He'll have it over to us this afternoon, just as soon as his electricity's turned back on and he can print it out. He swears Corey Haim's attached."

"Corey Haim's in rehab."

"No, that's Corey Feldman. Corey Haim's the sober one."

"Well they should both be in movie jail anyway for a lifetime of cinematic affronts. Listen, Don, I'm not feeling so well. . . ."

"And I have to call and schedule lunch today."

"Y'know, Don, if there was any way we could do this another day . . ."

"So, where do you want to go?"

"Don, I don't feel good."

". . . I was thinking, maybe Hamburger Hamlet . . ."

"Don, listen to me. I'm dying here."

". . . Maybe Numero Uno . . . oh, I forgot—you hate that place."

"Don . . ."

"He's coming up from Manhattan Beach, so maybe Barney's Beanery. It's a little farther west. . . ."

"DON!!!"

He looked up at me startled, making that weird sucking noise with the straw he always does when he reaches the bottom of his Big Gulp. "Something wrong?"

This wasn't going to be easy. But the idea of going back to bed, tanking up on Nyquil, and passing out in a hazy catatonia until this diabolical condition passed was just too enticing.

"Don, I think I'd rather not go to the lunch today. I mean, who is this guy, anyway? I know it's probably important, but I think I need to go back to bed and go to sleep."

Silence. He looked at me with that jaw-tightening look that said, "You're not doing what I want, and I'm unhappy." I hated that look. Don had a way of making you feel really lazy and trivial under such circumstances, and probably with some justification. But his not-so-passive-aggression only served to make me knee-jerk angry and defensive.

"Goddamn it Don, every day it's some loser. Someone who claims to have money to make movies, and he's just jerking us off. Someone who says he's got Pacino attached to his script and he doesn't have cab fare. I mean, I know we have to follow it all up, and you're really good at pursuing every lead, but Christ, I'm sick. Can't you just let me feel bad?"

I could see his entire frame swelling with self-righteous indignation. "This is for you, you know. This is about *your* book. I just thought it might be a chance to get it made—this guy swears he can get his next movie financed for three or four million dollars."

The book he was talking about was indeed something I was passionate about. *Budding Prospects*, written by T. C. Boyle, the story of three college boys who face the wilderness trying to grow pot unsuccessfully in Humboldt County. When Don and I had partnered up to become producers out of USC film school the year before, we'd shared with each other the things we dreamed of making into movies. Don had supplied me with a stack of comic books, everything Frank Miller and Alan Moore had ever done; I'd given him a novel about '70s surf culture by Kem Nunn called *Tapping the Source* and James Ellroy's *The Big Nowhere* in addition to *Budding Prospects*. And although it was great that Don was trying to get people interested in *Budding Prospects*, there were two key problems that he was overlooking, and they were doozies. Number one: The guy he had in mind was some geek friend who had never directed a movie, had never even written anything that had been made, he was just running around saying he was going to direct a movie like every other wannabe in Hollywood. And the past year had taught me that 99 percent of these people were full of shit—the other 1 percent were on their way to solid careers, and wanted nothing to do with us. The other thing that Don had conveniently skipped over, as Don was wont to do, is that *we didn't own the book.*

We had no *hope* of owning the book. Somebody else had the rights to turn it into a movie. And even if the rights had been available, we couldn't afford them—we were "butt poor," as Don put it so eloquently. Neither of us came from money, we both worked side jobs to pay our expenses—me as a temporary secretary and Don in a comic-book store. We were lucky to make our phone bill every month, let alone shell out thousands for a book option. Love Don though I did for his conviction that we would succeed or he'd kill everyone who stood in our way, he could not will those rights into our hands for no cash.

"Don, I just don't see that much potential in this particular situation." I was careful to be as diplomatic as possible—not, as you might assume, out of fear for my own safety, but because it was enthusiasm that fueled Don's tenacity. And although he could be occasionally uncouth and frequently unreasonable, at that moment, Don's tenacity may have been the biggest asset we had.

But no matter how hungry you are for success, no matter how much you yearn for it and lie awake at night tortured with fear that you'll wind up begging quarters and washing windshields at the local 7-Eleven, sometimes the uninterrupted banging of your head against the wall makes you want to give up. As I skulked away to my bedroom to swill Nyquil, I tried to tell myself that the worst of it was over, I'd faced Don's disappointment, and now I could just get on with being sick.

I knew Don was being pointedly unsympathetic to my ailments, was trying to break me with his will the way he did the rest of the world. And if I'd had a better excuse for being sick, I'd have felt fine telling him where to get off. But as I lay there in bed, still hearing Don pound away at the world despite the doors that were constantly being closed in his face, I knew I was in this predicament because I'd been drinking like a fish at some dingy L.A. club watching unmemorable bands the night before until 3:00 in the morning. You know how it is when you've had a couple of cocktails and suddenly you don't feel sick anymore? And you're eventually drunk enough you convince yourself that the alcohol is killing the germs, and you'll be fine the next day? Well, Don deserved better than that, and I knew it.

So at about 12:30 I emerged from my room.

"What are you doing all dressed up?" asked Don, seeing me in heels and stockings and makeup and a dress.

"You don't think I'd let you go alone, do you?"

So it was more out of loyalty to Don's spirit than any hope for *Budding Prospects* or the loser who'd be eating lunch on our dime that I dredged myself out of bed, still feeling like shit, and packed myself into his VW Rabbit on that Tuesday afternoon. By grace of an open window, a fresh breeze, and a natural embarrassment born of a genteel upbringing I managed to keep from regurgitating on the drive up Highland Avenue to Hampton's, a burger joint near Sunset Boulevard.

Life with Don Murphy was fraught with unpleasant predicaments, but none was worse than the necessity of eating with him every day. For Don lives (if you can call that living) on a diet of hamburgers and pizza, fries, and garlic bread. I've seen a vegetable pass his lips only once, when my mother tried to get him to eat a tiny piece of cooked carrot one day. Don was gagging for the rest of the afternoon; you'd have thought she dosed him with Drano. Feeling like Chinese, Thai, Italian or Peruvian? Don will cut loose with a strident, childish chorus of "I can't eat anything there." Today, however, I was more than willing to use up a tolerance chit on dining at one of Don's intolerable eateries, since eating was the last thing I had on my mind.

When we got to the restaurant, we found that the guy was already there. A bad sign—people who arrive early to lunch in Hollywood usually do so because they have nothing better to do. Worse yet, his whole physical presence said "geek." I think he wore big turquoise pants and a Hawaiian shirt, and as the outfit was hanging on one of those bodies that didn't look like it saw the inside of a gym with any frequency, he wasn't exactly the kind of guy who could make anything look good.

Whatever. I was here to see if I could outlast the ride. Almost instantly, the guy began talking at a blinding speed that made Don look a bit palsied by comparison. Worse yet, he had the habit which slightly nauseated me at the moment of waving his hands manically as he spoke. He seemed to be doing this almost uncontrollably.

I stared at Don long enough to make sure he was looking at me before I pasted on my most impenetrably charming smile. If I was going to put on the performance of my life, I wanted credit for it.

"So, Don tells me you hope to direct a movie this fall."

Now the guy got *really* lathered up. I thought he was going to become airborne with all the flapping about he was doing. He'd written this movie, see, about these guys and this heist gone bad, and it was told novelistically, you know, with time folding back on itself, not linearly like most movies, which he was really fascinated with, and on and on until my head was spinning just trying to keep up with him.

And then a funny thing happened. Suddenly, I became kind of fascinated just watching this guy. He might be the king of the geeks, but there was something really interesting about his energy. He wasn't brilliant, but he was somehow—I don't know, *right*. You know when you're tired of everything out there, be it TV shows or music or shoes, and someone comes along at the right time with the right idea, and suddenly it's exactly what you were hungry for without even knowing it? Well, that's how I felt about everything this guy was talking about.

As I ploughed through piles of unworthy scripts every day, I had been searching for something special to fall in love with that could justify all the energy and intensity you had to work up in order to get a film made. Sure, we could go looking for the next big action script, but guys like Joel Silver and Simpson/Bruckheimer already did that pretty well. Nobody needed us to do it. Besides, Don and I knew we'd probably have to end up shooting our first film for under $100,000, and it's a little hard to pull off gunfights and explosions that don't look incredibly silly on a budget that finds your mom cooking food for the crew. I'd always used *sex, lies, and videotape* as a model for what I was looking for: something that was limited in production scope, but was fresh and energetic and a little shocking in its subject matter. Something you could be clever about shooting for scant cash, which would hopefully get some attention, and would launch you onto bigger things where you could hopefully pay your bills. Everything this guy was talking about seemed to be ripe for this kind of scenario. And by the time we left our lunch, I was more interested in what he had to tell me than anything I could have told him.

My illness seemed to have abated in the midst of a peculiar enthusiasm as Don and I got in the car. I was no longer overcome with the urge to spew all over him as he pulled out onto Highland Avenue.

"He was interesting. I liked his ideas," I told Don as he chauffeured me home. "I want to read that heist script he was talking about."

"I think there's already a producer on that one."

"I don't care, I'd just like to read it anyway," I said.

"Well, we don't have that one. But there's this other script he wrote. It's been sitting on your dining room floor for almost a year. I keep meaning to read it, but never do."

Big miracle there. Don was short-attention-span boy; people regularly got angry at us because Don would canvass enthusiastically for scripts which he promised to read overnight, and then would forget to give to me. He wasn't lying; he just regularly got so caught up in his own enthusiasm that he wouldn't think about the unlikelihood of actually coming through on his promise.

Which called for me to attack Don's pile of spooge with a fervor upon our return to my apartment. I withdrew a script from the bottom of the heap—it was covered with dust and badly mangled, having been shifted around for a year in Don's attempts to look like he was actually doing something with his junk.

"What was that guy's name again, Don?"

"Quentin. Quentin Tarantino."

"Was the script called *Natural Born Killers?*"

"Yep, that's the one.

An hour and a half later, I walked out of my bedroom—and I had no doubt that it was, indeed, the one. In fact, I'd never been so certain of anything in my life.

At this point, you might be asking yourself how Don and I came to this unlikely arrangement, and you would not be alone. I asked myself the same question every day. And there was only one answer—I had talked him into it.

We'd met at USC film school in the fall of 1987, and at the time Don had wanted to be a writer/director. Most of the people in film school thought Don a bit of a goof. His appearance certainly camouflaged his intelligence; he habitually wandered around campus sporting a crap hair-cut, pizza stains running down the front of his superhero T-shirt, a jacket with the lining hanging out of the sleeve that looked like a dog had been sleeping on it for several years, and jeans worn shiny from compacted dirt and negligible laundering. He was a far cry from the rich, polished, Ivy League degree–clutching, Armani-wearing, studio president's kid whom everyone looked to for surefire success in the movie business.

Unlike Don, I was attending a program within the cinema school that focused on training producers, rather than writers and directors. Whereas the bulk of the school was devoted to training people in the technical craft of filmmaking, my program was quite small and dealt with the business, financial, and logistical aspects of making a film. Don knew where to put a camera; I knew how much it would cost. Don could coax actors into delivering their lines; I was trained to draw up contracts that would ensure they'd never see net profits until the next millennium. So when Don was getting ready to write and direct his thesis film, he went to the head of my program and asked for a recommendation, someone who could produce the thing for him so he could focus on the creative aspects. She recommended me.

"I'm looking for someone to produce my thesis film," said Don, when he introduced himself to me. "Kathy Fogg said you'd do a good job. I want to do it feature length, 35mm."

"No," I said flatly.

"But I'm—"

"No."

"Don't you even want to read the script?"

"No. I don't want to. And you shouldn't do it, either; it's too damned hard. Believe me."

I told Don that I tried to do a feature film before for no money, and failed miserably—there was no way I was lining up to do it again. But despite my flat-out rejection of him, Don was undeterred, even after I tried to explain in detail that the problems involved in shooting a 35mm feature film for scarce cash made it damned near impossible. It was the first demonstration of a quality that Don Murphy has that is absolutely sterling in this business: a mule-stubborn refusal to ever take no for an answer. Raised on Long Island, Don came to USC because he loved films so much, he couldn't imagine a life outside the movie business. And as I spoke to him, I discovered that what Don lacked in social graces he made up in razor-sharp smarts. My reluctance to produce his movie for him was in no way going to derail his efforts—Don ultimately decided to produce the thing himself by default. I thought it was a doomed venture; you had to be one thick-skinned sonofabitch to keep all the disparate elements in line and make a film that ambitious when you weren't paying anyone any money, then have the presence of mind to go on a set every day and be creative.

For the next six months, my phone was ringing off the hook. Almost every time, it was Don Murphy asking me another question, and usually in a panic. Don never seemed to be worried that he was bothering me. It never occurred to him that I might think him an incredible pest or an imbecile. "How do I get free cameras? Where can I get cheap film stock?" he wanted to know. But one of Don's great gifts is complete obliviousness to what anyone thinks about him. And unless you came right out and told him to fuck off and die, it would never occur to him to stop calling. I found that quality sort of endearing, even inspiring. His other strength, as I discovered, was an absolute willingness to admit when he had no idea what he was doing, and ask for advice. Worried that people would think he's an idiot? Not for a second.

The following summer, I packed myself into my car and drove out to an elementary school in Pasadena where Don was, indeed, directing the first day of his shoot of *Monday Morning*. When I pulled into the parking lot, I was stunned. The level of production resources Don had managed to garner was outstanding. He had truckloads full of expensive equipment at his disposal, a crew of about forty people, and technical apparatuses like dollies, silks, generators, the works. It would have been a full-time job for several people to fast-talk all this stuff here for no money, and indeed, I wasn't the only person Don had pestered incessantly for the past year—he must've been on the phone constantly bugging everyone he knew in order to get all this crap at his disposal.

But even once the shoot was finished, the hardest part—as I had learned—was ahead of him. You can basically get through production for very little money; but when it comes to postproduction equipment and facilities, you have to pay and pay and pay. While Panavision may have an old 35mm camera kicking around that they'll lend you for no money, the minute you want to edit, you've got to rent a flatbed, and those start at $800 a month. Mixing sound? Well, the facilities are booked by the hour, and it takes two to three mixers working for days to mix the sound on a 35mm feature. They're pros, and they don't work for free. If Don could pull this off for no money, after having already done a job that would have exhausted a mere mortal, he would have to be superhuman.

After having spent more time with Don Murphy than most people can even conceive of, I can, indeed, attest to the fact that he *is* superhuman. He came up with a solution to the postproduction "pay as you go" problem that was as inspired as it was outrageous. He conned Universal Studios into giving him three editing rooms in order to cut his film there for the next six months. And he literally moved in. Then he took the student-loan money he was supposed to be living off, and put it into finishing his film. Around the campus, we began referring to him as "the homeless director."

Stories abound about Don's residency at the Universal editing rooms. Jeff Burr, a friend who was editing *Stepfather II* in the same facility, tells the story of how he was cutting sound effects of screaming and knife slashing into his film one night until the wee hours of the morning, when suddenly Don showed up at the door in his pajamas.

"Could you keep it down in there? People are trying to sleep."

Did the Universal postproduction guys know this was happening? Almost certainly; there was no way you could ignore the smell that was coming from a place where someone was living that had no ventilation. Did they care? Well, I think they started hinting to Don; but as I've mentioned before, Don's not really the kind of guy who responds to either subtle or not-so-subtle hints. (As our friend Dave Veloz puts it so eloquently, "Don just lives in a different emotional matrix than the rest of us.") I think that he finally moved out on his own steam, but not before he'd gotten them to give him a day of sound mixing in return for his departure. Once the student loans ran out, he paid for finishing most of his film by selling off the excess mag tape he found lying around in the hallway.

We were the unlikeliest of friends, even more implausible allies. Don's salient qualities were an encyclopedic knowledge of *Twilight Zone* and comic-book arcana, an affection for junk food and '70s bubble-gum music, Nintendo, and pinball machines. I had edited a punk-rock magazine in my teens, I liked big-block American muscle cars and macrobiotic food, Harold Bloom and Dogen and Dostoyevsky. I wouldn't be caught dead at a Star Trek convention. Don never smoked or drank or took drugs; I made up for his abstinence on all fronts. Don had a slightly naïve "lost boys" never-never-land demeanor that foretold he'd probably never grow up. As a slightly rebellious and unrepentant minister's daughter, I'd probably grown up too fast. What, then, did we have in common? Easy. Blind, burning ambition.

As graduation drew near in the spring of 1988, I'd grown increasingly antsy (okay, paralyzed with fear) about how exactly I would go about launching a successful assault on Hollywood. I knew at the time that I needed a partner, and although I liked working with women, having one as a partner wasn't a practical choice. For all the posturing about supporting strong roles for women and enlightened feminist principles, the entertainment business is one of the most sexist and discriminatory industries in creation. It's a world ruled by short, bald men with too much money and way too much power, who are driven equally by the universal desire to get laid and punish the women who wouldn't fuck them on a bet when they were nobodies. (My personal theory is that everyone who comes to Hollywood does so not in order to create beautiful, soul-searing works of art, but to get laid by a better class of people than they could ever hope to otherwise. While it may not be a completely comprehensive theory, you will not fall far wrong if you assume that this is the imperative that everyone — including myself — is working under on some level or another.)

It didn't take tremendous powers of observation, either, to realize that the world of Hollywood belonged not to the deep, penetrating, provocative thinkers; it belonged to the cantankerous sons of bitches who were willing to risk any humiliation, broach any authority, get on the phone and scream until they got what they wanted. And if you doubt my word, line up the top producers in Hollywood, one next to the other, and you will find each more aggravating, more exasperating, more stubborn and willful than the one before.

Which left me with two choices. I could either turn myself into someone who could be like that — because despite my talent for rebellious, obstreperous, devious, and manipulative behavior, I'm pretty nonconfrontational — or partner up with someone who possessed those qualities inherently. I didn't much relish the idea of pushing myself into being something other than I was — not because I was unwilling, but because I believe that people are more likely to make it if they find out what they do best and then do that. What I needed was someone who was as driven as I was and shared my megalomaniacal desire to go all the way to the top. I was someone who held my cards close, listened attentively, thought things through meticulously before acting. I didn't like putting myself on the line for fear of seeming needy and making a fool of myself. What I needed was someone who was just my opposite. Who could sell refrigerators to Eskimos. Who had no fear of making a fool of himself because he had no awareness that anyone might think he was a fool. Someone like—Don Murphy.

I remember sitting around the Formosa Café on Santa Monica Boulevard with some of my USC classmates one night, tossing back beers and wondering what we were going to do with our lives now that we were graduating. Sitting with me were Paul Simmons, an Amherst graduate and one of my closest friends; David Hartwell, a promising young writer/director; and Jim Slocum, another production graduate who was in the process of raising money to shoot a feature film independently.

I'll never forget the look on Paul's face when I told them I was going to ask Don to go into business with me. His beer practically came up through his nose.

"Jane, that's ridiculous," said Paul. "Don doesn't even want to be a producer."

"I can change that," I said.

"He's not exactly Mike Ovitz," said Hartwell, referring to the slick, well-manicured head of Creative Artists Agency (also known as "the Armani Army"), the largest agency in the business.

"All he needs is a little polishing. I can do that, too."

"But Jane, even if you dress him up, he'll still be *Don Murphy*," said Slocum.

"That's what I'm counting on," I said.

Undeterred by the fact that my classmates clearly thought I was out of my mind, I arranged to meet Don at Barone's Italian Restaurant in Toluca Lake, near Universal, where he was still living on the floor of the editing room. I told him my proposal.

"We become partners. Have a company. Fifty-fifty."

"What exactly would we do?" Don said, through a mouthful of half-chewed pizza.

"We'd option scripts, take them around to companies, try and get them made as producers."

"But I want to write and direct."

"Don, I'm going to tell you something here. Do you trust me as your friend to tell you the truth?"

"Sure."

"Okay. You are a good journeyman writer and director. You could definitely have a career at that if you tried. But you are, without question, the best producer I've ever seen. Whatever the salient qualities are that belong to every big-time Ferrari-driving, model-dating, Morton's-dining hotshot, you have, and you have in abundance. If you became a producer, you'd be the biggest producer in Hollywood, especially with me behind you. You're fearless; I'm devious. You're good at bullying people into doing what you want; I'm good at spotting people's weak points and knowing when they're vulnerable. You're headstrong, and you let your passions get in the way of your objectives; I'm cold-blooded and pragmatic. You're the perfect complement for me. I'm intuitive, and I overthink everything to the point where I can't speak, I get tongue-tied when I'm on the spot, and I hate the telephone. You speak first and think about it later, if at all. We're the perfect match."

It was one of the few times I've actually seen Don stunned. Nobody had ever come to him and told him he was good at much of anything; his producing achievements had been completely overlooked because his peers were all aspiring writer/directors who were judging his work on a creative level. I was looking at it from a completely different angle.

"I'll have to think about it," said Don.

And he did. For almost a year, while I went off and worked as a production assistant for Danny DeVito on *The War of the Roses*, then produced *American Summer*, Jim Slocum's direct-to-video film.

That Christmas, I was in Texas visiting family for the holidays when I got a call from Don.

"So, if we're going to do this producing thing, how would we start?"

In January 1990, Don and I first set up shop in my dining room. I'd love to tell you what we did in order to rudimentarily equip our so-called "office," but I don't think the statute of limitations has passed.

Cabin fever first struck in those early days. It describes what happens when Don and I sit in a room together too long. We'll get restless and bored and stir up trouble just to amuse ourselves. Or, more accurately,

Don stirs it up in order to amuse me, because if you can follow Don's rapid-fire verbal assault (and it isn't aimed at you), Don's probably the most savagely funny bastard in the world. His wit is razor sharp. He has reverence for nothing and no one. "When I want your opinion, I'll give it to you," he'll fire off at someone offering an unsolicited critique of one of our scripts. And although I scream and yell, it's hard to reprimand someone convincingly when you're laughing uncontrollably.

The term "cabin fever" was bestowed by our friend Peter Rice, who had been Don's first—and probably worst—victim. I'd met Peter when he was nineteen and working as an intern in the 20th Century Fox marketing department. Don encountered him when he was trying to get distribution on *Monday Morning*. Peter now had a job in the Acquisitions Department at Fox, where he was responsible for seeing every independent film that made it onto celluloid. He struck up a friendship with Don because even though there wasn't much he could do with *Monday Morning*, he was one of the first to appreciate Don's chutzpah. "Don Murphy will make it because he has to," Peter said. Over the years, he's been our best friend in the business, has talked Don down out of numerous emotional trees, and has always been a tremendous supporter. He would frequently say to Don, "You call me more than my parents do—and I always phone you back because it's the only way I can get you to stop calling me."

Our adventures as novice producers began with a couple of so-so scripts tucked under our arms as we made our first venture to the American Film Market. At the time, it took place each year at the Beverly Hilton Hotel, and it was (and still is) without question one of the most astonishing parades of international sleaziness I have ever witnessed. In the early '90s, when we started going there, many low- to medium-budget movies were being financed by "preselling" the foreign and video rights. While studios completely finance their own product, and control both domestic and foreign rights to their titles, many independent companies had to depend on the three annual film markets: Cannes, Milan, and the AFM—to be able to finance production of their films, where they would sell off movies' rights to distributors in individual countries. So the whole AFM was basically a hotel full of "hospitality suites," where buyers from across the world came not only to prebuy the rights to movies not yet in production, but also to have sellers try to palm off the Sri Lankan rights to old Stacy Keach made-for-TV movies.

The lobby was packed with drunken foreigners from around the world leering down the ample cleavage being displayed by "actresses" who came to try and meet producers and show them their "portfolios" (or so the story goes). Since Don and I were new in the business, we thought our best chance at getting someone to roll the dice on a couple of newcomers like us was at the low-budget end, and this was low-budget heaven. Everywhere you looked, there were Tanya Roberts and Wings Hauser movies; Robert Davi and Michael Ironside are *huge* overseas, don't you know, said the international sales representatives, the lot of whom managed to make it look like hawking for strip clubs would be a respectable step up the ladder.

Since we didn't have the $200 to buy a pass, we had to sneak into the thing. (Don Murphy is an expert at this, a talent that continues to come in handy.) It was the first time we had to walk up to people cold and say, "I'm a producer." That alone took a shitload of nerve since every sleazeball in every bar in Los Angeles is a "producer" once he's had a few cocktails. Walking through the halls, I was simultaneously consumed with nausea and fascination; if I'd only had to look at the whole thing, I could have enjoyed it as some sort of macabre theater, but we were actually here to introduce ourselves to these people.

I will always love Don for the complete fearlessness and zeal with which he forged into each crummy little room. Armed with a brochure containing a map of all the hundreds of rooms and sales organizations, Don walked into every last one of them, diligently and tirelessly, extended his hand, and said "Hi, I'm Don Murphy and I have this script. . . ." After making some small talk, he would write down the name of the person who was in charge, hand them our hastily printed business card, and then check the little box on his map. Almost everyone was a stranger to me, but Don knew a few of these people from his attempts to sell *Monday Morning*. We went there for six harrowing days, in which I swallowed my fear, and tried to find a way to work in tandem with Don. He was the one getting away with being direct to the point of abrasiveness, and I was there to laugh and try and spin it if it didn't go over too well. It was probably at the AFM that I first uttered the line "Oh, that's not *really* what he meant. . . ."

During the AFM and beyond, we pounded the pavement incessantly, taking meetings with anyone who would talk with us. We learned several hard lessons that way. Namely, that there were many people running around out there who made outrageous assertions about their important industry connections and claimed to have vast sources of independent financing. But something was always wrong—their telephone was turned off suddenly, they looked like they'd been sleeping underneath bus-stop benches, or had white powder dripping out of their noses. We couldn't figure out what they gained from leading people like us on, but let me tell you, there are about a zillion of them. As Keith Gordon, the actor/director, is fond of saying, "Most people who claim to have independent financing turn out to have metal plates in their heads." As a result of this, we developed our "no bozos" rule; although Don Murphy became absolutely diligent about following up any potential lead, if my internal "bozo" warning bell went off for any reason, he'd stop wasting his time.

In the first interview we ever did, Don commented, "If I'd met myself at the first AFM, under the 'no bozos' rule, I would have ignored myself." This became clear to me slightly before it did Don, as I was watching him stand next to Trimark's immaculately dressed chairman, Mark Amin, trying to sell him one of our scripts. Mark looked as though he thought Don potentially dangerous; and if there was any way he could have escaped, he would have. Now, Don's a big guy with a strong presence—at one point, my sister Pam snatched her infant son away from Don, claiming he was too intense for small children—but I had the feeling that Mark's trepidation was based more on Don's film geek/slacker appearance than it was on his personal mannerisms. What worked just fine for Chris Cornell simply wasn't going to work for a guy asking for millions of dollars. As grateful as I was to have Don there with me, I realized that I was going to have to broach the painful subject of his personal style before we were ever going to get anywhere.

Don had one suit, which his parents had bought him during his undergraduate years. It was an ill-fitting Haggar double-knit number he'd picked up on the cheap at Sears. He brought it over to my house/our office to show it to me one day.

"Don, what's that hole in the sleeve?"

"That's where the price tag used to be. I ripped it out the day I got it."

This was not going to be easy. In addition to being remarkably smart and absolutely tenacious, Don Murphy is also unbelievably cheap. At this particular time in our partnership, there was good reason for being cheap.

But my mother had been a successful businesswoman, and she'd always told me that in business you had to convince people you didn't need money in order for them to give it to you. Therefore, looking good was critical. Having a great pair of pantyhose was more important than eating. Quite fortunately, I had an internal "mom" that told me you should sooner slit your wrist than walk into a meeting without looking impeccable. How was I going to impart the importance of looking like a million bucks to Don, when we had no money to even pay for gas, let alone decking him out in designer duds?

Thus began the longest and biggest series of fights Don and I have ever endured during our partnership. And believe me, when Don and I fight, nobody wants to be in the wake of it.

"Don, I think you need a new suit," I ventured with trepidation.

"What's wrong with the old one?" he asked, immediately stiffening at the prospect of spending money.

"Well, quite frankly, it looks like Sunday go-to-church at the homeless mission."

"WHY ARE YOU ATTACKING ME? YOU'RE ALWAYS ATTACKING ME! It's just like last week, at the New Line party. . . ."

And suddenly we're fighting about something completely different. This is Don's standard tactic; confuse and disorient your opponent into complete exasperation. I soon become enraged when he won't address my point, as we segue off into seven different long-standing arguments that Don dredges up to push my buttons and keep me off the topic. And then things really get heated.

It took me two months to finally get Don to cave on the suit front. During that time, I became a complete pain in the ass, a shrill harridan that just wouldn't shut up until he gave in. I think we broke up the partnership no less than four times. I became furious and threw Don out at least twice, whereupon he'd begin calling me incessantly until I unplugged my phone. Minutes later, he'd come beating at my door, and I'd retaliate by throwing all his crap out my second-story window and onto the lawn. He'd relent every time, promise to get a new suit, but something always went wrong: he'd lost his checkbook, his sister was coming into town and he didn't have time, and one shopping trip after another got canceled due to Don's incessant stalling.

Finally, I refused to take another meeting unless he had a new suit. There are just so many times you can walk into a room with a guy who looks like a used-car salesman and maintain any sense of self-esteem.

"Okay, let's go shopping," he said, at last defeated.

I knew I'd never get him into a store by myself; so, along with our friend Lauren, I physically dragged Don into the Bullocks Beverly Center. (He lost his nerve at the top of the escalator, arms and legs flailing in a panic as he tried to turn around; but between the two of us, we managed to haul him cussing and screaming into the men's department.)

"I hate it!" he said to everything he tried on, as if by driving the poor salesgirl into a fit of hopeless desperation, he could get off the hook.

"You love it," I said finally. "I love it. Lauren loves it. You look good. We're taking the blue Hugo Boss jacket. And the two pairs of pants. Where's the shoe department?"

But the suit was only the tip of the iceberg. There were many more fights ahead. Don regularly avoided haircuts at any cost. He'd also accustomed himself to once-a-week showers when living in his Universal Studios digs, and didn't really see the point of wasting that kind of time on a daily basis. He also had this really weird mustache that grew orange on one side and blond on the other. When I finally got him to shave it off, all his friends thanked me for not having to look at the ugly thing anymore. Even now, years later, the fight continues. Don has a troublesome affection for argyle socks, despite the fact that I've bought him boxes full of Calvin Klein dress socks over the years. I've threatened to come over and burn the damned things, so now he only wears them to the gym.

In addition to decking out Don for the part of the big Hollywood mogul, we also had to figure out our strategy for getting our films made. I wish I could say we had a clear idea going in, but a lot of it was trial and error, a process of butting our heads against the wall over and over again until it finally crumbled.

I had picked up one piece of wisdom while working as a secretary that partly guided our efforts in the beginning. When Mike Ovitz was an agent at the William Morris Agency, he'd gotten the idea to splinter off with a bunch of other agents and form CAA, which—before too long—had not only overtaken every other agency in town in size and power, but had changed the role of the agency to such a degree that they now held the studios themselves under their thumbs.

Ovitz's idea had been simple: The best way to control Hollywood is to control the material, and to control the material, you have to control the writers. So when CAA opened its doors, they went after every major writer in the industry. Traditionally, writers are the doormats of Hollywood, so having someone court them was an amazing lure. Sure enough, once the writers came, the talent came, too, because talent stays hot by working with good material. And once he had the talent—well, Mr. Ovitz and his buddies knew the studios were nothing without the stars. As someone who sussed out how to throw the studios into a collective hammerlock in a relatively short time, Ovitz was—and remains—one of my true inspirations.

Well, there was no way that Don and I were going to get million-dollar writers like Ron Bass or Joe Eszterhaus to write a script for us. (On the latter count, sometimes poverty is a blessing.) Our only hope was to get writers who didn't even have agents yet, to discover them before anybody else did; because once they had an agent, you'd have to call that agent up. And when you told them you were nobody, they'd promptly hang up on you. (Trust me, it's an exercise you can try yourself.)

So in the beginning, every day I would turn my apartment over to a scene that went something like this:

9:30 A.M.	Jane emerges in her bathrobe, eats an orange, and plunks herself down on the couch to begin reading bad scripts.
10:00 A.M.	Don arrives, begins loading up on Coca-Cola and pretzels before launching into "super phone boy" mode.
11:00 A.M.	Don has called anyone who will talk to him, and many who won't.
11:15 A.M.	Jane awakens from her mind-deadening bad-script stupor to yell at Don for being incorrigible on the phone.
11:30 A.M.	Don yells at someone's secretary for refusing to put him through.
11:45 A.M.	Jane yells at Don for being mean to a secretary, who is only doing his/her job. (Jane has spent the past few days pounding a typewriter at the Bank of California, and is overidentifying with Don's unfortunate victim.)
11:50 A.M.	Jane begins to clean up for lunch with someone who will inevitably reveal himself/herself to be a worthless loser.
12:00 P.M.	Jane to Don: "You're not going looking like *that?*"

12:20 P.M.	After 20 minutes of fighting, Don finally gives in and changes his shirt.
12:30 P.M.	Leave for lunch.
1:00 P.M.	Lunch with worthless loser who claims to be fabulously wealthy/well-connected/extremely talented/far more important to their company than they actually are.
2:30 P.M.	Don whines all the way home about how much the lunch cost.
3:00 P.M.	Aspiring writer Don has dredged up arrives with bad haircut/high-wader pants/body odor to put another script in Jane's script pile.
3:30 P.M.	Don angry about everyone who hasn't called him back from that morning, so he calls them again.
4:00 P.M.	Don interrupts Jane to strategize; becomes enraged when she suggests he won't be able to get a $500,000 fee on a $1 million movie.
4:30 P.M.	Deriving no satisfaction from fight with Jane, Don calls Peter Rice at Fox to wind him up. In order to get him off his back, Peter gives him a lead for some other worthless loser who might make one of Don's pictures.
4:35 P.M.	Don begins two-hour phone search trying to track down Peter Rice's lead—if Peter's smart, he hasn't given Don enough information, and this will keep Don busy for a while.
5:00 P.M.	No longer able to read with Don's relentless bellowing in the background, Jane gives up and goes down to get the mail, which is full of nothing but bills. She promptly throws them all away.
6:00 P.M.	Most civilized people go home.
7:00 P.M.	People who don't really want to talk to you begin calling you back, figuring you'll be gone. Ha ha ha. Don Murphy is still there.

Things worked like this for about a year. But all that came to an end as *Natural Born Killers* entered our lives.

Chapter 2

If You Don't Listen, You Won't Worry

"Okay, so here's the sketch," Don said one morning.

I was giving him only about 10 percent of my attention at that moment, just enough to know he was babbling again. The other 90 percent was devoted to a much bigger problem: For the third time that week, our computer had exploded, and I was currently standing over the shoulder of our resident computer expert, Don's friend Bernie, as he tried to salvage the antiquated pile of silicon chips that should've been scrapped years ago.

"I had a brainstorm. Go with me on this one," Don said. "I think I can get Michael Heuser to take the test footage to Milan, he presells the rights to a couple of worthless South American territories . . ."

"What *are* you talking about?" I asked, swiveling my full concentration around to him at last.

Don rolled his eyes in exasperation. "You know, the ten minutes we promised to shoot. That's the deal that Quentin has with Rand. He has to shoot ten minutes in the next three months."

"Okay, I'm starting to recognize names here, Don. Quentin—Quentin Tarantino. I guess we're talking about *Natural Born Killers*, then."

"Of *course* we are," said Don.

In fact, we weren't. We'd been discussing motherboards and micropro-cessors and buses and other things I'm vaguely afraid to know too much about for fear that pocket protectors and Coke-bottle glasses will not be far behind.

"Was there some segue I missed?" I asked. "I thought we were talking about the computer. Bernie, weren't we talking about the computer?"

"We were talking about the computer, Don," Bernie said.

"Oh, great, another country heard from. You shut up and keep working," said Don. "You know, you've got to learn to follow these things," he fired off at me. "If you can't keep up, I can't be held responsible."

It takes less effort to end world hunger and achieve international peace than it does to follow Don's conversations. Most people simply shake their heads, exhausted and puzzled, when he drives off on one of his rants. But after having spent ten hours a day in a room with the guy for almost a year now, I was a regular fucking Sherlock Holmes when it came to making sense of the bizarre detours his brain was always taking. What I concluded from this exchange was that (a) Don had talked to someone about producing *Natural Born Killers*; (b) Quentin had some sort of preexisting agreement with someone regarding the rights, and (c) Don was already racing ahead to how he was going to finance the movie based on some piece of film he'd give to someone he barely knew through a process he barely understood. By Don's standards, this passed for coherence.

This left me with only one question. "What's a Rand?" I asked.

It was Bernie who chimed in with a response. "Rand Vossler," he said. "He's a friend of mine who works as an assistant to Lewis Chesler, a TV producer. He's one of the regulars at Games Night."

Uh-oh. This was not a good sign. Bernie was a sweet guy—in fact, he was probably Don's best friend—but he was one of those hopelessly doomed characters who are forever floating around in the cesspool of the Hollywood underclass, and his friends tended to be equally suspect. Bernie was probably in his early thirties, but his premature hair loss and Ward Cleaver fashion sense pegged him a good ten years older. Don referred to Bernie as "The Alien," and kept him around partly because he was good at fixing our ever-combusting computer, and partly because Don enjoyed abusing him mercilessly. Bernie never seemed to care, or even respond with anything that could be characterized as an emotional response. Don accused him of coming from the planet Shrug. "Bernie, do you want a million dollars?" Shrug. "Bernie, do you want to be gang-raped by a bunch of large, angry men in prison?" Shrug. He'd never had a real job as far as I could tell, and made his living as a kleptomaniac. (I always think it's great when people can support themselves by adapting their emotional problems, but he and his friends were nobody that I particularly wanted to be in business with.)

Bernie was also the undisputed king of the cinema-geek network, and when he wasn't trying to bail himself out of jail, he spent most of his time trying to sneak into every free screening in Hollywood. Every Friday night, he'd host a gathering known as "Games Night," where fifteen or so people with limited interpersonal skills and circumscribed social lives would get together to load up on soft drinks that Bernie had spent the week boosting from various 7-Elevens around town and play games like Pictionary, Trivial Pursuit, and Jeopardy. Don had been a member of this group for years, which was how he got his hands on the NBK script in the first place. If this guy Rand was a member of that crowd, my internal bozo alarms were already going off at top volume.

"Rand has been trying to make NBK for almost two years now," said Bernie. "He was going to produce, and Quentin was going to direct."

"I tried to help them get the money one time, remember?" said Don.

"No," I said.

"Sure you do. Remember Chris Ruben, that guy who was running around town telling everyone he had access to millions?"

"You mean the guy you used to call the Fat Piece of Shit?"

"Well, never to his face," said Don. "But that's the one. He said he knew a couple of bodybuilding twins who wanted to get their SAG cards, and were willing to put up the $250,000 to get a film made if they could have a role in the movie. I turned them on to Rand and Quentin. They were buffoons, and I guess they never came through."

As it turned out, the reason that Don had never read the NBK script—aside from apathy and a general inability to concentrate—was because the whole scheme sounded incredibly dubious, even to him. People in Hollywood will try almost any scam to get their film made, but the idea that someone would pop for $250,000 to get their SAG cards was ludicrous. SAG was the Screen Actors Guild, and getting a SAG card simply entailed getting cast in a movie or a TV show or even a commercial that was signatory to the guild. Since almost every production in Hollywood with any kind of budget at all is signatory to SAG, even if they're not signatory to the technical unions, a SAG card is not that tough to get if you're a bit bright, and even if you're not. If these guys were saying they would come up with that kind of dough simply for a SAG card, they were clearly less than not-bright. (The only person you could accuse of being stupider was someone who believed that a questionable scam like this would work.)

"I guess when the twins didn't come through, Quentin gave up hope and let Rand have the script," said Bernie. "He went off to write *Reservoir Dogs*, which looks like it's going to get made."

"So let me get this straight," I said. "If we want to make *Natural Born Killers*, we have to take this guy Rand as a producer?"

For some reason, Don began signaling frantically to Bernie, but Bernie didn't seem to notice.

"Oh no," Bernie went on. "Rand wants to direct it now."

"WHAT??" I screamed.

"You shut your cake hole and go back to fixing your computer!" shouted Don. "Nobody asked for your two cents."

"Don, are you telling me this guy is attached to *direct?*"

Don smiled sheepishly. "Oh, did I forget to mention that?"

"No, unbelievably, you left that out."

Don was always skipping over key details that he knew would set me off, and this bit of news was a guaranteed bomb detonator. It's one thing to take someone on as a piece of producing baggage, because we knew that we could handle that aspect of a production ourselves. But it's easier to talk Sylvester Stallone into taking a supporting role behind Schwarzenegger than it is to break a new director in Hollywood, and there's good reason for that. No matter how strong your script is, once you get out on the set, everything is resting on the director's back. If he (or she) craps out, you've wasted everything. And until someone's been tested over the course of a shoot and on into the editing room, there's no way to know whether they've got the emotional resilience, the drive, and the vision to hold it all together.

"Don, let me ask you a serious question here. Do you have any—and I mean any—reason to think that this guy can direct?"

"Details, details," said Don, who I could see had conveniently hurdled over all these obstacles and was already writing the *Variety* review in his head.

"Don . . ."

"Okay. Well, why don't we get together with Rand and talk to him? Then you can judge for yourself."

In retrospect, I probably should have had the common sense to bail on the whole thing then and there. The trouble was, since reading the script for the first time, *Natural Born Killers* had really gotten under my skin. In the first incarnation I ever read, *NBK* was the story of Mickey and Mallory Knox, two lovestruck outlaws who kill her parents and go on a cross-country killing spree before they are hunted down and apprehended. They become media darlings, murdering sweethearts, lionized by a character named Wayne Gayle, a Geraldo Rivera–like tabloid host hungry for ratings points. Against all the odds, they break out of jail and reunite, taking Wayne hostage and killing him in front of his camera before they escape into a happy ending. Vile as Mickey and Mallory are, they stand out as sympathetic against all the corrupt institutions—the prison system, the police, the media, even the family—from which they are trying to escape.

The script had a kind of relative morality that really intrigued me. In the '60s, Bonnie and Clyde paid for their crimes in a bloody shoot-out at the end of the movie, and justice triumphed. Today, they'd wind up with a lucrative book deal and pump their story on *Oprah*. We all love to swell with indignation watching *A Current Affair* or *60 Minutes* as Mike Wallace sweats some loathsome bastard who's guilty up to his eyeballs. (I do, anyway.) We're duped into believing that these shows represent some kind of objective journalism, rather than the shamelessly manipulative ratings vehicles that they are. Artistically, *NBK* was sort of a mess, but it was spot on about something that was in the air—the criminal-as-celebrity would soon become a rising star in a world that couldn't tell the difference between Richard Ramirez and Antonio Banderas.

In fact, *NBK*'s provocative (and prescient) subject matter had been inspired by an episode of *A Current Affair* which Quentin had seen detailing the posttrial exploits of Richard Ramirez. Known as "The Night Stalker," Ramirez had broken into homes and killed thirteen people before being caught in 1985. When he went on trial before the TV cameras, America got a chance to see that Ramirez was actually a pretty good-looking guy. We might shake our heads in abhorrence, but nobody was switching channels as the lurid details of the case were laid out. Women thronged to the courtroom and would sit there every day like groupies at a Metallica show. They began visiting Ramirez in jail, fighting amongst themselves for his attention, pledging their undying love even as he was found guilty and sentenced to life in prison. When asked how she could be attracted to a man who had raped and killed so many, one of the women responded: "When I think about him, I like to think about Richard the man, not Richard the murderer."

In addition to exploring America's perverse attachment to violent characters, *NBK* had an entertainment quality that really worked for me. Personally, I'd rather watch *The Terminator* than *Gandhi* any day; if it was possible to be provocative and scathing within a context that was fun to watch, so much the better. I also had a disturbed identification with the character of Mallory Knox, a woman who could smile charmingly in one moment and rip your head off in the next if you rubbed her the wrong way. The dialogue within the script was sharp and furious and funny, and the story moved at such breakneck speed that it didn't have time to stop and hit you over the head with a message. It simply cast its characters in a *Badlands* riff that was thrilling and hilarious over and above its themes.

My favorite scene in the script, as it turned out, was the one that had been written for the two bodybuilding twins to play. I later discovered that it had been written by Roger Avary, Quentin's friend and collaborator from the days when they worked at a Manhattan Beach video store called Video Archives. Although Quentin was the credited author of *True Romance*, *Pulp Fiction*, and *NBK*, they were all born out of his creative musings with Roger when they had nothing but time to kill in those early days. Originally, Roger had written a script entitled *The Open Road*. Quentin had then taken that script and expanded it into a wild, unruly 400-page opus. It told the story of the character who would eventually become Clarence, one of the main characters in *True Romance*, who writes a script about himself and his girlfriend, Alabama, when they're on the run, romanticizing themselves in the characters of Mickey and Mallory Knox. Roger and Quentin then stripped it down to what would become the foundations of *True Romance*, and over the next year they rewrote the version that would finally become the shooting script. Later, Quentin went back and took what was left over from *The Open Road* and fashioned *NBK*; he also pillaged random bits for *Reservoir Dogs* and *Pulp Fiction*.

The bodybuilders' scene in *NBK* appeared during a segment of *American Maniacs*, the tabloid TV show hosted by Wayne Gayle, in which he interviews two bodybuilders who had almost been killed by Mickey and

Mallory. In the midst of taking a chain saw to their legs, Mallory recognizes them as B-movie stars. "Oh my God, Mickey, it's the Hun Brothers!" she cries. "We're your biggest fans!" Upon this realization, she and Mickey call 911 in order to save the two, and then split. Despite the fact that their legs have been amputated up to the knee, the two—when questioned by Wayne on television—champion Mickey and Mallory, whom they feel have passed their "fighting spirit" on to them. It was an absurd moment that parodied the celebrity factor that TV bestowed upon the most heinous of criminals, to the point where the victims themselves buy into the mythology.

NBK was the kind of movie I wanted to make. It was the only thing I'd read up to that point that seemed worthy of spending two years of my life trying to bring to the screen. So launching my better judgment down the drain, I agreed with Don's request to meet up with Rand on the off chance that this whole endeavor wasn't completely doomed, and we could find a way to make it work.

We arranged to meet with Rand at El Coyote Mexican restaurant on Beverly Boulevard, renowned for its cheap margaritas and rock-'n'-roll clientele. He appeared to be somewhere in his late twenties, and looked like he spent half his time ironing his jeans into polite creases; he must've spent the other half pulling his hair back into a ponytail that curled pristinely at the end. He seemed anal retentive in a way that made for an unlikely pairing with Quentin, but hey, I was sitting there with Oscar Madison at my side, who was I to talk.

When Rand spoke, he hunched emphatically over his food, delivering each sentence like a carefully pointed missile across the table. "So the first thing you must know," he said, "is that I'm absolutely *passionate* about *Natural Born Killers*. Quentin and I worked on the script together for years, refining every detail. It's my sole mission in life to see that it gets made."

"What parts did you add, Rand?" I wanted to know.

"Well, you know the courtroom scene, where Mickey acts as his own attorney and kills Grace Lovelace when he's interrogating her on the stand? When Quentin wrote it, it was all just dialogue. I'm the one who added all the details of how it's supposed to be shot. When the ring falls off her finger and rolls across the floor in slow motion—that was my idea." He beamed with pride.

Okay. A lot of people in Hollywood thought they deserved screenplay credit for adding appropriate punctuation—at least this guy knew what a camera angle was, even if my personal feeling on the subject was that this hardly represented a significant contribution.

I could see Don getting bored and impatient beside me, eager to get down to business. "So here's the deal," he said. "You can correct me if I'm wrong, Rand. But the agreement you have with Quentin says that you can have a free option on the script if you can shoot a ten-minute segment from the film within the next three months. After that, if you can get the movie fully financed, you can buy out the underlying rights to the script for $40,000. Is that right?"

"Absolutely," said Rand. "Since I'm now moving over into the director's seat, I'm going to need someone to handle the producing responsibilities. I don't know you, Jane, but I've known Don for quite a while, and I know he's someone who gets things done. If you guys would like to work on it with me, maybe we can come to some kind of arrangement."

"Rand, let me ask you a question," I said. "Have you ever directed anything before?"

Rand began to shift uncomfortably in his seat. "Well, no, not exactly. But I'm absolutely passionate about this script, and I know every single detail of how it should be shot. I've lived with it for the past two years, and I know I'm the only person for the job."

Not the answer I was looking for. It was my turn to squirm nervously in my seat. "Well, let me ask you this—do you have this agreement with Quentin in writing?"

"Yes, absolutely," he said. "I made him sign a written contract."

"Did you have an attorney write it up?" I asked.

"No, I did it myself."

Uh-oh. "Did you ever have an attorney look at it?"

Rand chuckled. "Well, I didn't. But you know, I have this friend who's an attorney who said to me one time, 'Rand, you know more about the law than most attorneys do.' I'm very good at these things. I make sure every single point is covered. You don't have to worry."

I worried. One of the first things Don and I had done when we went into business was find the best entertainment attorney we could afford, a young Harvard Law guy named Karl Austen. We knew that in the movie business, you couldn't just have any shyster represent you; the entertainment business is a very specific business whose laws and conventions change almost daily. If you're represented by someone who doesn't know what they're doing, your contracts are going to leak like the *Titanic*. Worse yet, they'll get taken advantage of by the sharpies they're going up against and give you bad advice that can cost you dearly in the long run. I had a master's degree in this kind of contractual crap, and even *I* wouldn't venture to draft a contract myself.

Don seemed blissfully untroubled by all of these issues. "So what did you think of him?" he asked on the way home.

"Well, he thinks he knows more than he does, which is always dangerous," I said.

"But he clearly is passionate about the script."

"My mother could be passionate about the script, and I don't think I'd let her direct, either," I said.

"Look, we could help him shoot this thing pretty easy. It wouldn't cost us much money, and then if it blew, we'd say '*hasta la vista*,' " said Don.

"I think you're wrong, Don. For one thing, it would take a shitload of our time and effort, which we could be spending on much less problematic projects. Secondly, if you're hoping to have a piece of film that you hope to sell this thing with, it's got to have a certain level of quality. Even if we got most of the stuff for free, I'm estimating it'd still cost us about ten grand."

Money—that stopped him in his tracks. But only for a second. Because once Don Murphy gets a plan in his head, it's hard to derail him. "I think we could come up with that," he said.

"What are you planning to do, rob a bank with The Alien?"

"No, The Alien only shoplifts. I don't think he'd be up for armed robbery. I've got a little bit of money coming in from *Monday Morning*, and we could go to our parents. . . ."

Ouch! "Our parents? Don, I'd rather shoot off my right foot. We already tapped them out during film school."

"I don't want to go to my family any more than you do. They'll just think we're bigger deadbeats than they already do. But we decided that *Natural Born Killers* is the thing we believe in, didn't we?"

Silence. "Yeah, we did," I said. "But I'm not sure I believe in Rand."

"Look, he's not an idiot, and directing isn't rocket science. We make sure we surround him with the best crew people we possibly can—how far wrong can he go?"

I thought about it for a moment. "Okay, but only under three conditions. One, you have to convince me that Rand has a valid agreement with Quentin. Two, I want to have some reason to believe that Rand can handle the job. And three, if we're going to put up the money to shoot this thing and it turns out to be a disaster, I want the script as collateral and an agreement that we can sell it in order to recoup our investment of time and capital."

A few days later, we got together with Rand and laid it out for him. "If we do this, we're really going on the line," I told him. "I just want you to know what the consequences are. We can't afford to be 'easy come, easy go' about that kind of money. If it doesn't work out with you directing, you're going to have to step aside and let us try to recoup the money we've lost by setting it up with someone else."

Rand scoffed, "Oh, I'm not worried about that possibility ever happening. I know if I can just get my shot, I'll do an *amazing* job. You'll see."

Well, I guess we would. I was glad that Rand, at least, was confident. But I, for one, was not blessed with his sense of manifest destiny in the situation. I'd had my ass handed to me producing a low-budget film with dicey characters once before, and I wasn't lining up to have it happen again.

Back when I was in film school, I had been assigned to an obligatory internship at a major studio during summer vacation, 1987. I was supposed to learn how the industry really operates by sitting in on all the so-called "creative" meetings that they held regularly. On the first day, they gave me my own office and handed me a script they all loved: *Stanley & Iris*, the story of an illiterate man (Robert De Niro) and the working-class woman (Jane Fonda) who teaches him how to read. I immediately concluded that they were all a bunch of wankers and decided to ignore them for the summer.

It was, however, a very nice office. And with all this free time on my hands, I decided that there was really only one way to put it to good use: I would produce a movie. I was a year away from my degree, and for all the time I'd devoted to making student shorts and studying contracts and marketing campaigns and distribution strategies, I still knew fuck-all about how to actually produce a feature film. It seemed like something I'd better learn, fast.

I got together with a friend of mine, a fellow film student named Everett Lewis who had written a script that he wanted to direct. *Lazarus* was the true story of a black woman in 1940s Los Angeles who cut the head off a chicken to cook it for dinner, but the chicken didn't die—it lived, head-less, for ten days. The members of her all-black church thought it was a miracle and named the chicken "Lazarus." It became a media sensation, and the white community galvanized behind the SPCA to put the woman on trial for cruelty to animals. I liked the scathing examination of racial dynamics within the script, as well as the absurdity of a story that was nonetheless true. But mostly, I liked the idea that it was *there*, and an opportunity for me to produce.

For weeks, I ran around trying to scare up everything we needed in order to shoot the film: cameras, locations, actors, costumes, crew members, film stock, transportation vehicles, food, processing, editing facilities, and everything else required to complete a 35mm feature. Let me tell you, it was no easy trick hustling all of this for no money. Fortunately, I had the help of one of my classmates, a business whiz named Jeff Montgomery, who came on board as executive producer. We were all set to go—one day before shooting—when we hit a huge speed bump. The guy who was the virtual emperor of the USC stockroom, who lorded over all the grip and electrical equipment we desperately needed to complete the damned thing, was Aziz Ghazal. He'd promised us use of all the equipment we needed—that was, until the last minute. Suddenly Aziz wanted to be a producer on the movie. If we didn't let him, we'd have no equipment, and hence no movie.

Aziz was someone who everyone at the USC film school had to go through in order to get their films made, and dealing with him was always touchy. He had great ambitions in Hollywood, and he tried to use the stockroom as his power base. Once upon a time, he'd produced *Zombie*

High, a perfectly awful film starring Virginia Madsen, that died at the box office when the distributor had the reels printed in the wrong order (not that I think anyone who saw the film noticed). But Aziz talked about it like it was *Dr. Zhivago.* He still ran a nice business on the side, renting out the equipment to people outside the cinema school and pocketing the cash, something all the students knew about but the administration seemed to be blind to. There was no higher authority you could go to in order to circumvent him—it was either deal with Aziz, or no dice.

When I got this bit of news, I came flying down to the stockroom to confront (and perhaps kill) Aziz. "This is really unfair," I said. "We've knocked ourselves out to bring all this together, and now you want to jump our credits?"

"You do not understand," Aziz went on to explain in his rapid-fire Middle Eastern accent. "I have experience that you do not have. I can be of great assistance. I have editing rooms in my garage that I set up when I produced my own film, *Zombie High.* I would let you use them for free. I would be an excellent producer. It would be very good for you to have my help on this film."

Suddenly I felt like I was bargaining for serapes in Tijuana or something. I called Jeff, and we got Aziz to agree to accept an "associate producer" credit for the time being if he'd let us use the grip and electrical equipment, with the possibility of being bumped up to a full producer if his contribution finally warranted it. Although I was suspicious of his acquiescence, I was just glad to have all the stockroom equipment at our disposal for the time being. I figured I'd worry about any potential fallout later.

Given our meager resources and the fact that I had no idea what I was doing, the details of the production were a nightmare. Along the way, I was chased down the street by the police, wound up coming home from fifteen-hour shoots to take up hems and pad out jackets and do most of the costuming myself, and spent my days halting traffic and forging location permits, and calming down enraged property owners who had no clue what they were getting into when they agreed to let a student crew shoot there in the first place. But in spite of all the bullshit, it was invigorating, exciting, and in comparison to the overblown corporate behemoth of modern Hollywood movie production, much more in the spirit of the original freebooting pioneers who had traveled out west to escape enforcement of Edison's patent when the movie industry began at the turn of the century.

The trouble was that despite Everett's talent as a director, he was sensitive and difficult. The necessity of shooting such an ambitious film under tremendous pressure with such limited resources was wearing him down emotionally. By the time we finished shooting and moved into Aziz's garage to edit the film, the trouble really began. Suddenly I began getting these hysterical phone calls from Everett, who accused me and Jeff of not supporting his artistic vision and trying to undermine him.

I called Aziz for help because I thought I'd become friends with him over the course of the whole endeavor. He had a beautiful wife named Becky and three great kids: two boys named Nazir and Chad, and a pretty young daughter named Khadijah whom I used to play with whenever I came over to the editing rooms.

"Aziz, can you talk some sense into him? Where is he getting this stuff from? We just want to see the film get finished."

"I will do what I can," said Aziz. "Everett is just under a great deal of pressure. I'm sure he will calm down."

Then—one day—Everett flipped. He took the work print of the film, put it in the back of his car, and drove off to San Diego to enjoy something along the lines of a nervous breakdown, muttering that Jeff and I were conspiring against him. Jeff was the first to smell a rat and realize what Aziz was trying to do: Now that he was with Everett daily, and the editing was being done at his house, he was trying to provoke Everett's natural paranoia and wind him up so he could move us out of the picture and become the sole producer. Well, I don't know how stupid they thought we were, but long before Jeff and I started putting our own money and time into producing the film, we'd made sure that the rights to it were controlled equally among Jeff, Everett, and me. Without either Jeff or me on his side, there was nothing Everett could do to boot us off. Aziz was furious when he found out. Everett withdrew into mute hatred and abandoned the project. Jeff was disgusted with the whole mess, and I was left feeling like I'd gone to all this effort for nothing.

Jeff once told me something that became my most enduring mantra in Hollywood: "The sign of a good businessman is the ability to know reality." Which means basically that you can't let your hopes and dreams skew your vision of what was really happening. I should have known that I was far too green and the personalities involved in the making of *Lazarus* were far too unstable to ever see the film through to completion, but at the time I was thinking with my heart and not my head. The next time out, I vowed I'd be sure that I had a venture that appeared viable from the outset, even if it meant demanding the answers to uncomfortable questions up front.

Before I finally committed to going ahead with our plans for *Natural Born Killers,* I wanted to hear from someone who could vouch for Rand's ability to handle the job of directing. And the most logical person to ask was Quentin. Since our lunch meeting at Hampton's, Quentin and I had become occasional phone pals; not really to discuss anything specific, just because we enjoyed talking to each other. I'd recommend books to him; he'd turn me on to the steady diet of Chinese action films and obscure '50s B movies he'd lived on during his days at Video Archives. So one day, I brought up the subject of Rand.

"Yeah, you know, it's kind of odd that you've been speaking to Rand about *NBK*, and we've never talked about it," said Quentin.

"That's mostly because I haven't decided if I want to be involved yet. It's going to take an awful lot of money and time, and I don't really know Rand well enough to tell if he can handle it. Do think he can?"

"Yeah, I do."

"I mean seriously—you wrote the script, and you've worked with him for years. He was acting as a producer before, and he hasn't ever really directed anything. Do you think he'd do justice to the material? Is this something you want to see happen?"

"That's why I let him have the script," said Quentin. "I think Rand will do a great job."

Well, he knew the guy a lot better than I did. *NBK* was his baby, and if he thought that Rand had the chops to make a go of it, I trusted his judgment better than I did my own.

So, based on Quentin's assurances, Don began to get into the legal aspects of the agreement. We had Karl look at the contract Quentin and Rand had drawn up between them.

"It's valid," said Karl, "but it isn't anything I'd want to test in court, since neither of them had legal representation when they signed it. I'd be a lot more comfortable if they could draw up a more comprehensive, binding agreement."

Rand called Quentin, who agreed to execute a more formal contract. It was great that he was letting Rand have an option on the material for free—it allowed us to put the money we would have otherwise had to pay for the script into a short film that could demonstrate Rand's ability to direct. Meantime, Don began negotiating a deal with Rand between him and us that would make him comfortable. Since Rand didn't have the money to pay an attorney, we paid his attorney's fees too, in addition to our own. All day every day for weeks, Rand was in my apartment niggling over every detail of the contract. He wanted every single contingency that he could possibly conjure up covered. I knew most of what he was obsessing over was bullshit; but if it made him feel good, it certainly wasn't hurting anything. Don was indefatigable. He talked all day and into the evening with Rand until he was happy with the terms. Since the clock was running out on Rand's original agreement with Quentin, we had to start prepping for production once Rand's deal with us was completed and we'd signed all of the contracts, but prior to Quentin's and Rand's agreement being redrafted.

I was thrilled beyond belief the day we finally hauled all our junk out of my apartment and set up digs in a crappy, dilapidated little office in the shade of the Culver City studios. This despite the fact that we were now spending money on rent, phones, gas and electric, supplies, office furniture, and production software. (Well, okay, we didn't pay for the production software—it just turned up mysteriously in our office one day, a present from The Alien. I simply refused to think about the time it had probably spent down his pants.) Down the hall, Wes Craven was editing *The People Under the Stairs*; across the way, Roman Coppola was directing some cheap Cassian Elwes straight-to-video venture. It had the atmosphere of a giant production dormitory, sans the beer busts and the panty raids.

My first job was to sit Rand down for a meeting on the section of the film we were going to shoot, and go through it scene by scene so I could create a budget and a schedule. Until you know how a director wants to shoot something, you don't know what you're going to need, how long it's going to take, or how much it's going to cost.

Knowing that Rand had probably never done this before, I tried to lead him through it.

"So in the first scene, how do you want to shoot it?" I asked.

"What do you mean?"

"Well, do you want the camera to be handheld, on a dolly, or a tripod? Is it a wide shot, where we have to clear and dress the whole area, or is it a series of close-ups?"

Rand thought about it for a moment, staring at the ceiling in professorial meditation. "I'd like to leave myself open, so I have all those choices once I get there."

"Well gee, that's great, Rand, but we don't have the money to have all that stuff there every day, so you've got to decide some of these things up front."

Rand scribbled down a note on his pad. "I'll have to think about it. Next question."

"Okay, well, is it something you think is going to need a lot of coverage, or is it just going to be a quick master? How many setups do you anticipate?"

"Oh, I don't want to decide that until I'm on the set."

"Well, I need to know if you think it's one setup or twenty-five, so I can schedule time," I said. "This scene could be shot in two hours or two days. If you don't make a choice now, you'll be limited in what you can do by the amount of time I schedule."

Rand scribbled on his pad again. "I'll have to get back to you on that. Next."

On and on like this for three hours, I tried to educate him about the technicalities of production. This was the guy who called himself a producer and had thought about every detail of the shoot for the past two years? This exercise was not inspiring confidence. People who were unprepared, who wanted to wait for the mood to strike them on the set for such decisions, often did so because they had no vision. On the set they'd be overcome by indecision—or worse yet, make decisions just to make them, without any sense of artistic coherence. They were low-budget horrors because they weren't imaginative enough to get around their limited resources and time in order to deliver anything that was even a little bit above the ordinary.

We were also troubled because it seemed to be damned near impossible to get a crew to work with Rand. Whenever we brought in our regular crew-member friends to meet with him, they always said something along the lines of: "I don't get the feeling the guy could direct traffic, let alone a movie." Around the office, evidence was mounting that this was, in fact, true. He wanted to spend his days calling all his friends, telling them he was now a real director; Don and I were left to answer the telephone and try to pull the damned thing together while Rand obsessed about having *NBK* crew hats made up. We had managed to get a casting director to work with us—a friend of Rand's named Russ Gray—but even he was pulling his hair out; Rand would schedule endless casting sessions, spend an eternity auditioning people who were clearly wrong for the role, back up the schedule by hours, then take off for a baseball game, leaving Russ to deal with a bunch of angry actors and their agents.

"I'm having a lot of trouble here," Russ finally told us. "I believe in you guys. I believe in the script. But the way Rand is handling this is starting to make me look unprofessional."

Meanwhile, Don had the unenviable task of trying to negotiate a revised agreement with Carlos Goodman, Quentin's new attorney. Rand's agreement with Quentin was known as an option. When someone writes something, be it a screenplay, a book, or a laundry list, under U.S. law it's considered automatically copyrighted by that person. The copyright owner (in this case, Quentin) controls whatever happens to it. He can sell it outright, he can license it, he can paper his bathroom with it if he wants to. And if someone wants the right to make it as a film (in this case, us), the copyright owner is probably going to want to be paid.

If a movie gets made for $5 million, for example, the screenwriter is going to want a good chunk of that. The trouble is that once a screenplay's been written, somebody has to go out and try to find that $5 million before they can pay the screenwriter the $250,000 or so for having written the blueprint for the movie in the first place. And that person is usually a producer. Rarely does someone want to plunk down that kind of cash for a screenplay that nobody might ever want to shoot, and there's no way to test out a script's viability until you put it out on the open market.

On the other hand, you don't want to spend a lot of time pimping a script you don't own, only to have someone come in and sweep it out from underneath you. Thus the option was born. For a much smaller fee—for example, $10,000, in this hypothetical budget range—the producer gets the exclusive right to shop the script for a period of time (say one year) and then pay the writer $250,000 in order to purchase the whole thing out-right. Hopefully, the producer will be able to set up the project and get a studio or a financing company to pay for the cost of producing the film. If not, at the end of the year, everyone takes their marbles and goes home. The writer gets his rights back, and he's free to do what he wants with it once again.

Often, these agreements are never memorialized on paper, and things run on verbal agreements and handshakes. But Quentin was getting hot—Tony Scott had announced recently that he would direct *True Romance*, and it looked like *Reservoir Dogs* was indeed going to get made. It didn't take volumes of common sense to realize that when a guy was getting a buzz behind him, you'd better get your agreements on paper, or your deals can go south real fast. While I liked Quentin as a friend and respected him as a writer, his relationship with Rand was shakier than I felt comfortable with. Quentin always said good things about Rand, but Rand was consistently bitter about Quentin's success. "He's jealous of me," Rand would say. "He thought he was the only one who was getting his break, and now he sees me doing well, he's jealous." Quentin and Rand came from a tight-knit bunch of friends; if I were Quentin and I heard this kind of shit coming back from a guy I'd quite generously just given a script to, I think I'd be pissed off and try to find a way out of it—which wouldn't be difficult to do, given the fly-by-night contract he'd executed with Rand in the first place.

When Don finally managed to get Carlos Goodman on the phone, Carlos had a news flash for him: whereas before, Quentin was willing to give Rand a free option if he could get it together to produce the ten-minute short, now he wanted a $10,000 option fee.

I fucking *flipped* when I heard that. I didn't know if this new development was a result of the stuff Quentin had been hearing on the streets regarding Rand's attitude, but whatever the reason, it spelled disaster for us. "You mean we've spent all this money, gone to all this trouble, gone merrily along based on everyone's verbal promises, and now we have to chase it with ten grand if we want to go forward?"

"Looks that way," said Don.

Rand was livid. He accused Quentin of betraying his friendship and the promise he'd made when they were "just a bunch of guys" trying to make a film. He held fast to the "Quentin is jealous" line of reasoning, saying, "Quentin is trying to stop me because he can't stand the competition."

Whether or not this was true, it didn't matter to us—we were now backed into a corner. We had to come up with even more cash if we wanted to salvage this thing. I grabbed Don by his designer lapels and pulled him outside to walk around the block so we could have some privacy while we discussed matters.

"What are we going to do?" I said. "We can't afford to pay that kind of money and finance the short, too. We were supposed to finance the short *instead* of paying an option fee. This is pretty shitty."

"I know." Despite his hyperbolic personality, Don is capable of getting extremely pragmatic when faced with the inevitable. "But Carlos is maintaining that the original agreement isn't valid, that when Quentin entered into it with Rand, he was a nobody, and his work wasn't worth anything. Now it is, and he wants to be compensated for it."

"But we got into all of this expense—the office, the production, everything—because he agreed to give us the option for free. We can't afford to let him go back on his word."

"I think we've got to pay it," said Don. "If we stand on principle, we'll lose it. Paying the option fee is going to be cheaper than filing a lawsuit. It doesn't really matter who's right in the situation—it's what you can get away with. If Quentin tried to contest the original agreement, despite everything he's said, we'll wind up having done all this for nothing."

His pragmatism only irritated me at the moment. But he was right. "Okay," I said finally. "But if we're going to pay all the money we borrowed for an option fee, I don't want to be contractually obligated to shoot the short as well. If we pay for the option, we assume it, with the same caveats. If we can't sell Rand as a director, we try and cover our losses by setting it up with an established director."

"Well, who knows?" said Don. "Quentin's getting some heat—maybe on the basis of that, someone will give Rand his shot without having seen any footage he's directed."

We went back to the office and told Rand what we'd decided: We'd pop for the ten grand for the option, but the idea of shooting the short would have to be nixed. We weren't Rockefellers, and we couldn't afford to do both. He stormed around the office for a while, burning with indignation that Quentin was trying to sabotage him, but he acquiesced to the new terms. "Actually, I think if we go straight to production companies with *NBK*, they'll want to finance the whole movie," he said. "The script is very good, and I think they'll be impressed with my passion and my vision for the movie."

And so we began sending the script out to studios and production companies, hoping that the recent interest in Quentin would incite them to read *NBK*. It did. And nearly every person we sent it to not only loathed it, but was completely offended by it. They all fired off angry rejection letters to us for having made them read it in the first place. Even though the buzz on *Reservoir Dogs*, which had just finished shooting, was great, nothing was going to get the studio people over the hump of the *NBK* story: a romance between two serial killers. At that time, nobody wanted to take a chance on releasing a violent, edgy, dark comedy that wouldn't fit neatly into anyone's distribution slate, especially if it was going to be helmed by an untried director. Most studio executives tend to be yuppies with Range Rovers and mortgages. While their first agenda is to make movies that make money, their second is to make stuff they like. *NBK* wasn't a guaranteed moneymaker in anyone's estimation; and while I was gratified on a personal level that most of these people found the subject matter reprehensible, it made me nervous on a business level. A couple of smaller companies were intrigued with the script and Quentin's style; but despite the "passion and vision" that Rand displayed when we met with them, they all turned us down.

Shortly thereafter, I got a call from a woman named Cathryn Jaymes, who was Quentin's manager. She'd heard good things about us from Quentin, and in addition to representing him, she also handled several actors she wanted to see cast in *NBK*. She asked me if I'd like to get together and meet for drinks, and I said yes.

"She's crazy," said Rand. When he heard about the rendezvous we'd planned, he tripped. "She just wants to find a way to latch on to the project. I don't trust her."

Well, I wasn't exactly taking my cues about whom to like and dislike from Rand Vossler—my instincts had served me quite well up until this time, and I got the feeling that Cathryn was holding something back on the phone, something she wanted to say that she only felt comfortable divulging in person. Despite his admonitions to the contrary, I agreed to meet with her and dragged Don along.

Cathryn actually turned out to be quite charming and lovely. She had been Quentin's manager for seven years now. She told us that he'd started out wanting to be an actor and had suffered through many years of unsuccessful, humiliating auditions before finally landing his big role as an Elvis impersonator on *The Golden Girls*. (Anyone who's ever seen Quentin's acting efforts will have no trouble believing that it was hardly something to bank a career on.) "He started writing and directing so he could cast himself in his screenplays," she told us. In fact, his first writing effort—a script called *My Best Friend's Birthday*—was something he'd written with Craig Hamann, another of her clients, and the two had actually shot it together on 16mm for no money. It was something they'd never finished, but it gave Quentin his first taste of the writing/directing experience. Cathryn was sort of unofficial den mother to a whole host of Hollywood hopefuls, including our director friend Jeff Burr; C. Courtney Joyner, the writer/director of *Trancers 3D*, Mark DaCoscos, a martial-arts star; and Linnea Quigley, "The Queen of Scream," just to name few. She had a big heart, and she supported Quentin in his acting career way past any level that common sense would have dictated, feeding him and paying his expenses when he couldn't come up with the cash. Needless to say, given his meager thespian abilities, there was no hope on the horizon of anything coming in to compensate her for her outlays.

After everyone had a couple of drinks under their belts, Cathryn's tongue loosened up and she got down to what I think she really wanted to say all along. "I have to tell you something," she said. "Quentin doesn't really want *Natural Born Killers* to be made. He doesn't think Rand can handle the job."

Don was already festering with some resentment against Cathryn that he'd borrowed from Rand. Immediately, his whole frame went rigid and he took on the posture of an angry dog. "That can't *possibly* be true," he said. "You can't possibly know that. It doesn't make any sense. You're just—"

"DON! Shut up, I want to hear this," I said, shooting him an I'm-dead-fucking-serious look that stunned him into a rare moment of silence.

"The only reason Quentin ever gave Rand that original agreement was because he didn't think Rand could get it together to shoot a short on his own," Cathryn went on. "At least then he could say that he tried to help Rand out. He was just trying to be a good friend. Then, when you two came along, and it looked like you had the intelligence and resources to help Rand get something made, Quentin decided to ask for option money, hoping that you wouldn't be able to come up with it. But you did, and now he has to go through on the deal; but he doesn't want Rand directing *NBK*."

Great. I'd been talking to this guy, I'd trusted him, we'd gone on the line based on his word, spent money, and now it turns out he thinks Rand's a goof.

Don fumed uncontrollably and leaped to Rand's defense. He thought of Rand as a friend and didn't like to hear anyone say anything bad about him. "Rand and Quentin have worked together and been friends for years," he said. "Quentin wouldn't just sell him out like that. I just don't buy it. It just doesn't make any sense."

"Look, Quentin just wants to be a good guy. He wants to support Rand," Cathryn said. "But I've known Rand for years, too, and I can tell you he never would have gotten anything off the ground if you two hadn't come along to help him."

Well, actually, if that was indeed what was happening, Quentin wasn't trying to be a good guy—he was just trying to look like one. I could understand why he didn't want to let Rand know he didn't have any faith in him, but I was more than a little piqued with him for encouraging us to go on the line while being something less than forthright in the situation.

Don stormed off to the bathroom in a disbelieving huff. Once his open hostility was removed from the table, Cathryn began to speak a bit more confidentially and openly. "You know, Jane, I really think you should get together with Quentin yourself," she said. "I think there are some things you need to talk with him about. He's under a lot of pressure these days, and I don't think he knows how to handle it. You should meet with him alone—he likes you. He doesn't trust Don."

Russ Gray had recently informed me that the William Morris Agency was no longer willing to send its actors out to audition for *NBK*. It didn't make any sense at the time, because they represented Quentin, but now it was all starting to fall into place. "Is Quentin having his agents at William

Morris go around telling all these companies that he doesn't want *Natural Born Killers* made with Rand directing?"

Silence. "If that were true, it would be something I couldn't tell you," she said. "You'd better ask Quentin yourself."

I told her I would and thanked her for her honesty, then swept Don out the door before he could act on any of the violent retributional fantasies I could see brewing behind his beady little eyes.

A nervous, angry sweat was lashing off Don as he piled into the car. "I just don't buy it," he said. "It just doesn't make any sense." He kept repeating this like an angry mantra as he interrogated me on the drive home, hoping to somehow prove that if something in the equation didn't fit, he could force it not to be true. I wished it didn't all make perfect sense to me, but it did. I reminded Don about our first production meeting, where Rand had flopped around like a beached trout when pressed for answers to questions he simply did not understand. Despite my repeated requests, he'd never gotten back to me with those answers he promised. If Quentin was running around telling people he thought Rand was a no-talent bozo, no wonder nobody was stepping up to let him direct.

"Oh this is just *hot*," I said. "We're caught in the middle of a personal battle between Rand and Quentin. Rand thinks Quentin's an asshole, Quentin thinks Rand is an idiot, and between all our preproduction expenses, our legal fees, and the option, we're out about thirty grand. We're doomed."

"You don't know that," Don said. "Cathryn Jaymes could just be full of shit. Maybe it's just like Rand said—maybe she's just someone who likes to stir up trouble."

Well there was only one real way to find out the truth in the situation.

"Guess I better call Quentin," I said.

I arranged to meet with Quentin for drinks not long thereafter at the old Gorky's, a restaurant and brewery just off Hollywood Boulevard.

He was in a good mood. He was editing *Reservoir Dogs* and was really pleased about the way the whole thing was going. After months of negotiations, with contracts going back and forth between lawyers for "i" dottings and "t" crossings, we'd finally paid him the option money for *NBK*, and he'd gone out and bought a '64 Chevy Malibu Supersport convertible with the money. (He'd ultimately use the car in *Pulp Fiction*; it was the one that John Travolta drives onto Eric Stoltz's lawn when Uma Thurman is OD'ing.)

"Quentin, I need you to be honest with me," I said. "We really respect your script and the work you've done, and our agreement is as much with you as it is with Rand—and for my part, probably a lot more. I know Rand's your friend and you two go way back, but I think I'm getting caught in the middle of something I don't understand, and you need to clear it up for me. Do you *really* want Rand to direct *NBK*, or not?"

Quentin gave a knowing inner smile, and was quiet for the first time since I'd known him. "When Cathryn told me about all the trouble you've been having with Rand, I immediately thought, 'Rand's being Rand again.' "

Great. So Rand was in over his head, and it was no surprise to anybody but me. Quentin went on to verify that, just as Cathryn had said, he gave Rand a free option only because he was abandoning the project and he felt badly about leaving Rand on his own. Since Rand had been trying to produce the script with astonishing lack of success for the previous two years, Quentin never thought he'd be able to get it together to produce a ten-minute short. And if Rand hadn't met us, Quentin maintained, he never would have. No, he didn't want Rand to direct his work—he'd rather see someone else at the helm. But it was something he never wanted to say to Rand, since he still considered him a friend.

"Do you want to direct it, Quentin?"

He thought about it for a minute. "I don't think so. It's kind of like an old girlfriend you don't want to go back to, you know? I feel like I've already directed it in my head so many times, I'm done with it."

Although I felt pretty duped, I didn't accuse Quentin of trying to work against our efforts. I didn't say that our failure to set the picture up with Rand directing was as much due to his duplicity as it was Rand's limitations, although I was certainly thinking it. There was no way to break a first-time director if the guy who wrote the script was running around telling people he couldn't handle it.

I took a deep breath and prepared to launch the bomb that I hadn't even told Don about yet. "Quentin, we've fulfilled all our contractual obligations to Rand," I said. "We busted our asses to put the script out there, and we've been turned down by everyone we submitted it to, and a few we haven't. There's just no way anyone is going to give Rand his shot on this one. We've got a lot of money tied up in this, and we agreed that if nobody would buy Rand as a director, he would have to step down and let us try to set it up with someone else. If that happened, how would you feel?"

"I'd understand," he said. "In fact, I'd be a whole lot more comfortable with someone else directing. I'd just like to stay involved, you know, and have some say-so over who came on board."

I breathed a horrendous sigh of relief. Now it seemed like there was actually some glimmer of hope on the horizon.

"We'd love to have you involved in the project to make sure that whatever happens to the script is in line with your vision for it." That was sincere. I genuinely liked Quentin, and despite my intermittent desire to panel him for getting me into this mess, I thought working with him could be fun. He agreed to be an executive producer on the project.

So we dropped the topic of business, drank more beers, and just had a lot of fun before calling it a night. Quentin walked me to my car and gave me a big hug in the parking lot; I think he understood I was in the middle of a big mess and was just trying to swim my way out of it. I also think he knew he inadvertently had created a lot of this and felt a bit bad about it, and was grateful that I wasn't calling him on it.

But as I got into my car, I knew the worst was yet to come. I had vague hopes that the big bomb would suddenly drop on Los Angeles, that I'd see the Four Horsemen of the Apocalypse riding past the Fatburger on Wilshire Boulevard on my way home. Because the thought of Armageddon finally arriving was far preferable to making the phone call I knew I'd have to make when I got there. What would happen when I told Don Murphy I thought we had to say *arrivederci* to his friend Rand?

Chapter 3

Keep Your Eyes Closed and Your Hands on Your Wallet

I doubt if Al Unser's fastest lap time at Indy could best the speed with which Don Murphy raced over to my house that night. It quite frankly astonished me that the four-cylinder motor of a VW Rabbit could rev that high without the pistons seizing up and cracking the engine block.

"This is all because you don't like Rand," said Don, storming into my apartment. With his face burning bright red and the hair of his neck standing straight on end, he looked like a giant, enraged porcupine.

"I'll admit it, I can barely stand him," I said. "I hate the way he leaves me to answer his phones and play secretary while he runs around getting silly hats made, and I think his self-absorption is annoying and his egotism completely unwarranted."

"So now we can only work with people you like? Is that it? If that's true, we're working off an awfully short list of people," said Don. "I don't know if it's come to your attention yet, but you like almost nobody."

"My dislike of Rand as a human being has nothing to do with this," I snapped. "If you could only work with people you like in Hollywood, you'd be working alone. But it's a lot easier to put up with the personally untenable if people are talented, and Rand is not."

"You don't know that," said Don.

"Look at the facts, Don," I said. "Everyone we've introduced him to say that they'd rather contract tuberculosis than work with the guy; not only do they think that *he* thinks he knows more than he does, they think he's arrogant in his ignorance. And you can count me as a member of that group."

"This is all Cathryn Jaymes's doing—I get it. She's stirred up this whole thing because she has some personal grudge against Rand. And you just don't see it."

"Well, how about Quentin? You can't deny that he's Rand's friend, and even *he* wants Rand off the project."

"Well, maybe it's just like Rand says, and Quentin's jealous." He looked at the wanton disbelief brewing in my eyes, and realized he'd just warped into the galaxy of the completely ludicrous. "Okay, scratch that one. But I still don't see any reason why Rand couldn't do a great job directing *NBK*."

"Yeah, well, you're also the guy who still believes in Santa Claus, the Easter Bunny and the Great Pumpkin. You can't make something true just because you want it to be."

We went on and on like this, around and around for hours into the night. Don finally had to face the fact that after my conversation with Quentin, I was now immovable on the subject. "We've fulfilled every promise we've ever made to the guy, contractually and otherwise," I said. "I know you like him. I know you think of him as a friend. But we just can't chase this project with more money we don't have. It's time to cut our losses."

Don slumped into my sofa like a giant bag of wet sand. Don's not stupid; I knew that the same suspicions had been plaguing him for a long time. All kinds of bills were now coming in that we couldn't pay, and there was no relief in sight. He kept hoping that everything would be all right in the end if he pretended that the problems would just go away. But now everything came bubbling up to the surface, and he was hating it.

"We can't just fire him," said Don. "He's the one who brought us the project."

"Well, that's a really generous sentiment, Don, but Rand's not the one who's into the project for thirty large. If he wants to pay us back all that money, he can have *NBK* back and do whatever he wants with it. But as it is, he's caught us up in a bunch of stuff he's either too unrealistic or too stupid to understand, and if he can't come to terms with that, then we're going to have to ask him to step aside."

Don and I fought like maniacs over the whole thing for days, during which time we talked with some people we trusted about whether *NBK* would be a viable project even without Rand. Nobody was very reassuring on that front, but Don finally had to accept my logic in the situation. I think he knew that if he didn't, he'd have to face the end of our partnership, because there was no way I was going to continue to chase rainbows with Rand on this thing anymore.

It's easy to look back now and say we were a bunch of greedy motherfuckers who simply wanted to fire Rand and get our hands on a Quentin Tarantino script and sell it for tons of money, but this conveniently overlooks the fact that at the time *it wasn't worth anything. Reservoir Dogs* wasn't even finished yet; Quentin Tarantino wasn't even Quentin Tarantino. Even people who were excited about *True Romance* thought *NBK* was loathsome. We still believed in the script (it would have been damned near impossible to do all of this if we didn't), but mostly we were looking for a feasible scenario where we wouldn't lose our shirts. There were hardly visions of big dollar signs in our eyes.

"Okay," Don finally said to me in defeat. I could see that his disappointment in the situation was bitter, and I knew that telling Rand what we had decided was going to hurt him more than anyone else. "But you've got to promise me that if we ask him to step aside as director, that we take him on as a full producing partner. We don't fire him; we let him share equally in any credit and money that we get."

Well, that wasn't part of our agreement with Rand; I certainly didn't think he deserved it. I still felt like he was a moron who had dug his own grave. (Don's right; I *do* tend to be on the uncharitable side when it comes to what I perceive as overt and unbridled stupidity.) But since it helped Don to feel better, I yielded.

Because of Don's friendship with Rand, I realized it was going to be a tough thing for him to face the guy with our decision, so I told him I'd tell him myself.

"No, we're partners," he said. "Whatever we do, we do together."

We walked around the block a few times to steel ourselves, because stuff like this isn't easy to do, even when you're a cast-iron bitch as I've been accused of being on occasion. We finally came back to the office and told Rand we wanted to talk with him.

"Look, Rand, we really like you," Don began, as gently as possible. "We want you to know this isn't personal. But as a company, Jane and I just can't afford to go on like this. Nobody is stepping up to the plate to make this film with you as a director, despite the fact that we've been trying as hard as we can for months. We want to ask you to consider stepping aside as director and come on board as a producer with us. . . ."

Well, Don got no further. Rand started to cry and went running out of the office. Don was really upset. He knew how much Rand had invested in the project emotionally, and that he'd just hurt his friend. But I stopped feeling bad real fast after this. As far as I was concerned, this was the response of a complete pussy. If Rand had really wanted to direct the thing, if he'd stuck around to plead his case convincingly and offered to go on the line with us financially in order to keep pursuing the project with him directing, I probably would've caved, especially since Don was on his side to begin with. But he didn't. To my mind, Rand had totally validated my concerns that he didn't have the bottle to direct a movie. This was business, I wasn't his mommy, and I wasn't responsible for paying to make his dreams come true.

Don called Rand for days, trying to get him to come back and work with us—at least discuss things—but Rand wouldn't even come to the phone. Don felt terrible, but I barely paid attention to his efforts, since I was concerned with other things. The time was running out on our option, we'd already run out of money, and we had to get this thing off the ground real soon, or it would all have been for naught. My first job was to call Quentin and tell him what had happened. He was happy that the whole thing had finally gone down.

"I have some ideas about other directors," he said. "In fact, my agents will probably be calling you real soon."

"Real soon" was a modest understatement. Almost instantly, the phone was ringing—it was Mike Simpson, Quentin's agent. As far as the Morris Agency was concerned, they now owned Quentin, and if there was a Tarantino project going out on the open market, and they were no longer under orders from Quentin to block it, they wanted to be the ones handling it.

They invited us down to their Beverly Hills offices for an "agency meeting," as they referred to it, although "dog-and-pony show" would've been a more accurate description. As head of the motion-picture division of the agency, Simpson sat at the head of the conference table and opened the proceedings. He was a native Texan, and compared with the huckster intensity of most other agents, he came off as almost soft-spoken. It was easy to see how writers and directors could be impressed with the sincerity and intelligence with which he came across; he didn't seem like the kind of guy who would auction you off like a used car. But I couldn't stop focusing on his unruly hair, which was cut in a bowl shape around his face, with errant tufts sticking up on all sides.

Also in attendance at the meeting were Beth Swofford, another agent from the literary side, who was responsible for handling Quentin's day-to-day business, and Glen Rigberg, an agent from the talent department who showed up to add their hosannas to the chorus. (The motion-picture divisions of most agencies are divided between "literary," meaning those who represented writers and, for some mysterious reason, directors and producers, and "talent," meaning actors. The two are supposed to work in tandem with each other, but frequently they're at each others' throats.)

"We just want you to know how excited we are about representing you on *Natural Born Killers*," Simpson said. "Quentin is one of our most valuable clients, and we think it's a great project. We don't think we'll have any problem setting it up."

Then almost immediately, he was out the door, having to attend to "pressing business." The rest of the meeting was presided over by Beth Swofford, who ran down a list of directors they thought would be interested in the project. Then Rigberg rattled off all the actors they wanted to show the script to. We sat there enthusiastically, glad at least that these people were no longer working against us.

When the meeting was over, we all stood up and shook hands. "So, we'll have the Business Affairs people call you and draw up the paperwork?" they said.

"Well, we've got to talk between ourselves first," Don said. "We're considering other options, so we'll let you know what we decide."

They looked like we'd just slapped them in the face with a big, wet fish—they'd gone to all this effort, put on this elaborate show, thrown out all these celebrity names, and we weren't going to sign the thing over to them on the spot? Well, uh, no.

We were anxious about making a move too hastily; not only because we were nervous about the people who only weeks before had been working against us, but also because we'd recently been contacted by another USC alumnus who had read the script and was interested in directing it. Albert Magnoli had been a real star at USC and had gone on to direct *Purple Rain*, a remarkably successful first film. He had then made the mistake of following it up by directing Olympic gymnast Mitch Gaylord in the perfectly diabolical *American Anthem,* and had been in movie jail ever since. (The term "movie jail," coined by Don, referred to people who'd made bad career choices and directed horrendous flops. The mere mention of their names in production meetings was guaranteed to make studio executives shudder visibly. Some people eventually get out of movie jail, like David Fincher or Terry Gilliam, and go on to successful careers. Others, like Michael Cimino, are occasionally let out on probation, but go back in quickly. Then there are some, like Elaine May, who are in for life.) Magnoli was making a bid to get out of movie jail. He liked the script and was willing to shoot it in the $2 million range, a level at which, practically speaking, we thought someone might be willing to take the risk of making it.

Since we'd agreed not to take on a director who didn't meet with Quentin's approval, we set up a meeting between the four of us at the Hamburger Hamlet on Hollywood Boulevard. Quentin and Magnoli liked each other. At one point during the meal, however, Quentin hit Albert with a bombshell.

"You know, when I first wrote the character of Wayne Gayle, he was supposed to be sort of a scumbag," said Quentin. "But as he developed, he turned into more of a guy like me—someone who just wanted to go out with a camera and shoot things, more of an investigative journalist. And I've been thinking—I'd like to play Wayne myself."

Magnoli's synapses stopped firing for a couple of seconds as he struggled to find an appropriate response. To his credit, he didn't say yes on the spot just to get the gig; he was extremely diplomatic. "I'd be open to it," he said, "but it's not a decision I'd feel free to make until things got a bit further down the line."

After Albert left, Quentin stuck around to drink a few more beers with us and talk things over. And then he hit us with another idea.

"I've been thinking that before I go out and do another full feature, I'd maybe like to shoot a short film," he said. "How would you guys feel if I wanted to shoot the *American Maniacs* segment from *NBK* as a short?"

Don and I looked at each other a bit puzzled. We didn't know how such an act would effect another filmmaker's desire to do the film, or how we'd even work such a thing. But if it was what Quentin wanted to do, we supposed we'd try to make it work.

"Sure," we said.

Meanwhile, since we now had Quentin's blessing on the Magnoli front, Albert set up a meeting for us to come down and meet with his new agents, Triad Artists. They were the number-four agency in town, behind CAA, ICM, and William Morris, but they'd been climbing up Morris's shorts quickly and challenging them enthusiastically for the number-three spot. We were escorted into the conference room on the fourteenth floor of their Century City offices. This time the meeting was presided over by their big gun, Arnold Rifkin, who was Bruce Willis's agent. It was the same parade of agents, all sitting around nodding in agreement every time Rifkin opened his mouth. This was starting to look familiar.

"Albert is a very important client of the agency," said Rifkin. "And we want you to know that if you sign over exclusive representation of the project to us, we think we'll have no trouble in setting it up."

The phone in the conference room rang, and Arnold answered it. "You'll have to excuse me," he said. "I've got to run — I have some very pressing business."

But before he could leave, this time Don found his voice. "So before you go, I just want to know — if we signed the project over to you, where would you take it?"

Arnold looked a bit stunned. He thought his appearance at this meeting was only going to be preliminary and pro forma; he had no idea he was going to have to defend this proposal to a couple of nobodies. Someone jammed a card into his hands hastily, and he ran down a list of companies that he assured us would be interested in making *NBK*.

"With all due respect," said Don, "we've submitted the project to half of those companies, and they all turned us down. The other half have run out of money and aren't even making pictures anymore."

Arnold pressed his hands together like a man summoning ultimate patience. "We can approach these people on a much higher level than you can. And I happen to know that they would all be enthusiastic about making this movie, especially with someone as talented as Albert attached to direct."

I was sweating like mad. At that moment, Arnold Rifkin looked like nothing so much as a human razor blade. I wanted out of the room in a serious way. I couldn't believe Don's nerve.

And I couldn't believe my *ears* when he kept going. "Well, if that's true, then why don't you attach an actor to the project that they can't say no to? Why don't you give us one of your clients like Bruce Willis or Brad Pitt?"

If Arnold could have thrown Don out the window and hurled him fourteen floors onto the street at that moment, I think he would have. He launched into a "we're professionals—you'll just have to trust us" speech, before excusing himself from the meeting politely. We could see the junior agents lined up at the table rolling their eyes in that "who do they think they are?" kind of way before we made our own "we'll have to think about it" speech, then bolted from the room.

I was desperately glad to get out of there. "Jesus, Murphy, I thought Rifkin was going to kill you," I said. "You showed some pretty big *cojones.*"

"I don't know, I kind of liked the guy," said Don. "If I was going to have an agent, I think I'd like to have Arnold Rifkin representing me—someone who seems capable of homicide could only be a good thing in the midst of a negotiation."

"So, what do you think? Should we go with them?" I asked.

"I don't know about this whole 'agency' thing," he said. "Every time we walk in, they tell us about all these wonderful directors they've got that they'll give the script to, but most of them are already committed to other projects, and they wouldn't have the slightest interest in ours, anyway. Then they tell you about the directors from other agencies they'd like to try and steal by baiting them with your script, all the actors they've got that they could attach to your project but won't, and all the people they don't represent but have 'great relationships' with that they could get it to. 'Oh, I hear De Niro's looking for something just like this.' It all seems like an exercise in how much bullshit they can throw at you before you run screaming from the room. I mean, we sign over the script to them, nothing happens, our option runs out, what do they care? Meanwhile, we've lost everything."

Don was right. Even though it was tempting to turn over our fate to the big guys and comfort ourselves with the feeling that we weren't a couple of zeros struggling on our own anymore, it was awfully risky.

"Okay, but before we give them an emphatic no, can we at least call around and see if Albert Magnoli as a director means anything?"

We did. We found out that the only thing people were less interested in than a script about a couple of serial killers was a script about a couple of

serial killers directed by Albert Magnoli. One company actually was interested in making the film with him. Brad Krevoy and Steve Stabler's Motion Picture Corporation of America, the guys who went on to make
Dumb and Dumber. But they wanted extensive rewrites and an ending in
which Mickey and Mallory die. Quentin nixed the whole idea, and we
turned them down. They ran around saying we were arrogant. Right.
Because we were nobodies and we didn't line up to hand over the script.
We were starting to sense a pattern here. . . .

It was all getting way, way too crazy. Now we had the Morris agency,
Triad, Albert Magnoli, and MPCA all pissed off at us because we weren't
doing what they wanted us to. Don was still feeling bad about Rand, and
Quentin was calling me constantly, suggesting the name of yet another
director whose work I'd never seen, sending me off to the video store to
watch truckloads of obscure efforts just to be able to have a conversation
with him. Yes, I liked *The Big Easy*; yes, I liked Jim McBride; yes, I'd seen
Breathless, but no, I'd missed *Glen and Randa*. . . . Don, I'm sure Rand
will get over it. . . . No, they can't have the script. . . .

Christ, could I just have something that *looked* like a vacation?

It was now January 1992, and the Hollywood community was flocking
en masse as they did every year to the slopes of Park City, Utah, in order to
prey on the young, the fresh, and the talented at the annual Sundance
International Film Festival, the self-proclaimed showcase for American
independent film. Ordinarily, I would have had neither the time, the
money, nor the inclination to attend, but this year was special. The big
film of the festival—the one everyone was rabid to see—was Quentin
Tarantino's *Reservoir Dogs*.

I came to Sundance with Cathryn Jaymes, Quentin's manager. Since
we were still struggling to mount production of the expensive potential
white elephant *NBK*, and as nobody had yet seen *Reservoir Dogs*, how it
played at Sundance was going to be very critical to our future. Since our
initial meeting, Cathryn and I had become good friends. I couldn't afford
the $500 for a ticket to the festival, so Cathryn paid it for me. It was an
extremely generous gesture, and for her part I think she didn't want to be
alone there. She hadn't been invited officially by Quentin and came to
Sundance on her own steam. Since William Morris had swept into Quen-

tin's life, they'd done a pretty neat job of excluding her from all his business—this despite her having lobbied long and hard for him to sign with them in the first place. She had to be feeling pretty shut out. We weren't invited to any of the fancy shindigs, which was fine by me, as I have a natural abhorrence for such events that continues to this day. So we managed to have a great time by ourselves, goofing around in the snow, and watching the efforts of guerrilla filmmakers working outside the Hollywood system. It was just what I needed at the moment, because when I arrived at Sundance that year, I was desperately in need of more than simply a good time—I also had a fierce need for some new inspiration.

I'd been working at this producing thing with Don for two years now. And, believe it or not, the whole Quentin/Rand/*NBK* thing was not what I was suffering from most acutely at the moment. Much more troublesome was my deep suspicion that I was simply in the wrong job. It just didn't seem like I had the right sensibilities for Hollywood. The people who were on the buying end of the business, the people who controlled the purse strings and could say yea or nay to a project weren't the sort that I could make understand what I saw in J. G. Ballard novels or Dario Argento films or Spacemen Three records.

Was it me? Was I just such an offbeat wacko that my tastes would never connect with an audience? I'd been trying for a long time to believe that studio executives with their Malibu homes and Jaguars and expense accounts and cell phones were the ones who were out of contact with popular tastes. But funny, they never seemed to agree with that assessment. I didn't know how much longer I could hold out in a business that seemed responsive only to easily marketable, incredibly stupid star-driven vehicles that I didn't have the first clue how to make. I needed to see some sort of sign that there was a revolution coming, or I was probably going to have to begin investigating career possibilities in real estate. Struggling along with no money is glamorous only for so long; once you hit thirty, you begin to look like a bit of a delusional wanker.

But suddenly at Sundance that year, I saw dozens—no, hundreds—of filmmakers who had flipped Hollywood the bird and found ways to make their movies outside the system. And people were loving them. The voices that these filmmakers were bringing to the screen could be outrageously dull and self-important, but they could also be fresh and energetic. Films like Christopher Munch's *The Hours and Times,* Bruce McDonald's *Highway 61,* and Tom Kalin's *Swoon* were willing to tackle the weird, the controversial, the taboo subjects in a radical style that Hollywood would shy away from in horror. It was my first indication that there was definitely a new spirit in the air, a hunger that Hollywood had not been feeding. A new young generation of filmmakers would soon have the skill, the talent, and the vision to step in and capture the public's imagination and leave Hollywood in the lurch if it didn't take notice.

It reminded me of the punk-rock revolution in the late '70s, when the music industry had become incredibly moribund, responsive neither to public tastes nor to new artistic impulses. In their arrogance, the record companies had spent hundreds of millions to acquire disco labels like RSO and Casablanca, only to find out that their artists were played out and their catalogs worthless. People wanted to hear The Clash; they had no more interest in Donna Summer. My personal idol, Malcolm Mc-Claren, had found a way to take them all to the cleaners with the hype he built around The Sex Pistols. Well, I had always wanted to be the Malcolm McClaren of the movie business. And it was starting to look like the time was ripe.

If that was true, then making the kind of movies that Don and I wanted to could soon become feasible in Hollywood in a way that it hadn't since *Five Easy Pieces* and *Easy Rider* had come along; if the industry was, indeed, ready to catch up to popular taste, then we were poised to be able to take advantage of that fact and push forward the kind of wild, edgy, controversial films we wanted to make. But was it really ready to turn? It was an awfully recalcitrant and conservative industry—*Honey, I Shrunk the Kids* was Hollywood's idea of a great film. Watching how all these people responded to *Reservoir Dogs* was going to be a big indicator of just how fast they were willing to change.

Despite all my efforts to stay out of all the industry schmoozing at Sundance, there were a couple of events being held in Quentin's honor that Cathryn felt obliged to show for. One was a soiree being throw by Live Video, the financiers of *Reservoir Dogs.* Cathryn wanted me to come as her guest; when her ticket arrived, however, there wasn't one for me.

Later, we were at the Sundance hospitality suite that served as a hangout for festival goers in between screenings, and a locus for journalists conducting interviews. Cathryn recognized Lawrence Bender, the producer of *Reservoir Dogs*, and dragged me over.

"C'mon, I want you to meet Lawrence," she said.

It was the first and only time I ever met Lawrence Bender. He smiled affably and shook my hand, and when Cathryn informed him that my ticket hadn't arrived, he said it was quite an exclusive party and he didn't know what he could do, but he'd try. Quentin was giving a radio interview over in the corner. Lawrence excused himself, saying he had to go help him, and he left.

"He's such a nice guy, he's so helpful," said Cathryn. "I'm sure he'll get you in."

I was barely listening. I was shaking a little bit, and my stomach had turned inside out. I couldn't tell you why. It had something to do with the color of his skin and the way his gaze sort of receded into some emotional abyss when he smiled or maybe it was the way his lips curled over his teeth when he spoke, but I had the terrifying awareness that I'd just been in the presence of a jackal. I'm sometimes tempted to color my stories for effect, but this time I'm not exaggerating. Maybe it was my religious background coming back to dog me—I didn't know—but I can't remember ever having been struck by that impression in anyone's presence before. There was nothing overtly hostile coming off Lawrence by any means. He'd been perfectly polite. But whatever interior landscape he was gazing across when he seemed to detach from the conversation, whatever city he went home to when he returned to his thoughts, I was sure it was sulfur-strewn and blazing. I had to get out of the room. I needed some air.

My ticket to the party never arrived, so I just decided to turn up with Cathryn, and had no trouble getting in. It was a slightly oily and creepy event in the way those things always are. Lawrence looked a bit startled when he saw me. I couldn't have cared less whether he wanted me there or not, but a vague suspicion was planted in my head at that time: Was this guy threatened by my relationship with Quentin? I had no desire to take over his place in Quentin's life, but producers who owe their careers to their attachment to one director—unlike Don and me, who liked the idea of working with different people on every project—tended to be sneaky and protective of those relationships. He had a lot more proximity to

Quentin than I did, and if he was nervous that Quentin still wanted to shoot the *American Maniacs* short with us, it wouldn't be unusual to try and disrupt our relationship with him.

I wasn't going to worry about it at the time. I was there to accompany Cathryn and maybe say "hi" to Quentin, which I did eventually. He was glad I'd turned up to support him, was heartened by the screening they'd had in Salt Lake City a few days before, but was still nervous about the upcoming screening at the Park City Egyptian on Friday night, which would be the one everyone turned out for. It's tough to be a filmmaker and know that your future is all riding on one night; Live had only about $1.3 million in the picture. They were principally a video distributor, and by the time Sundance came around, they'd sold the domestic theatrical rights to Miramax. But the amount of money and effort that Miramax would put behind that release was largely dependent upon what the Sundance response turned out to be.

The night of the screening came. We got there early, to assure that we got good seating, and found the place packed. Monday night at Mortons has quantumly less schmoozing than was going on that evening. I saw my attorney Karl, who could barely keep his eyes on me when we were talking for looking over my shoulder to see who was walking into the room. (An onerous quality, I know, but it's what I paid Karl for—because he does it, I don't have to.)

The lights went down. The film went up on the screen and, to my mind, it was a pretty good little film. Having read the script, I don't know what I was expecting; the performances were good, save Quentin's (I now knew how I'd come down on the issue of his playing Wayne Gayle), and although I thought the directing was working a bit hard to call attention to itself and was sometimes at odds with the performances, over all I thought it was a remarkably self-assured first directing effort. There was no question that the guy had a career. Hopefully, the word of mouth coming off the screening would be good enough that we could get someone to pay attention to *NBK*.

The cheer from the audience at the end credits was deafening. And when Quentin went up on the stage, it was the first time I ever saw the Quentin that was soon to invade my television set, my living room, my life—that slightly smarmy, falsely modest Uriah Heep character constantly turning verbal cartwheels in an attempt to make people keep looking at him. I thought he was never going to get off the stage.

"What do you think about violence in film?" came a question from the audience.

"I think it's great!" said Quentin. "I think there should be *more* violence in movies!"

Anything he said brought down the house; he could've said "shoehorn" and the agents I was sitting amidst would've crippled themselves laughing. I could only imagine what kind of effect this would have on a guy like Quentin, a geek from the Valley who'd never had much attention for doing much of anything.

Well, time would tell.

When I came back to the office from the airport after the festival, I found that Don was not alone. Bernie was there with him, sitting in a corner watching TV.

"What's going on?" I asked Don.

"The Alien's working for us now."

"Do we really need someone sitting around watching reruns of *Three's Company?*"

"I'm kind of helping him out," said Don. "He got busted stealing a shirt at the Costa Mesa Mall in Orange County."

"I'm not even sure I should ask, but I'm going to, anyway," I said, dropping my bags on the floor.

"Well, it's kind of like this," said Don. "If you got busted sticking five Nestlés down your pants, the cops would call it petty theft and probably just write you a ticket. Blow me, they wouldn't even care—although I might worry about you. But if you've spent any time in the system, like he has, it becomes petty theft with priors, and that's a felony. So The Alien got forty days in a halfway house, but he can get out during the day if he has a job to go to."

"There's no way he's gonna sit here eight hours a day, Don. What happens if they show up to check on him and he's out filching Chee·tos?"

"He committed the crime in Orange County, so we figure they'll probably never show up to check. The worst they'll do is call. Anyway, we've got someone here to answer the phones for free. So how was the festival?"

"Just splendid," I said. Don had a way of staggering you senseless with his bizarre, twisted logic; although it's almost certainly rife with holes, it always seemed better not to dig any deeper, or you were sure to unearth even more crap you're simply better off not knowing.

"*Reservoir Dogs* must've gone over like gangbusters," he said. "All day long, the phone's been ringing off the hook. Everyone who hated *NBK* before has been calling, wanting to know if it's still available."

"I hope you haven't been telling everyone they're all full of shit," I said.

"No way. Who cares if they're disingenuous bastards if they've got money?"

Don was right. On the heels of the Sundance screening, a weird and miraculous phenomenon had occurred—"Quentinmania" was now in full bloom. Indeed, everyone was whistling a different tune. "Remember that script you sent me? You know how much I liked it. I just couldn't get anyone over here interested in it before, but now I think I can." Well, that was a crock. Young development people might be into *Reservoir Dogs*, but the people at the top of the studios, the middle-aged guys who were into Meryl Streep movies and keeping stock prices up, were still not going to bet the farm on some guy named Quentin Tarantino, even if he was the flavor of the minute. People forget that even after the limited success of *Reservoir Dogs* (it had only done $2 million at the box office), *Pulp Fiction* was turned down by every studio in town before Miramax finally made it.

But through a circuitous and complex series of events that are too boring and involved to relate here, our attorney Karl managed to get the script into the hands of a guy named Paul Feldsher, an ex-ICM agent who had recently been hired to head up the new American division of the French company CIBY Pictures. CIBY was owned by François Bouygues, a rich industrialist most noted for controlling the construction company that built the Channel tunnel. Buig was in his eighties, and before he kicked he decided he wanted to drop a couple of million bucks making movies, and CIBY went on to finance Jane Campion's *The Piano*, David Lynch's *Fire Walk with Me*, and Jim Jarmusch's *Dead Man*. Feldsher wanted *NBK* to be the first picture he made, and as an ex-agent he had great avenues for getting the script in the hands of talented directors who could really do something with it.

"I'd really like Brian DePalma to do it," said Feldsher. "And I think I could get him to read it."

We were thrilled. Up until this time, we still thought we'd be lucky to be shooting *NBK* for $1 million; if someone like Brian DePalma came on board, we were looking at a big-budget film with a major studio release. I also knew that DePalma was one of Quentin's idols, so I called him to tell him the good news.

"That's great," said Quentin—somewhat more coolly than I would've expected. He had seemed a bit withdrawn every time I'd talked to him since Sundance; I attributed it to being overwhelmed by the task of being the Next Big Thing, so I hadn't bugged him too much. Yet I still didn't want to do anything without his approval. He told me to let him know what happened with it, and I agreed.

We went to meet with Feldsher shortly thereafter. Feldsher was a good guy, had some smarts, and we liked him for his willingness to take a chance the first time out in his new job. But when we walked into his office, he seemed worried.

"I spoke with DePalma's agent today," he said. "Quentin had gone in to meet with him, and he told DePalma that if he made the movie, Quentin would picket the theater."

"That's impossible," I said. "I just talked with Quentin a few days ago and told him we were going out to DePalma, and he thought that was great."

"Is Quentin really behind this movie?" Feldsher wanted to know.

"He's calling the shots, Paul. I promised him he had approval over what we did with the project every step of the way, and we haven't made a move without telling him."

"I got a call from Quentin's producing partner, Lawrence Bender," said Feldsher. "Lawrence said that Quentin doesn't want the movie made, and that he'd like to talk to me about it."

Don was livid. "That's bullshit," he said. "That guy's just nervous because he's only got a career as long as he's got his teeth in Quentin's butt, and he's worried because Quentin likes us. In fact, Quentin wanted to shoot the *American Maniacs* segment from *NBK* himself, with us producing. If there's anything out there with Quentin's name on it, he wants to be the one producing it."

We went flying back to the office, me to try and get Quentin on the phone and Don to call Cathryn Jaymes. In recent weeks, since the whole Rand fiasco, Don had done an about-face on the Cathryn front, and had come to respect her as someone who played straight and was supportive of us. "Sounds like Lawrence," she said. She'd grown somewhat more skeptical about him since Sundance. Did she think Quentin said anything like that to DePalma? She didn't know.

I got Quentin on the phone. He denied the whole thing. Oh, no, he'd never do anything like that. Of course not. Did he ask to talk to Feldsher? Yes, but only because he wanted to have some official say in the project, he didn't want anything to be done with it without his knowledge—after all, it was his script. Like a credulous fucking boob, I believed him.

Then, one afternoon in March while we were sitting around the office, this guy we'd never seen before walked in wearing one of the "NBK" baseball caps Rand had had made up. He was carrying a picture of Don and me. He handed Don an envelope, asked him to sign for it, which Don did. Then he took off.

Don opened up the envelope, and stared at the document for a few minutes. "Motherfucker!"

"What is it?" I asked.

"Rand's suing us."

If you've never been sued before, let me tell you, nothing can quite match the wild disbelief that courses through your whole body when you realize someone's going to take you to court.

"Jesus, what the hell does this mean?" I said.

"I know a good attorney . . ." said The Alien.

"Shut up, doofus, we don't need a public defender," said Don. "We need Karl."

We faxed the documents over to Karl immediately. He looked them over and called us back.

"What in God's name is Rand trying to claim here, Karl?" I asked.

"Well, here's the problem," said Karl. "If Rand wants to sue you guys, simply saying that you've violated your contract with him, all he can sue you for is damages, which doesn't do him any good, since you'll still have the script and you haven't got any money, anyway. The only way he can get at you is to try and prove you committed fraud, and then he can have the contract rescinded."

"WHAT FRAUD?" Don screamed.

"He's asserting that when you signed the contract with him, you never intended to let him direct the film, and you defrauded him out of his property."

"That's ridiculous, Karl," I said. "We did months of work. There are dozens of people who can attest to the fact that we knocked ourselves out trying to make this work. We have rejection letters we can virtually paper the walls with to show we made every effort to set it up with him, and nobody wanted it."

"Rand's also alleging that he never knew he could be removed as director," said Karl.

"Oh, he can just fucking blow me," said Don. "He signed a contract to that effect, in front of Quentin, you, us, God, and everyone."

"Well, now he's claiming that he never saw that in the contract," said Karl.

"That's bullshit," I said. "He niggled over every single fucking comma in that contract for weeks before signing it. And he was represented by a lawyer of *his* choice—we never even met the guy."

"Rand's got a new lawyer now, and he's saying that the lawyer who represented him on the original contract was incompetent and never advised him of that fact."

"Gee, whatever happened to 'you know more about the law than most attorneys, Rand'?" sneered Don.

"What does this mean to us, in terms of setting up the project?" I asked. "It's clearly a frivolous lawsuit. Nobody's going to take it seriously."

"Well, here's where you guys get fucked," said Karl. "Since the chain of title for *NBK* came *through* Rand, no company is going to invest millions of dollars in the project unless they know they can have clear rights to it. And although the claim seems frivolous, you never know what can happen years down the line when the thing finally gets to court, so you're going to have to settle the suit before you can set it up with anyone."

"And what if we don't settle with him and our option runs out before it even gets to court?" I asked.

"I hate to tell you guys, but you're screwed," said Karl.

"Oh, this is just fucking *peachy*," said Don. "So, Karl, how much is it going to cost us to defend this thing?"

"For starters, it's going to cost about $10,000 for our litigators to respond to the claim," said Karl. "And then if they start filing motions, and we have to start taking depositions and going to court, it's going to get really expensive."

"Let me ask you this, Karl," I said. "How is Rand intending to back up his claim that we defrauded him, considering he has no evidence to that effect?"

"It looks like his good friend, Quentin Tarantino, is willing to come forward and say that you told him that you'd never intended to use Rand as a director before you even signed the contract, Jane."

You know that feeling you get when something is so awful you just can't accept it? I steadfastly refused to believe that Quentin was behind this until I heard it from him with my own ears.

I called and called and called Quentin until he finally picked up the phone.

"What's up with this lawsuit, Quentin? Did you know about it? Are you really supporting this?"

Quentin said—and I'll never forget it, "Jane, I've decided I don't want *NBK* to be made. What about if I gave you the $10,000 back in exchange for the rights?"

"Quentin, we're into *NBK* for a lot more than ten grand, and we can't just walk away. We've got our professional reputations on the line, not to mention the fact that we took a chance on this project when nobody else believed in it. We went through hell with Rand, we've staked our whole career on this, and we're not about to walk away now."

"Well, I just don't want it to be made," he said.

"And so you're going to back Rand? Are you *really* willing to assert that we defrauded him? That's a fucking lie and you know it, Quentin. The reason we did what we did with him—the only reason we've done anything—is because *you* wanted it to happen. We've done *nothing* without your permission. And now you're turning on us?"

All he could say, over and over, was that he "just didn't want *NBK* made." I hung up the phone stung, feeling like a complete fool, knowing that we were now going to be cast as the villains in the whole situation. Worse than that, we now had to defend a lawsuit.

We called Paul Feldsher to tell him what had happened and find out what his response would be. We discovered we were the second people to call him with this particular news flash—the William Morris people had already called to let him know. (A lovely little practice we saw as "interference with potential business interest," but the least of our problems at the moment.)

Feldsher told us what everyone else would say eventually: "Even though Rand's lawsuit is spurious, the chain of title came through him, and you've got to settle with him before anyone will touch *NBK.*"

"Paul, there's no way this guy is going to settle with us," said Don. "He'd rather have a hot poker stuck up his butt than even talk with me. This is all about revenge."

"Look, if Rand ties this thing up until your option runs out, it goes back to Quentin, and he has no claim on it, right?" said Feldsher.

"That's right," I said.

"So maybe, if he's smart—"

"He's not," I said.

"But if he can be made to see that the only way he gets anything out of this whole situation is if the film gets made before the option runs out, he'll settle. Since he clearly hates you guys, maybe he'd talk to me?"

"Paul, if you could do that, I promise to name a few of my children after you," I said.

"I don't know what I can do, but let me give it a shot."

We called Karl and told him what Feldsher was going to attempt. He told us that was great, but that we still had to respond to the claim Rand had filed against us within a certain period of time, or he'd win the lawsuit by default. Rand had gotten some recent law-school grad to take the case on contingency, so it wasn't costing him a dime. We already had outstanding bills with Karl we hadn't been able to pay, to the tune of $5,000. Karl was a prince. He went to his bosses, told him that he believed in us, and got them to agree that if we simply paid the money we already owed them, they'd respond to the claim without making us put up the ten grand first.

Which meant doing something I never, ever wanted to do again—I had to call my mother. I swallowed my pride, picked up the phone, and dialed Seattle.

"Hi, Mom, how you doing?"

"Just fine, honey. How are you?"

"Oh, okay, more or less. What have you been up to?"

"Well, this morning I went to a meeting at the Assistance League, and this afternoon I've been puttering around the house—it's your cousin's birthday tonight, you know, so I've been doing some baking."

"That's great, Mom. Wish her my best. Listen, I've got sort of a problem here. . . ."

"It sounds like something's troubling you," she said.

"Mom, I'm being sued by Rand Vossler over *NBK*. He's claiming we defrauded him, and if we don't come up with the money to defend the case, we lose the project."

"How much do you need?"

"I hate this, Mom—I know I've asked you way too many times for help, but"—I winced—"five thousand."

"I'll have it wired into your account this afternoon."

I breathed a guilty sigh of relief. Mom was retired now—it wasn't a sum of money she could easily afford to lose, but it was either go to her or give up.

"There's just one thing," she said.

"Anything, Mom." I thought that now would be an opportune time for her to suggest I make a career switch.

"Promise me you won't quit until you pound that little bastard into the ground."

God, I love that woman. And they wonder where I get it from. . . .

The whole situation was ugly. Since all we could do was wait and see how Feldsher fared in his conversation with Rand, Don and I had nothing to do but sit around the office and worry.

"I don't get it," said Don. "Rand would never have the guts to do this by himself. It's been four months since he walked out of here. Why now?"

"I'm not sure," I said, "but it has to be because Quentin put him up to it."

"But *why*? You've been really good to Quentin through all of this. Why would he do that?"

"Well, here's the only way I've been able to figure it," I said. "So you're Quentin Tarantino. You've been a big goof sitting on a sofa watching videos for most of your life. You don't even have a car, but you get yourself a job in a video store with a bunch of other geeks like yourself, and you all sit around musing about the movies you'd make if you had the money. With your pal Roger Avary, you jerk off this 400-page mess called *Open Road*, and out of that you carve *NBK*, *True Romance*, and parts of *Reservoir Dogs*—the rest you rip off from Chinese action films."

"And the only thing you've ever written by yourself is this lame vampire movie called *From Dusk till Dawn* for some special-effects guy who pays you $1,500," says Don.

"Right. So boom, *Res Dogs* comes out, and it's a phenomenon. Boom, *True Romance* comes out; it could be better, but everyone's calling you a genius. Suddenly the onus is on you to follow it up. And in your heart of hearts, you know that you're a one-trick pony—you've got the same characters, the same scenes appearing over and over again in *Res Dogs*, *NBK*, and *True Romance*. You've never really written anything on your own, except for one weak script. What are you gonna do for a follow up? The last thing you want is for someone else to be doing your hyperviolent, digressive dialogue stuff and playing it out before you can do that yourself. How do you keep that from happening?"

"I get it," said Don. "Suddenly you've got Rand Vossler calling you, whining because Jane and Don done him wrong. He doesn't know you put them up to it, but if you can get pathetic, weak Rand to think you're behind him, he'll find some loser wannabe lawyer to file a suit. He hasn't got a case, but maybe he'll tie the whole thing up long enough so their option runs out and you get it back. Rand gets nothing. Jane and Don get nothing."

"And you buy a little time before anyone realizes you haven't got an encore," I said.

"And let's not forget the Lawrence Bender factor," said Don. "That fucking former ballerina is probably winding him up every day, whispering in Quentin's ear that Jane and Don are bad juju, so he can be the only barnacle attached to Quentin's ass."

"It's classic," I said. "Quentin is getting hot, and suddenly he's surrounded by a bunch of people who think it's more important to stay in his good graces than to tell him something he doesn't want to hear, so Lawrence, his agents, his lawyers, everyone who hasn't got a conscience—with the exception of Cathryn Jaymes, that is, and that's probably why she's on the outs—are doing nothing but acting like a bunch of sycophants and boosting his ego. He can be a complete dick, and everyone around him will tell him he's justified; in fact, they'll ask how they can help. And he's someone who's never developed the maturity or the social skills to know what's happening to him."

"I think that's being a bit charitable," said Don. "I think he's basically just a prick."

"Well, you're not going to get a big argument out of me on that front."

Feldsher finally got together with Rand and had to listen to about an hour of his drivel as he jumped up and down like a whiplash victim grabbing his neck, screaming about how he was a "passionate artist" and how he'd been mistreated. Paul didn't care—all he wanted to do was negotiate a settlement with Rand so we could all go forward and make the fucker. Well, it turned out—to everyone's surprise—that what Rand wanted was not to get the rights back to *NBK* so he could direct it. No, the thing that would make Rand feel better and repair his wounds was cash. Lots and lots of cash. Paul got him to agree to a settlement whereby, when the film got made, Rand would get a large chunk of money—which would come out of our fees, but we didn't care. All we wanted to do was to make the damned movie.

It looked like all systems were go. Then one day we called Feldsher's office at CIBY and found that an answering machine was now accepting Paul's calls. Further perseverance located his assistant at home; she told us that Paul had shown up for work that day to find himself locked out of his office, with security guards posted there. The French broad who was CIBY's Paris representative got on the phone with us and told us that Mr. Feldsher was no longer employed at CIBY, and the company was no longer interested in pursuing *NBK*.

And then things got worse. When Rand found out, he went back to pursuing his case with a vengeance. Karl called to tell us his attorney had filed a motion for a summary judgment.

"Karl, I don't mean to sound stupid, but what's a summary judgment?" I asked.

"It's where they ask the judge to decide that there's so much over-whelming evidence in his favor that he decides on the spot that they win," he said.

"Oh, like *that's* going to happen," said Don. "Who would be so stupid?"

"Someone who knows that you've got to pay an attorney to go to court and defend it," said Karl.

That shook Don for a moment. "Then I guess it's not so stupid. How much is this one going to cost?"

"About another five grand," said Karl, whom we were already into for $10,000 we couldn't pay.

It was Don's turn to go back to the parental well. We paid Karl, responded to the motion, and showed up at court. One of Rand's claims was that he hadn't been able to work because of all the emotional damage and depression he'd suffered as a result of the whole thing, yet Bernie had a picture of Rand dancing like an idiot in a top hat at a friend's wedding the week after he'd walked out of our office in tears. Don had it blown up and pasted it on top of the folder he carried into court, with the words "passionate artist" scrawled underneath. It probably wouldn't win any points with the judge, but it'd sure bug the heck out of Rand.

Rand turned up at court looking like a completely overwrought, de-feated, self-righteous loser. All I could think about was the fact that he'd finally found a role in life he could play convincingly. But the judge wasn't impressed. He laughed at their motion. But he also dismissed our request that they be required to pay our legal fees for having dragged us into court for this charade in the first place, saying that the "chill factor" would be too great.

"What the fuck is a 'chill factor,' Karl?" I asked.

"Well," said Karl, "even though the judge thought their motion was a joke, judges almost never make the people who are pursuing a lawsuit pay their victim's court costs because it will make them afraid to pursue their cases."

"That's the whole fucking point!" I screamed. "If some whore's son is filing a motion just to make me pay to defend it, even though it's prepos-terous, he should be forced to pay if he's found full of shit!"

Karl just shrugged.

Don and I looked at each other for days as we sat there in defeat in our office. We'd won our initial court battle, but it was a Pyrrhic victory. Things had never looked bleaker. We'd called our families for their support way past anything they should've given us, and now we had no place else to go for money to keep the goddamned judicial system from being manipulated against us.

But we kept going out there every day, taking meetings, trying to pretend nothing was wrong as we continued to try and set up *NBK*, even though we knew how dangerously close everything was to exploding in our faces. Everywhere we went, William Morris was right behind us, telling people not to do business with us. The whole thing just seemed completely doomed.

But shortly thereafter, we got a phone call. From Thom Mount, someone we didn't even know.

"Guys," he said, "Oliver Stone wants to direct your movie."

Chapter 4

Do You Think He Even Understood What He Just Said?

No matter how choked and congested the streets of Los Angeles become, Don Murphy can navigate from point A to point B in half the time it takes anybody else. By now, you can probably imagine how this feat is accomplished; it requires the services of a new set of brake pads (both front and rear) every six months, and a white-knuckled conviction on the part of anyone in the passenger seat that the car eventually *will* stop.

On the day we were supposed to meet Oliver Stone, traffic was hellacious; worse, Don was nervous, and had some excess aggression to burn off. Amid all the chaos that was going through my mind about whether this whole Oliver Stone thing was a big yank, and how were we going to wrestle all the flailing tentacles of this project to the ground, it crossed my mind fleetingly that it would be a shame to die in a wicked conflagration of twisting metal just as there seemed to be hope in the air.

"Yeah, yeah, the horn works," Don said dismissively as he cut off a Volkswagen full of hippies. "So listen, what are we going to say to this guy?"

I paused to let my heart climb down from my throat and looked back at the hostile contingent Don had left in the wake of that horribly illegal maneuver. Cars were sliding and jamming on their brakes. People were leaning out their windows and shaking their fists. Nobody seemed to be injured.

"I don't think people like us say anything to Oliver Stone," I said somewhat haltingly. "I think he does the talking."

Indeed, after our two years scraping across the bottom of Hollywood, we'd never met anyone even close to Oliver Stone's stature. Such unlikely pairings up, with the balance of power so completely unequalled, simply didn't happen; he had more Oscars than Don had matching pairs of socks. The fact that my opinion about his filmmaking abilities was inconsequential did not make it any less ardent. I wasn't particularly a big fan of his movies; I thought he tended to be a heavy-handed propagandist, and the women in his films made Barbie look like Sylvia Plath. Although I admired much of *Salvador*, that had been years ago, at the beginning of his career, before he became OLIVER STONE. I couldn't figure out what he saw in *NBK*, but if he was interested in it, we'd certainly listen to what he had to say. When someone as powerful as Oliver Stone calls, people like us show up. Besides, at that point, what did we have to lose?

In addition to his remarkable driving abilities, Don has also been blessed with this amazing gift we call "parking karma"; any time we pull up to a crowded area with no parking in the same hemisphere, something miraculously opens up right in front of where we're headed. I think it has something to do with the complete lack of guilt with which Don approaches the task of driving; without either the burden of fear or responsibility lying heavily on his conscience, he's Kierkegaard's "authentic man," and the streets of L.A. just open up and offer him their bounty.

So inevitably, Don saw a parking space open up on the other side of the street. "Do we tell him anything about Ponytail Boy?" asked Don, invoking the name he'd been using recently when referring to Rand. Before I could answer, he whipped the car wickedly into an opposing alley in order to back out and grab the space.

An unfortunate woman in a blue Renault was also turning into the alley behind Don; unlike Don, however, she had no desire to back out, and with her car sitting there, his egress was blocked. He rolled down the window and shifted the full force of his imposing frame right through it.

"MOVE YOUR FUCKING EUROPEAN SHITBOX!!!" he screamed. The woman in the Renault started shaking so badly she couldn't seem to find reverse. "Personally, I don't think we tell him a thing until we find out if he's for real," Don nonchalantly said as he climbed back into the car. "I think it's all going to turn out to be bullshit, anyway."

Trying to pretend that the whole traffic incident simply wasn't happening, I attempted to focus on the business dilemmas that stood ahead of us before we got into Oliver's office. "There are several big problems in store for us if he *does* want to do it, even without the Rand situation," I said. "We haven't hung onto this fucker so hard for so long just to turn it over to somebody else to produce—and Oliver's worked with the same producer, A. Kitman Ho, ever since he did *Salvador*. I don't see him boning the guy anytime soon just so he can hand the job over to us."

"There's a worse problem than that," said Don. "Guys like Oliver Stone and Martin Scorsese and Sidney Pollack and Steven Spielberg buy scripts like you or I buy toilet paper, thinking that maybe one day they'll wake up and want to direct them. It took Redford eight years before he finally made *A River Runs Through It*, and by that time the guy who wrote the book was worm food."

"I just don't get why he's even interested in *NBK* in the first place," I said. "I mean, is he just latching onto the Quentin phenomenon? This script doesn't have anything in it that says Oliver Stone—it's got no Vietnam, no sixties themes, no conspiracy theories, no acid flashbacks, nothing. Why the hell does he even like it?"

"Well, I guess we'll find out," Don said, as he wrenched up the parking brake. We got out of the car to discover the parking meter blessedly busted.

Unaccountably, we arrived at Oliver's office without killing anyone. It was located above Arnold Schwarzenegger's famous Schatzi restaurant in Venice. In fact, Arnold owned the building and had situated his own office on the top floor, which he shared with Oliver. Getting off the elevator, we were greeted by posters for *Terminator*, *Predator*, and *Commando* to the right; to the left (and with no small amount of irony), *Salvador*, *Platoon*, and *JFK*. It was vaguely like walking into the Emerald City. The floor was vibrating with the kind of charisma, fame, and power we'd only been witness to as spectators in a movie theater or casual readers of *People* magazine. It was what we aspired to, I guess; only just not so silly and macho.

Oliver's office was much more casual and grungy than I expected. It reflected someone who was in production a lot, which made sense, because Oliver makes about a picture a year. Production offices—which are put together for the purposes of making a movie, and then dismantled— tend to be sort of grimy and prefab as a rule. These were certainly not the dwellings that would typically accommodate anyone as famous and wealthy anywhere else in the world; they reflected the gypsy soul of someone with a bivouac mentality. Well, this was the man who directed *Platoon*, after all, and production—as we knew all too well—was a much closer cousin to war than most people would imagine.

Thom Mount was already there. Mount was famous for once running Universal Studios, producing *Bull Durham* and *Tequila Sunrise*, soaking some Japanese conglomerate for a lot of dough, being Roman Polanski's best friend, and dating fabulously beautiful women. Several people had told us Mount was also habitually full of shit, which was why we were seriously doubting his word when he told us that Oliver Stone was sniffing around *NBK*. In order to flush him out, Don told him, "Okay, let's meet the man." But up until the time we walked into the office, I think we were both completely unconvinced that this particular encounter would ever happen.

Mount had a great handle on the situation as we walked into the lobby, spotting me for cheeky but intimidated and Don for blustering and paralyzed with fear. He did his best to soothe our nerves and take us down a few notches before the big encounter awaiting us.

"Guys, Oliver is a fair man," he said. "You should just be up front with him in the situation, tell him what you want and what you expect in the deal, and he'll respect you for it."

Oh, yeah, like that was gonna happen. I looked up on the wall, to a hideous green painting that was supposed to be Post-Impressionist but was mostly just an awful portrait of Oliver as the lizard king. Me and Oliver Stone? Geesh, it just didn't seem a likely marriage. As I was casting around for a picture of Jim Morrison exposing himself to Miami or some equally ludicrous totem to confirm my suspicions, my eyes fell on the man himself, coming out to greet us.

"Oliver Stone," he said, extending his hand. It's always weird when you meet people in person who have saturated the media; somehow, you feel like you already know them, but when you come face to face with them you realize that only a fragment of who they are ever comes across in print, and even less through a cathode-ray tube. He was much less pretentious, a good deal less cartoonish than he seemed when viewed through those flawed mediums. Yet there was something incredibly powerful about him; and although he was very casual about it, he seemed to be in firm control of that power.

I think I expected him to be snorting coke, waving guns and bouncing off the walls or something. He was much more subdued, affable, and casually charming than I expected. He ushered us into his office, with its walls covered in Hollywood trophies bagged over the past twenty-five years. Photos of young Oliver in Vietnam and with stars like Michael Douglas and Tom Cruise and Charlie Sheen. Books he'd authored as companion pieces to *JFK*, an American flag, posters of The Doors and, of course, the Oscars. All kind of thrown together with no thought to order or impression, which made them all the more intimidating. It looked like more of a warehouse than an office. The general sense was that this guy had not only lived and collected all this crap, but that he didn't give a shit.

I'd seen Oliver once before at USC, in a class where film critic Charles Champlin had filmmakers down to show their works every Thursday before the cinema school. It turned out Don had been there that evening as well, although we hadn't met each other at that point. Oliver was accompanying *Platoon* before its opening. After the film was shown, there was a question-and-answer period moderated by Champlin, in which the students got to have a go at the filmmakers. I remembered this guy Oliver Stone, whom I knew vaguely for writing the first *Conan* movie, sitting up there sweating like Albert Brooks in *Broadcast News* and completely freaked because he couldn't slow his own brain down enough to answer the questions posed to him in any coherent fashion. Well, as I sat down in Oliver's office, I realized that the awkward novice who brought *Platoon* to USC was long gone. The sweating, the nervous stutters and pauses had been ironed out. This man was clearly at home being in public. And he was having no trouble talking to us.

"So, I read *NBK*, I liked it, and I'd like to direct it," he said. I had a brief flash of Glinda, the Good Witch, waving her magic wand in our faces and making all our dreams come true. Then it was gone. Imposing as he was, we'd been bullshitted before in Hollywood way too many times in order to fall at his feet credulously.

"Why?" I asked. "What is it that you like about *NBK*?" I wanted to know.

I was expecting some big convoluted left-wing conspiracy-laden nut-job answer. He took me completely off guard when he said, "Everyone expects me to be the guy with the message. I just want to do something that's completely nihilistic."

Well, that shut me up. Here was this guy with all this muscle who can do anything he wants, and what he really wants to do is confound his critics and take a big chance? He talked about wanting to explore the violence in his past in a new way, and I'll admit I'm talking more from how I understood him than to the words he actually used, but what I heard was a desire to strip away the politics of war and law from the basic human impulse to violence and look at it in its most raw and primal and unapologetic form. I didn't expect to be impressed with him; I thought he would be some bombastic prick trying too hard to blind us with smoke and mirrors. And although I was completely green and abundantly more impressionable than I am now, I still remember feeling that it wasn't like he was plotting a smart career move. There was sincerely something in *NBK* that he wanted to explore, for better or worse. And I don't think he knew what he would find on the other end; there was no point he was trying to make. I found myself won over by his infatuation.

But I don't think Don cared a hang about his artistic impulses at this point. He was worried about something else.

"So, when exactly did you think you wanted to shoot it?" he asked.

"Well, I'd like the freedom to do it as one of my next four or five movies," Oliver said.

Sounded okay to me. The guy was prolific and he shot fast. At the very least, we'd have the resources to try and strike a deal with Rand (who seemed to just want a lot of cash at this point).

"No way," said Don. "Frankly, I'd rather shoot it for $50,000 now if the alternative is sitting around picking my nose for the next five years. I'm not willing to do that. Either you shoot it after *Heaven and Earth*, or no deal."

I panicked. I was afraid to breathe for fear it would plant any more disruption in the room. After all, this was a project with A LOT OF PROBLEMS. In fact, if you started scratching, they'd never stop rising to the surface. We couldn't afford to play hardball in the situation; there was too much on the line. And yet here was Don, going for broke.

Mount, who had been silent up to this point, seemed to perk up, too, seeing a potential deal go spiraling down the drain because of Don's chutzpah. But Oliver was even faster. He mused for a couple of seconds, then said, "Okay."

The rest of the meeting was a blur. Don went on about how we really wanted to produce it—we didn't want to be producers in name only—and Oliver nodded respectfully. Mount joined in to say how smart we were, how young and energetic and on top of it, and I couldn't get over the fact that my bullshit meter should have been picking something up in the air (well, okay, Mount a little bit, but you could excuse that on a "glad to have a deal" basis), and it just wasn't. This guy Oliver Stone seemed to be completely on the level. It was outside my experience, he didn't seem to be holding anything back. I scanned frantically for subterfuge in his brow, for deep reservations he wasn't expressing in his cadence, for out-and-out lies in his smile, and there just weren't any. He seemed periodically to go home mentally, check with his gods, and come back with a decision almost instantly. And the decision was he wanted to do *NBK*. Well, I must be off today, I mused, because things this big just don't happen this way. Not to people like us.

As the meeting ended (for Oliver decided it had ended) I stood up sort of reeling and incredulous. I remember his taking my hand across the desk and holding it as we both walked down its length toward the door.

"Good face," he muttered from nowhere.

Don and I walked out of the office in a daze. We giggled and laughed all the way home in the car at the utter unreality of the whole situation.

"I don't get the feeling many people talk to Oliver Stone like you just did, Murphy," I said.

"It was easy," said Don. "I never believed he was serious in the first place, so there was nothing to lose."

I combed the event over and over for places to plant my skepticism, and found none. I was pretty sure that this was only because I wanted to believe so much at that point. But maybe—just maybe—wanting to believe would be enough to carry us through this time.

The fragile hope we were nursing in the situation, however, existed in complete denial of one critical factor: What would happen when Rand found out?

"Maybe he won't," said Don. "Maybe we can get Karl to get him to accept the same settlement Feldsher negotiated with him before he finds out Oliver wants to do *NBK*."

"You're in never-never land again, Murphy," I said. "It'll only be a matter of time before word gets out on the street, and someone who already has visions of green in their eyes will simply go orgasmic when they hear the name 'Oliver Stone.' "

"Yeah, but Rand's not connected, and neither is his creepazoid attorney. They wouldn't know if a bomb dropped on Burbank and wiped out half the studios in town until they heard it on the eleven-o'clock news."

"I think you're forgetting about our friends at William Morris. Even though Oliver wants to keep this quiet, it'll be on every agency's e-mail faster than The Alien can slip a can of Cheez Whiz down his pants. And you can bet the first thing they'll do is be on the phone to Rand."

Don thought about it for a moment. "Look, Rand hates me, and he's a pussy anyway, so he's not going to talk to me. But his lawyer may just be greedy enough to work out some kind of settlement if I got together with him and tried to work things out. How does that sound to you?"

Since I'd been responsible for handling the Quentin part of the deal and felt like I'd bungled the whole thing so badly, I wasn't trusting my own judgment very much at that point. "I'm gonna leave this decision up to you, Murphy," I said. "If you think it might work, go for it."

Don called him up and arranged to meet him for drinks at The Grill in Beverly Hills. Seemingly flush with the thrill of serious impending cash, Rand's Kmart Johnnie Cochran forced Don to endure hours of self-righteous bluster. The way the judge had laughed his case out of court during the summary judgment had clearly been an affront to his professional pride, so he was going to barrage Don with volumes of claptrap before he let him make his case. Well, we were already well aware that Rand had us over a barrel, but it was a time barrel, not an ethical one; had we had all the time in the world to take the thing to court, we knew we would've won. But we didn't. So Don bit his tongue and stomached all that swaggering bullshit (during which time I would've lost it and paneled the little fucker, lawsuit or no) before he could finally get down to business.

"Yeah, yeah, your burning rage is great," said Don, "but where are you going to get paid off for all your time and effort? If you're thinking of trusting Quentin Tarantino to take care of Rand once he gets his script back, you're in outer space, pal. Just ask Rand what a loyal friend he thinks Quentin's been to him in the past. And if Quentin bones Rand again, boom, your Christmas is canceled. Your only hope of ever cashing a check is if the film gets made. So what's it going to be? Are we going to have a deal, or more burning indignation?"

The attorney didn't have to think about it very long. It was partly his visions of a big payday and partly the fact that Don was Don that made them decide to settle. I think Don had quite frankly scared the crap out of Rand by that point. He had stayed in Rand's face every day for months, calling anyone who'd ever met him and getting statements from them; Rand couldn't shit without running into Don Murphy's trail. There was good reason to believe that if we lost, Don would've gone psychotic with rage. Rand later went on to state, in one of the many premature Tarantino biographies, that he would've stuck with the case if Quentin hadn't abandoned him. But Quentin was having trouble with his creative juices now that *Reservoir Dogs* was a hit, and had pissed off to Amsterdam, leaving Rand to fight it out himself. Rand claimed he had been suffering under the "financial burden" of having to mount a lawsuit. Since his lawyer was working on contingency, that always gives me a good laugh. The settlement Don negotiated with the lawyer called for Rand to get much more money than either of us did, and a coproducer credit to boot. But in the end, I think the biggest gift we gave Rand in the whole situation was the great excuse he needed in life to be what I saw him as: a failure and a loser.

Then we had to deal with the fact that eventually Oliver would have to find out about the whole mess. We were working with Karl to approach Oliver's attorney, Bob Marshall, with an overall proposal that included the settlement before the whole legal miasma was exposed. But once again, the William Morris Agency was one step ahead of us. One day, as we were sitting around our fleabag Culver City offices, we got a phone call from Oliver.

"Mike Simpson called me," he said. "He told me there's some guy named Rand Vossler who says that you guys ripped him off."

Don went white with anger and aggression. I cut him off before he could speak; nothing makes you look guilty faster than sputtering self-consciousness in the face of an accusation.

"Oliver, we have an agreement with Rand, legal and binding, signed in front of everyone, with all our attorneys present," I said. "Quentin realized somewhere along the way that all he could do was rip off his old material for new scripts, so he decided to put this guy Rand up to suing us and clouding the chain of title. We've already been to court, a judge threw out their summary motion as spurious, and the fact is that Quentin and Rand are just a couple of greedy, lying bastards. Anything anyone else tells you is bullshit."

There was a pause on the other end of the phone. How was this man we barely knew, who held our fate in his hands, going to react? "Simpson told me that if I simply waited until your option runs out, he'd sell *NBK* to me without you two attached, for more money. If I didn't, he said Quentin wouldn't support the project."

I worked up every bit of nerve I had. "And what did you tell him, Oliver?"

"I told him that was completely unethical," he said. "I told him that Jane and Don had brought me the script, and I couldn't do something like that."

I'd been in Hollywood long enough to know that the more powerful people were, the more entitled they felt to step over anyone they chose in order to get what they wanted. And at that point, it was a lot more important for Oliver to stay in Quentin's good graces than ours. But he didn't accept Simpson's offer to sell off Quentin's approbation like he was some kind of medieval pardoner. Oliver told him to go fuck himself, and ultimately he would pay a big price for that decision. I think that was the moment where a bond was formed between us and Oliver that wouldn't break, no matter how many times we've wanted to strangle each other over the course of the ensuing years, and they were numerous. But what else can you do when you owe a guy everything you've got?

In my favorite episode of *The Simpsons,* Marge develops a gambling addiction and begins spending nights in the local casino. Homer is left to take care of the kids. One night Lisa comes into his room to tell him she's been having nightmares.

"That's okay," Homer says paternally. "Tell me all about it."

"Well," says Lisa, "I know it's ridiculous, but the bogeyman—"

"THE BOGEYMAN!" screams Homer, leaping out of bed in a panic and running into Bart's room. "Quick, boy, I'll get the gun—you board up the house!"

By the time Marge gets home, Homer is hiding behind a mattress with the kids, having riddled the house with shotgun holes. "It's all your fault," he moans to her pathetically. "If you had been here to keep me from acting stupid, none of this would have happened."

I frequently found myself in the position of having to play Marge to Don's Homer. Never was this more clear than when we were finally managing to tie all the loose strings of *NBK* into a less-than-neat but still-cohesive package, and close the deal once and for all.

Bernie the Alien had been busted again, this time for stealing $11 worth of 7UPs and batteries in Santa Monica. "Grocery stores are his downfall," said Don. "The problem is, he's still on probation for the Orange County bust. But he's learned our ways. We earthlings haven't mastered communication between courthouses, so he's been dragging the Santa Monica case out long enough to go to the Orange County judge and ask him to let him off probation before the Santa Monica case comes to trial."

"How's he gonna pull that one off?" I asked.

"He's gonna tell the judge that his brother wants him to come to Toronto and work with him, and he doesn't want to break his probation by failing to report to his probation officer like he's supposed to."

"Good fucking luck," I said.

The day of Bernie's court visit in Orange County arrived, and the judge bought his story. Bernie was so happy that he stopped on the way back to the office to steal a color printer to celebrate his good luck. I went down to his car to look at the new piece of equipment he'd just "bought." (Amazingly, Bernie didn't think I knew about his thieving habits.) I found it sitting in the back seat of his automobile, which Don fondly refers to as the "Alien Attack Vehicle," a late-'70s Toyota station wagon covered in what looks to be black bondo. (I asked Don what that was: "Re-entry burns," he muttered.)

"Don, I'm worried," I said when I came back in to the office.

"Just a sec." Don was typing away furiously at the computer.

"Don, this is important. It's about Bernie," I said.

"Okay . . . just a minute . . . do you think 'retrading bastard' or 're-trading motherfucker' is better?"

"If Bernie doesn't stop, I'm afraid he's going to wind up doing hard time in county lockup, and I just don't think he'd do very well in that kind of . . . what exactly are you doing?"

He put a few finishing touches on his opus. "I'm typing a letter to

Oliver's lawyers," he said. "We just got a copy of the contracts they sent us, and none of the points we asked for, about Oliver doing *NBK* as his next picture or us being hands-on producers, are in there. So what do you think? Personally I think 'motherfuckers' is a bit strong. I went with 'retrading bastards.' I think it's both fair and accurate."

Don has a habit of preempting your rage and disbelief by taking things even a step further than you would have thought possible, and leaves you gasping for air as you try to catch up. I was breathing hard as I looked over the contracts, and discovered that Don was right: they'd left out all of the points that we'd asked for. I was murderously pissed off as well—I'd really believed all of the things Oliver had told us, and it didn't make sense that this was happening.

"Retrading" is a particularly unethical Hollywood practice, whereby a project goes out on the open market, and several companies express initial interest in it. One company makes a big bid for the project and effectively gets rid of the other ones. Then, as time goes on, contract negotiations get dragged out, and they take back one deal point after another. Since the other parties have moved on, and are no longer interested in the project, the one you're negotiating with is now the only game in town. And if you want to make your movie, you're forced to "retrade" all the points you thought you'd already agreed to, only this time under much less favorable terms. It's what Don was now accusing Oliver's attorneys of doing.

"I think we have to send this," said Don. "If they're going to hold to this, we need to know right away, because we haven't got much time. I want to fax it to Oliver's attorney, Bob Marshall, tonight."

Fucking hell, what was I supposed to do? Kamikaze Murphy may have been right in the situation, but what if they came back, said he was insane, and decided that they just didn't want to deal with us? I'd just started sleeping again, thinking that it was all going to work out after all. Now this.

This was frequently my relationship with Don; he was out there with his butt flapping in the wind because he knew I'd pull him back if he went too far. Was this too far? We didn't have any experience in waters quite this deep. Was Don being tough or foolhardy? It was on me to decide what to do: to pull the trigger or rein him in.

I decided that he might as well. If they came back tomorrow all full of aggro, I would just laugh and say, "Oh, that Don, what a card, don't take him seriously."

"Send it," I said.

"And I want to fax a copy to Oliver, just to make sure he knows what's going on."

Oh, why not. "Go ahead," I said.

This was not an easy job.

The next day, a conference call was set up between Joe Rosenberg, the agent at ICM we'd finally gotten to represent us on the project, our attorney Karl, us, and Bob Marshall. I figured Marshall would tell us all to take a hike after Don's blistering fax of the night before, which was my cue to chime in with "Oh, that Don . . ." But one by one, as Joe and Karl read down our list of points, Marshall rolled over. Yes, Oliver would agree to do it as his next picture. Yes, we would be the producers. We were all shocked.

Later, Don found out what had really gone down. "I guess when Oliver got my fax, he put a saddle on Marshall and rode him around the office a few times. He told him to stop being such an attorney and screwing up his deal."

What could have been a huge disaster turned to our advantage, because I think Oliver decided we were completely insane at that moment, and that was a quality he admired. He began inviting us over to his office, wanting to know who and what we thought was new and hip and hot, not only in terms of books and scripts and directors but young actors and actresses as well. Not being stupid, we saw that we could cement a position on the film and in Oliver's life as the people who could satisfy what was clearly an insatiable appetite on his part for the radical, the wild, and the new.

When the deal was finally closed, we came over to bring Oliver a present in celebration: a bottle of Nighttrain, a clown painting by John Wayne Gacy, a copy of the Richard Ramirez *A Current Affair,* and a pack of serial-killer playing cards. "Have a white-trash evening," said the enclosed card.

"I'm leaving for Thailand to shoot *Heaven and Earth,*" announced Oliver, who didn't seem to know what Nighttrain was, "and while I'm gone, I want you to bring in one of your wild and crazy friends to do some work on the script, since I'm not going to have time to touch it until I get back."

What? Since when does Oscar-winning screenwriter Oliver Stone need any help with a script? Oh, sure, we had wanted to produce the picture and all, but how were we supposed to handle this curveball? We didn't even know any professional screenwriters at that time—all we knew were film students and waiters and word-processing temps who simply hoped to be screenwriters one day. It was obviously a test; he wanted to see what we could do when left to our own devices. And if we fucked up, we might well seal our fate as active producers, and could soon find ourselves relegated to a "thanks for the check, see you at the premiere" position.

"Um, Oliver, exactly how much money do you want to pay this person?" asked Don, trying to ascertain what level of professionalism he was looking for in a writer.

"Oh, about five thousand dollars or so. What do you think?"

We gulped. "That's not even WGA scale," I said.

"We'll do it through your company. You're not signatory to the guild, are you?"

"No," said Don.

"Then great. Get me some scripts written by people you like. I need them right away, before I leave for Thailand, so you better hurry."

We left the office in what could be mildly described as a state of complete perplexity. What was going on in Oliver Stone's head that he'd plunged into an amped-up, nihilistic joyride of a film like this in the first place, and why was he asking us to find a writer to work on the script? Clearly Oliver must be bored off his skull, and we were like a ball of yarn being tossed around by a very big cat.

"Five grand," Don said disbelievingly, over and over again. "Five grand. Where are we going to get a writer to work for five grand?"

"The way I see it, there seem to be three criteria for choosing a writer," I said. "One, they've got to be willing to work for nothing and like it, which means they've got to be desperate, so it'll probably be someone we know from film school."

"Well, there's no shortage of people like that," said Don. "That's almost everyone we know."

"Two, they've got to be good with character, because from what I can tell, the big problem with trying to match up a Quentin Tarantino script with an Oliver Stone movie is that Oliver likes to explore his characters' depth, and Quentin's characters have none. The basic weakness of *NBK*, as it stands now, is that Mickey and Mallory are pretty much cardboard cutouts who simply have a lot of neat dialogue."

"And three?" asked Don.

"And three, they've got to be able to handle a lot of insanity. Because the more we get to know Oliver Stone, the more I'm sure he's a madman."

I combed my brain day and night trying to figure out someone who fit the bill. Finally, I narrowed it down to one choice.

"I have an idea, Murphy. Dave Veloz."

He looked at me like my brains had suddenly started leaking out my ears or something. "Have you lost your mind? Jane, Oliver Stone is expecting us to bring him someone 'wild and crazy.' He wants some biker to walk in covered in tattoos and BO. Dave Veloz is a Mormon. He's married with two kids. He doesn't even drink tea. And you want to fix him up with *Oliver Stone?*"

"Okay, I'll admit there are flaws to my plan. But Dave is extremely talented, he's got a really distinctive voice, he just graduated from USC, and he's desperate for his first writing gig. I can't explain why, but it's an emotional matchup that just feels right."

Don shrugged. "Well, it's not like we have anybody better. But Dave's a friend. I just hope Oliver doesn't put the poor guy into a mental institution."

I took a couple of Dave's student scripts over to Oliver that Friday afternoon, hoping to say hello to him at the same time. I'd been sitting in his lobby for about fifteen minutes when his assistant, a smart young recent UCLA grad named Azita Zendel, came out to talk to me.

"Oliver would really like to see you," she said, "but something very important has come up, and he won't be able to." She seemed like someone who was desperately trying to hold it all together at the moment.

Just then, I saw a very pretty and rather famous young actress go flying out of Oliver's office, scrambling with her belongings as she dashed for the door. I glanced at Azita, who looked like she was on the verge of panic.

"Is everything all right?" I asked. "I could wait—"

"No, no, that won't be necessary. Everything is fine. I'll give the scripts to Oliver, and I'm sure he'll call you about them soon." She grabbed the package from my hand and rushed back into Oliver's office.

I didn't know what was going on, but I was sure that it was probably business as usual in the life of a superstar director. I expected that Oliver would get back to me in a few days after he'd had time to read Dave's scripts. But the next day, I got a call from Oliver.

"I'm sorry I couldn't see you yesterday when you came by, but I'd taken some 'smart drugs,' and I passed out," he said. "They had to call the paramedics. I didn't remember anything until I woke up in the hospital this morning and this nurse had her hand on my cock." Then he let out this maniacal laugh.

This was more information than I either needed or wanted. "Are you okay?" I asked. All I needed was for Oliver Stone to die on me right now.

"I'm fine. And I've read those scripts you brought me. I think they're *terrible*."

Holy shit, this guy was insane. This morning he's in the hospital, and this afternoon he's reading scripts? More than that, if he hated David's work, I didn't have a backup. I was thinking frantically, trying to calculate a fallback position, when he preempted my next move.

"So, do you think David could come in and meet with me on Monday?" he said.

I could tell that Dave Veloz was probably sticking his finger in his ear to pull out the wax that had built up and was clearly blocking his hearing when I called him that afternoon.

"You want me to *what?*" he said.

I hadn't told him about sending his scripts over to Oliver, since I didn't want to get his hopes up for nothing. But now that Oliver had read his stuff and wanted to meet with him, it seemed like a good time to fill him in on what was happening. I decided it was wisest to leave out the bit about the nurse, however.

"He wants someone 'wild and crazy' to come in and do some work on *NBK* while he's shooting *Heaven and Earth*, so I sent him some of your scripts," I said.

"And he liked them?"

"Well . . . uh . . . well, he wants you to come over and meet with him. I guess that pretty much says it all, doesn't it?"

Dave stumbled around for a few moments, trying to come to terms with the weirdness of the situation. Sure, he'd been looking for his first writing gig, but he never expected anything like *this*.

"Okay," he said.

"That's great," I said. "So listen, Dave, here's the drill. He wants a résumé from you."

"It's pretty short. It's just got my screenwriting degree, the scholarships I won, the script that got optioned to Warner Brothers. . . ."

"Huh?"

"It was part of the scholarship—Warner Brothers automatically got an option on the script that won."

"See, there's kind of a problem here, because Oliver wants someone who's completely outside of Hollywood. I kind of took the liberty of portraying you as this crazy Mormon out in Canyon Country who couldn't find Hollywood with a map. You must've done something else to earn money while you were in school."

"I painted houses."

"That's good—I like it."

"Would you like me to show up barefoot and wearing overalls?"

"Nice touch," I said. "See you at Oliver's office Monday at two o'clock."

Listening to myself on the phone, I started to wonder. Was whatever Don Murphy had contagious?

Don has this rather peculiar habit of waving things manically in his right hand whenever he's nervous. Books, CDs, videotapes—anything will do. At 2:30 the following Monday afternoon, Don was frantically ventilating the lobby of Oliver's office with a copy of *Time* magazine, while I sat nearby pulling my hair out in clumps. For the first and maybe only time in his life, Oliver Stone was on time. David Veloz was not.

Oliver kept walking out of his office, shouting, "Where is he? Is he here yet?" When Dave finally showed, he was completely cool and collected. Don and I were both ready to clobber him with hostility when he arrived; his excuse had something to do with traffic. He wasn't bothered by our anxiety, or by his impending meeting with Oliver. Dave has an unflappable exterior that shields some really dark and complex stuff, but at first blush, he looks like a big, affable mountain man who's uncharacteristically contemplative about everything he says.

Oliver liked him immediately. "So, Veloz, are we going to make this 7-Eleven movie?" was the first thing he said when we all sat down. A bit of chitchat was exchanged, typical in a meeting with Oliver, during which time I've concluded that he not only asserts his command of the room but also sizes up the weak points of his prey, tucking them away for future use.

"Tell me what you think of the script," he finally asked Dave.

"Well, I see Mickey and Mallory like wolves," Dave said. "They're predatory, and they mate for life. They might kill each other in a fit of anger, but they wouldn't let anyone else—they'd protect each other to the death."

Oliver seemed to like this. "I'd like to explore Mallory's past. Her relationship with her family, her father. It's something that Tarantino only hinted at in the script." Indeed, in the original Quentin draft, we get only a brief flashback of Mallory's father and mother as they're being killed, before Mickey and Mallory take off on their spree. Oliver wanted to look down into what motivated that moment, to get at "the darkness of their souls," as he put it.

Dave agreed to give it a shot. Oliver told Don to do the deal with Dave, and then sent us all away.

I honestly don't think Oliver was expecting anything to come of Dave's work. He told him at the time that if we wound up using any of his material, we'd bump him up to WGA scale and give him a screenwriting credit, but he wasn't promising anything. Dave understood this and was pretty realistic about the whole situation. For him, it was an opportunity to get to work with someone like Oliver Stone; he knew that whether anything came of it or not, it would be an interesting experience.

But we were both worried about the direction Oliver was pushing the script. The one thing we'd agreed on, after Dave read the script and before we went into the meeting, was that WE DIDN'T WANT TO MAKE AN OLIVER STONE FILM. What was fresh and exciting about *NBK* was that it wasn't full of whining, apologetic I'm-a-killer-'cos-Daddy-spanked-me bullshit. I think Quentin wrote the script the way he did because he thought it was cool to have unapologetic violence on the screen, but for Dave and me, it was an interesting challenge to cast someone as the hero of the script who had dark impulses, and then make an audience identify with them. It'd been done before, in everything from *Richard III* to *The Honeymoon Killers*, but it was definitely an out-of-fashion dramatic practice in a Hollywood that wanted likable protagonists who made the audience feel good about themselves and the state of the world. Well, the state of the world was fucked—maybe no more or less fucked than it's ever been, but fucked nonetheless—and it wasn't getting any less fucked by pretending that characters like that didn't exist. It looked like *NBK* might be taking a dire turn into a whinging social-commentary film we just weren't interested in making.

"So, uh, what do you think, Dave?" I asked when we got out of the meeting.

"I don't know," he said. "Let me take a stab at it."

It only took two weeks for Oliver Stone to reduce Dave Veloz from a stable, reliable churchgoing Mormon to a borderline psychotic Pepsi-swilling mess, rolling around the floor in his boxer shorts and wondering if he'd ever be able to do anything right again for the rest of his life.

Oliver took off for Thailand. Within a few days, Dave had delivered twenty pages that Oliver loved. He began to expand the characters of Mickey and Mallory and give them a real flesh-and-blood relationship. It was Dave who conceived of presenting Mickey and Mallory in an ordinary domestic situation. Mickey gets mad at Mallory for taking off her wedding ring when she washes her hair. The whole thing seems perfectly romantic and sweet, until you pan over to the corner and see that they've got a female hostage tied up in the background. It was also Dave's conceit that Mickey Knox, as someone who was playing to his outlaw image in the media, would remember his past as if it were a television sitcom; but the painful reality of the family situation, with its domestic violence and child abuse, would keep breaking through the canned laughter and the bland video surface. Thus was born the Rodney Danger-field scene, which most people credited with being the most inspired scene in the film. (They credited Quentin, who had nothing to do with it.)

Initially, Dave felt great. Oscar-winning screenwriter/director Oliver Stone loved his work. Then he sent another batch of pages, and this time the phone calls in the middle of the night began coming from Thailand. "What are you doing? You're ruining my script!" Oliver would scream at Dave. "What's all this romantic shit? I'm making a prison-break movie!" Then the next call: "What do you think this is—a prison-break movie?" Dave didn't know what to think. He'd call me up and I'd talk him down for hours on end, trying to help him figure out what Oliver wanted. But I was just as stumped as he was.

"Maybe he's just been doing so many 'smart drugs' again that he doesn't remember what he's saying from one time to the next," I told Dave.

But I wasn't sure about this last point, and I told Don how I really felt. "It seems too calculating. Oliver's way too savvy and too much of a provocateur to dismiss that easily."

"What do you think he's doing, then?" Don asked.

"I don't know, but I know he likes to push people's buttons," I said.

"No shit," said Don. "The way he called us up with that Mike Simpson news—I almost exploded."

"It's kind of Zen," I said.

"Get out of here!"

"No, I'm serious. In Zen practice, it's the teacher's job to push the student into realization by contradicting everything he thinks he knows. Kind of like taking the cane away from a blind man, then turning him around and pushing him down. Every time Dave thinks he's got it, Oliver pulls the rug out from underneath him."

"Have you been doing some of those 'smart drugs,' too?" Don asked.

"No, look, he's driving Dave crazy, but he's also getting better work out of him than anyone ever has. Dave keeps reaching deeper and deeper inside himself to find something that will make Oliver happy again, and regain the approval that made him feel so good in the first place."

"So what you're saying is that Oliver Stone gets really good work out of people by torturing them."

"Well, kind of, yeah, I guess."

"Oh, I can see right now that this whole thing is just going to be a fucking *picnic*," he said.

In addition to trying to keep Dave Veloz glued together during this time, we were also worried about something else—namely, how to keep Oliver interested in *NBK* while he was halfway around the world shooting another movie. He was nothing if not impulsive. What happened if he decided he wanted to do something else when he came back? Studios regularly pay millions to develop movies they never make—paying us off wouldn't be unheard of. And, after all this, we wanted to make sure that *NBK* got made.

So I decided to provoke him, just like he was provoking Dave. Knowing that Oliver was not the greatest feminist in the world, I sent him *Bricks Are Heavy*, a CD by L7, my favorite all-girl band. It was full of angry female anthems and lyrics. I attached the following note:

> *Dear Oliver: This is the music I see for NBK. You'll probably hate it. I certainly hope so. —Jane*

At least it would get his attention.

Around that time, **Reservoir Dogs** was beginning to develop a reputation as a cult film, and Quentin became the idol of hundreds. No one idolized Quentin more than Ella Taylor, a writer for the *Los Angeles Weekly*, who wrote a cover story on him in which she ranted, "Quentin Tarantino *is* Los Angeles." It was tough to look at every street corner and see his ugly mug looking up from the cheap newsprint, even as we were counting the moments as the documents were being passed back and forth between Rand's and Oliver's and our attorneys and agents and anyone else who thought themselves worthy of an opinion on the subject before we could finally be sure we'd actually pulled the whole thing off.

Then one day Karl phoned us to say that the papers had finally arrived, Rand had signed off on his settlement, and all we had to do was come up to his Century City offices and execute the documents. I remember sitting in his conference room as I signed the contracts, and feeling like I was floating on a cloud of euphoria and disbelief. Was it really over? Had we really won? Did we really beat the odds, hold out against some of the meanest, greediest, low-blowing motherfuckers in Hollywood? Well, it looked like indeed, we had.

We were elated. We were dizzy with the thrill of success. We were writing *Variety* headlines in our heads for our mothers to read and boast about over bridge. We felt like we could breathe. We could begin to enjoy our lives. And in that moment, we instantly became mature, responsible adults, sobered by the weight of the sacred trust that had been placed in our hands as serious producers. We gave up our willfulness, our petulance, our jocular precociousness and became respectable members of society. We put aside our anger at everyone who had ever vexed us, and looked forward to a future that was bright, hopeful, and socially responsible.

Well, if you believe that, you obviously haven't been reading very closely. We were still Jane and Don of course, the disobedient film students we'd always be. Giddy with victory, our imaginations and energies liberated from the burden of fighting off our enemies, we were suddenly stuck in an office waiting for Oliver to come back from Thailand so we could get going on *NBK*. Picking our noses, playing video games, with too little to do and too much time on our hands, our minds inevitably turned to amusing ourselves. And revenge.

Too many people had treated us like shit, walked all over us just because they thought they could and, worse yet, acted like we were stupid. Sometimes we're too busy to worry about this kind of stuff, but cabin fever was raging and we were bored. It was inevitable that one day something would happen.

"You know who pisses me off the most?" Don said one day as he was sitting around playing with his new action toys. "Lawrence Bender."

The name still made me shake. "Why?"

"Because he fucked us and he didn't have to—we never did anything to him. The only reason he did what he did was to suck up to Quentin. I hate people like that. He fucked with us just so he could sink his teeth deeper into Quentin's butt; because without Quentin, he's just a vampire looking for a place to land."

"People think he's ridiculous," I said. "My friend Vicky was doing publicity for *Reservoir Dogs* up at Sundance, and she said that when even Quentin did an interview, Lawrence threw a tantrum if he wasn't interviewed, too. It made her life hell because nobody wants to talk to the producer."

"Roger Avary said he was like that on the set," Don said. "Running around like he owned the place, telling the grips where to set up the C-stands and stuff. They used to get rid of him by making him go order the takeout food."

I looked over to the copy of *L.A. Weekly* and the photo of Quentin's big face that was sitting on the floor; you could see the self-importance taking over his entire being. I'd read the article. It was revolting not only in the praise it heaped on Quentin, but the way he now seemed to expect nothing less. "Bender must be pissed off at the article," I said. "It doesn't even mention his name once."

I could see the wheels turning in Don's head as he sat down behind the computer, that murderous little smile on his face. A few minutes later, the printer was humming:

To: Ms. Ella Taylor, L.A. Weekly
Dear Ms. Taylor,

It was with great dismay that I read your recent profile of my business partner, Quentin Tarantino. As one who believes very strongly in accuracy and ethics, it is imperative upon me to set the record straight.

First of all, without me, Quentin would still be working in a video store and riding the bus to work. Being Quentin's boss and guidance counselor is a 24-hour job; he needs constant hand holding and ego-stroking. It is for this reason that my deal with Quentin requires a fifty/fifty split of all revenue no matter how allocated, for example, in the Jersey Films/Pulp Fiction deal you cite, I split all fees evenly with Quentin. This is why my name appears equally with Quentin's in all of Miramax's ads for Reservoir Dogs, and why Quentin singled out my name for mention on The Tonight Show.

Which is why I was shocked to see my name omitted entirely from your profile. I read the script and gave it to French-loved film director Monte Hellman. I okayed the use of Harvey Keitel; Quentin wanted Steve Guttenberg. I did everything from make sure lights got moved to go out and pick up the falafel.

I urge you to correct this glaring error in the next edition of your otherwise excellent periodical. Only once my essential contribution to the success of Quentin Tarantino is finally acknowledged can the critical role of the producer in the filmmaking process be recognized.

I appreciate your prompt attention to this matter.

Sincerely,
Lawrence Bender

He handed it to me. "What do you think?"

He was looking for me to be Marge Simpson, of course. To pull him back because he'd gone too far. But the letter satisfied something deep inside me, and it was far too perfect to crumple up and throw in the trash can.

"It's brilliant," I giggled with glee. "It captures all of Lawrence's arrogance to a T. He'll be furious."

"You mean I can send it?" He was somewhat taken aback.

I handed it back to him. "I think the punishment should fit the crime."

It wasn't long before we got a call from Cathryn Jaymes. "There's a problem," she said. "Somebody sent a letter to the *L.A. Weekly* from Lawrence Bender, saying all these ridiculous things, and it almost got printed."

We were stunned—we sent the letter as a joke, thinking it was so outrageous that everyone would know it wasn't for real. But when the *Weekly* had checked it out with Quentin's publicist, she had told them it sounded just like Lawrence, and they were going to go to press with it. It was only at the last minute that somebody tripped to the fact that it was phony, and they'd pulled it. Of course, we were the immediate suspects— it didn't take a rocket scientist to figure out who hated those guys, and who was capable of something like that—so William Morris, still smarting because of our refusal to lie down, coupled with their inadequacy in Quentin's eyes for not being able to crush us like they must have said they could, brought in the famous private investigator Gavin DeBecker. He traced the fax back to us through a gob of dried white-out on our fax machine that they matched up with other faxes we'd sent during that time.

"They're talking about pressing felony charges," said Cathryn. Great— Mike Simpson, the guy who deserved to be shot for interfering in our business, was threatening us for pulling a practical joke? Was that the best thing they could find to nail us on? It made them look like the sad, scrambling bunch of losers they were. To this day, "Lettergate" is still the only thing they can pin on us, and the way they talk about it sounds like we were responsible for the S&L scandal or something. Well, aside from a serviceable set of ethics, it looked like they were also in desperate need of a sense of humor.

Don wrote a letter of apology which Karl drafted for him. They were all hopping mad that in the face of Don's admission they couldn't do much to nail him, so Simpson did the only thing he could think to do that could hurt us: He called Oliver to tattle on us.

Of course, Oliver had to call and wind us up about the whole thing. "You're supposed to be producers, not a couple of junior-high students playing school pranks."

"Oh, Simpson's just pissed because he can't get a decent haircut," Don said.

"What?" said Oliver.

"Nothing," said Don. "I was wrong, wrong, wrong. It was a bad thing to do. It'll never happen again."

"It better not," said Oliver. "I can't have you working with me as producers if you're going to go around pulling shit like this."

But secretly, I think Oliver was chortling about the whole thing. He'd been fucked over in Hollywood enough times himself to appreciate Don's response to the cheap, thuggish tactics they'd pulled on us from the start. If he hadn't been, I'm quite certain he would've laid into both of us a lot harder.

And in return, I was starting to have some respect for what he was trying to do as well. As I looked over where he was leading Dave with the script, I was starting to like it. He was obsessed with making Mallory's character a strong and vigorous one. In one of Dave's drafts, Mickey rescues a helpless Mallory from her prison cell. Oliver didn't want that. "Mallory should save herself," he told Dave. Since he'd long been criticized for having female characters in his films that were not the strongest or best-drawn people in the world, I really respected him for not only being conscious of his weak points, but trying to address them. Even though I was sorry that some of the ease and wit of Quentin's original script was disappearing, what was happening felt good. I started to see how Oliver invested himself in his work and, in doing that, created something he could get passionate about. Because if you didn't believe in what you were doing, as we were quickly finding out, this whole Hollywood thing was just too damned hard.

Chapter 5

We Wanted to Do This All Our Lives, Right?

Up until the time Oliver returned from Thailand, the encounters I'd had with him had been limited to the occasional brief meeting and the inevitable windup phone call. But one day soon after his arrival back in Los Angeles, I got my first dose of the full-on, up-close-and-personal Oliver Stone experience.

"I've got an extra ticket to the Keith Richards show at the Universal Amphitheatre tonight," he said one Saturday afternoon. "Would you like to go?"

Well, how could I say no? Bonding with your director, someone you'll soon be living with night and day for months, could only be a good thing. Besides, seeing a legend like Keith Richards with self-appointed sixties spokesman Oliver Stone would undoubtably be a kick in the pants.

"Sure," I said.

"Then be at my house at seven."

I arrived at his house in Brentwood to find that he wasn't there yet. I was greeted at the door by his wife, Elizabeth, a pretty blonde who invited me in and offered me a glass of wine. The house was much more modest than I would've expected; the only way you could tell there was serious money in action came from the two hideous Julian Schnabel broken-crockery paintings at the end of the living room. Stone and Schnabel. The perfect macho pair.

In the kitchen, Elizabeth introduced me to a guy named Richard Rutowski, who would also be accompanying us to the concert. I pegged him in his mid-forties. He would not have been a bad-looking guy, save for the fact that his face looked like a beaten leather road map, destination fast lane. Think Jan Michael Vincent, without the eye patch.

"Nice to meet you," said Richard, pouring the wine.

Just then, Oliver came roaring up the driveway at about eighty miles an hour in his late-model Mustang convertible. Looking through the kitchen window, I could see that he barely missed the narrow walls of the overhanging porch that so many Los Angeles homes sported. They had been built in the '40s to accommodate the much narrower vehicles of the time.

"He does that every day," Elizabeth said. "Half the time he knocks the side-view mirrors off the car. That's why he likes the Mustang. He can get them replaced easily."

Oliver came into the house. "Sorry I'm late," he said. "I just got finished seeing *Body of Evidence*."

"I heard it was garbage," I said.

"I thought it was *great*," said Oliver. "I loved it. But Madonna's got no subtlety. There's never going to be any depth to her performance."

Everyone in Hollywood knew that Oliver had long been toying with the idea of directing *Evita*, and had stated publicly that he wanted to do the movie as a tribute to his mother, Jacqueline. (Mercifully, no one in the press ever asked why a musical about a whore who slept her way to the top and then raped her country was a tribute to his mom.) I supposed that he'd seen *Body of Evidence* in order to assess Madonna's acting abilities. What I didn't know then—but know now—is that Oliver goes to such things because he *loves* crappy movies. As Don puts it, "Oliver makes quality movies, but he loves shit."

We all piled into a big four-wheel drive and took off for Universal. Oliver took up his position in the van's passenger seat, reached into his bag, and pulled out a tape. Ever since my incendiary CD gift to him in Thailand, Oliver had decided that I was Music Girl. In fact, he'd called me from Thailand to ask me to put together more music for him, stuff that I thought would be good for the movie. In the original draft of *NBK*, Quentin had called out his predictably Quentin music—seventies stuff like "Groove Me" and "I Only Want to Be with You." Which were by no means bad songs, but I had different ambitions. When I didn't deliver the tapes to Oliver quickly enough, he called me on Christmas Day and told me I should be working faster. I got them to him just before New Year's. But it was now late January, and since that time, I hadn't heard anything more about it. Which was typical of Oliver. If he wasn't into something you gave him, he simply never mentioned it again.

Suddenly, one of the songs I'd sent to him came over the stereo: the Cowboy Junkies' melodically hypnotic version of "Sweet Jane." "I really like this," he said.

I thought that he was responding to the song because it was an old Velvet Underground tune he remembered from the '60s. "Yeah, it's a great song," I said. "In fact, it's the only other recording of the song that Lou Reed likes."

Oliver turned to me, puzzled. "You mean there's another version?"

I had assumed all along that Oliver was a complete '60s music freak, and that was why we were going to this concert. But I discovered over the course of the trip up to Universal that he barely even knew who Keith Richards *was*. Later, his assistant Azita—who could always be counted on to give you the real scoop—would tell me that Oliver knew almost nothing about music, and that the songs he put in his films were all chosen by his music supervisor, Budd Carr. "Oliver didn't know anything about music in the sixties," she said. "He was too busy in Vietnam."

When we got to the Amphitheatre, we drove up to the backstage parking area, where celebrities usually park so they can enter the theater through the back door unmolested. But Oliver's name was not on the list. I was actually pretty surprised when Oliver told the guard quite graciously that he'd be happy to park in the general parking lot; even Don Murphy would've tried to bully his way in that situation.

Once in the parking lot, Richard went to the back of the van and retrieved a bottle of tequila. Oliver and he both took a swig, then told Elizabeth to put it in her purse. I still thought we must be going in through some special celebrity entrance because I knew there was no way the Universal security people at the general admission gates were going to let someone in with *that*.

But we didn't. We walked up to the general-admission turnstile. And sure enough, the security guards searched Elizabeth's purse and confiscated the bottle.

"I'm sorry, but you can't bring this in," they said.

Richard and Oliver looked at each other in bafflement. I think the guards were a bit embarrassed. Obviously, they recognized Oliver, and they didn't want to be responsible for pissing him off.

"You can drink it here before you go in, if you like," one of them said to him, handing him back the bottle.

And, to my utter and complete astonishment, while hundreds of people were thronging through the turnstiles and watching them, Oliver and Richard stood by a nearby wall and guzzled the bottle of tequila.

"That really pisses me off," said Oliver. "Now we're not going to be able to drink at the concert."

"But they *always* search people for alcohol at concerts," I said.

All three of them turned and looked at me in disbelief. "You mean you *knew* they were going to do this?"

"Well, sure," I said.

"You should have told us!" Now Oliver was mad. "Why didn't you warn me?" I didn't even have a response. When was the last time this guy had been to a fucking concert?

We finally got to our seats without further turmoil. Before the concert began, Oliver had some news for me.

"I've been meeting with actors for the role of Mickey," he said, "and I think I've found someone I like."

"Who?" I asked.

"Woody Harrelson."

I think I laughed out loud. "Woody Harrelson? You mean the Woody Harrelson from *Cheers?*"

"You don't like him?"

"No, I . . . it's not that I don't like him, Oliver. . . . It's just that it's . . . it's just that it's so . . . *weird.*"

"Well, who do you see in the role?" he wanted to know.

"I don't know," I said. Since we'd never envisioned doing the movie for more than $1 million, the kind of actors he was now considering weren't the kind of people we had ever thought about. "I kind of like Ray Liotta. But I realize that maybe he's a bit too on the money for the role."

"No, Mickey has to be sexy, and Ray Liotta isn't sexy," said Oliver.

Elizabeth and I looked at each other, sharing that "men don't know, but the little girls understand" kind of smile. "Oh, yes he is!" we both shouted with libidinous enthusiasm.

Oliver leaned across Elizabeth and leered into my face. "You just want to get fucked by greasy garage-mechanic types," he said.

"Well, nothing wrong with that," I said as the lights went down.

Keith Richards came onstage and was great. Everything he played sounded like "Happy," but it didn't matter, Keith was Keith. Oliver, how-ever, was still Oliver, and along with Don Murphy, he shared a notoriously short attention span. After about four songs, he was ready to go.

On the way back to the parking lot, Oliver and Elizabeth began bicker-ing about something between themselves, so I was left to talk with Rich-ard, whose function in Oliver's life I still couldn't quite figure out.

"So, I hear you're into Buddhism," he said.

"Yeah, well, I have some interest in it," I said.

"Oliver and I are into tantric sexual practices," Rutowski said sugges-tively as he grabbed me in a tango hold and dipped me toward the pave-ment.

I struggled to disengage myself and get back on my feet. "Your mother must be so proud," I mumbled. I later discovered that Richard was a member of that group whose motto was "Ask a hundred women to fuck you, and one of them will say yes." He was something less than selective about his female companions, but they were legion. Well, I was perfectly happy being a member of that unlucky 99 percent.

When we got back into the van, Oliver whipped out a joint. Not being much of a pot smoker myself (it makes me paranoid), I was hesitant when he handed it to Elizabeth and me in the backseat. But what the hell— there was no way I was going back and telling my friends I had the chance to smoke pot with Oliver Stone and said no. It was like snorting cocaine with Hunter Thompson, something you'd want to tell your grandkids about one day. So I took a hit.

And lost my fucking mind. I don't know what the hell was in that dope, but whatever it was, it was all I could do to keep from drooling and stammering on my way back to Oliver's house. Every time I was asked a question, I struggled desperately for some kind of command over the English language. I was freaking out and in a complete panic as I tried to maintain—it wouldn't look too good to Oliver Stone if his new producer suddenly turned into a complete idiot after one hit of pot.

When we arrived back at Oliver's, I stumbled out of the van and said my good-byes, thanking them for the ticket. Richard kissed my cheek and told me he was sure we'd be seeing each other real soon.

I staggered into my car, turned it on, and eased it out of eyesight from Oliver's house before I stopped it and passed out. And there I slept for the next six hours, until I could sober up and get enough control over my faculties to drive myself home.

"So, how did it go?" Don asked, when he called me the next morning.

"Oh, Hollywood, you know," I said. "It's such a glamorous town."

There was no question about it. At some point, my business partner was going to have to be sent to reeducation camp with regard to big-budget film decorum before this whole thing was over.

"We're the producers on this movie. Who does Oliver Stone think he is?" said an outraged Don when I told him that Oliver had met with Woody Harrelson and decided to cast him as Mickey.

"Oh, I don't know, Don—he's only won three Oscars. Where he gets the gall to think he can do anything without asking you first is beyond me."

Don's naïveté on the subject was reflective of where we'd gotten all of our previous experience as producers—film school, a place where sets are nothing short of anarchic and almost anyone feels they can yell "cut" at any moment. But it was also indicative of a problem we were both having now: as things moved forward and millions of dollars started being spent, we had to acknowledge that we weren't calling the shots anymore. For so long it had been just him and me, sitting around in some semblance of an office, and the only person we had to consult whenever we made a decision was each other. Now it came time to hand over the reins to Oliver and his crew—because when you took on Oliver Stone, you took on all of the people he worked with on film after film as well. We were definitely the new kids on the block. And even though it was everything we'd ever wanted, it was tough for a couple of control freaks like us to admit that we were now acting at somebody else's behest when it came to *NBK*. Don had a particularly rocky time adjusting to that fact. His motto in life had always been "It's a Don world—you're just living in it."

When we'd first brought *NBK* to Oliver, he had wanted to cast Michael Madsen (of *Thelma and Louise* and *Reservoir Dogs* fame) in the role of Mickey. Let it be known here and now that when he told Warner Brothers and New Regency, the financiers of all his films, that *NBK* was what he wanted to do next, they were somewhat less than enthusiastic—in fact, Warner Brothers cochairmen Bob Daly and Terry Semel openly despised the script. But if that's what Oliver wanted to make, they didn't want to lose him as one of their prize filmmakers, so they acquiesced to financing it. However, they had little faith in Madsen's ability to pull audiences into the theaters. So if Oliver was going to insist on Madsen, they were willing to pump only $10 million into making it. And although Oliver had at one point toyed with the idea of making the movie down and dirty for a low budget, when he finally took a good hard look at what he wanted to do creatively with the film, he realized that such a limited budget would leave his cinematographer and production designer without the resources they needed to create something as bold and experimental as he envisioned.

So Warners sent over a list of actors they'd approve for a budget of $35 million, the amount of money Oliver now felt he needed in order to make the film. Woody Harrelson was on that list. Did the Warners guys really see him as a serial killer? I think their faith in Woody was due partly to his rapidly climbing box-office potential (*White Men Can't Jump* had just been a big hit), and partly because they thought that someone who had a light comic appeal could alleviate some of the brutally violent impact of a movie they were so afraid of in the first place.

"I hate this idea. It just sucks," said Don. "Woody is just some sitcom guy who made the studio a hundred million dollars jumping around with a basketball. He's all wrong for the role of Mickey Knox. Oliver made a terrible creative compromise with the studio just to get his film made."

"I dunno, I kind of like the idea," I said. "I think the studio brass feel that Woody will lighten up the picture, but I think it's going to backfire on them—offering America up its beloved fair-haired boy next door as a sadistic serial killer makes the whole thing even more perverse," I said. "It certainly lends another layer of meaning to the sitcom scene."

"Well, I'm going to have a word with Oliver about it," said Don.

"Suit yourself," I said.

"And *you're* coming."

Even though the Thailand portion of *Heaven and Earth* was done, Oliver still had to shoot numerous scenes in Los Angeles before principal photography would be complete. When Don requested an audience with him over the Woody situation, Oliver had us down to his set in the San Fernando Valley in order to speak with him.

Oliver loves to have meetings on set when he's shooting. I think he feels like Rommel in the middle of the desert, surrounded by his troops and in complete control. When we got there, we were greeted by Clayton Townsend, who had been Oliver's production manager for years, and had recently been upped to the role of producer when Oliver had a falling out with Alex Ho in Thailand. Oliver had called us at the time to tell us that we'd now be sharing our producing responsibilities on *NBK* with Clayton, since Alex Ho was history. Well, that wasn't part of our contract. The terms of our deal stated specifically that we would take a third producer on board with us only if the person had received the credit before, which Alex Ho had and Clayton Townsend had not. We grumbled a little bit about the exception, and Oliver threw a fit.

"If you don't accept Clayton as a producer right now," he screamed from the rice paddies of Thailand, "I'm not going to do this picture. I can't work if I don't have my people."

Eventually, we relented. And when we finally got to meet Clayton, we were kind of glad he was going to be working with us instead of Alex Ho, who had a reputation for efficiently manipulating Oliver's natural paranoia to keep anyone he saw as a threat out of the picture. We were pretty sure that once *NBK* got going, Alex would have tried to swat us away like flies. Clayton seemed an affable enough guy, and had an easygoing manner that probably acted as a good counterbalance to Oliver's endemic mania. At the moment, he was in the process of trying to pay off all the shop owners on the street who were claiming that the shoot was disrupting their business, and saw a way to grab a couple of bucks out of the situation. Clayton was handling the whole thing pretty calmly.

"Ollie is on the set right now," he said, after he had disengaged himself from the production fray. "But he'll be with you guys in a few minutes."

Which gave Don some time to load up on diet Coke and raise his intensity level a few notches before Oliver finally arrived, looking pensive and deep in thought as he came from the set.

"These people, they drive me crazy," he muttered. "They think they can get some money off of you if they raise a big stink."

"So, Oliver, it's good to see you," said Don.

"Good to see you, too."

"Well, the thing Jane and I wanted to talk to you about—"

"I had a meeting with Tarantino yesterday," said Oliver, cutting Don off before he could even get started, as if he hadn't heard him in the first place.

Oh, Don just became completely *unglued* at that piece of news. Whatever words he'd been preparing virtually froze in his throat. "You WHAT?" he sputtered. "You . . . you met with the guy who tried to fuck us over, you . . . you didn't even tell us. . . ?"

"Don, whatever your battles with Tarantino are, I'm not going to carry them on for you," Oliver said. "I met with him because he asked for the meeting, and because I feel that it would be good to have his support for the film."

I could see Don was about to spontaneously combust. And I could also see that behind Oliver's slightly annoying, patronizing tone, he was completely digging the response he was getting out of Don.

"Actually, I kind of liked him." Oliver smiled amiably. "He reminds me of myself as a young man."

Don was ready to go for Oliver's throat, playing right into his games. I didn't want Oliver to think he could manipulate us so easily, so I gave Don a swift kick in the shins to shut him up.

"Well, I hope the two of you just had a *lovely* testosterone festival," I said, digging back at Oliver.

He leaned down into my face, smiling wickedly. "You're just jealous because you don't have any."

I smeared a big grin across my face and stuck it right back in his. "I probably have more than *you* do."

That got a laugh out of him. Which managed to diffuse the ticking bomb that was Don Murphy, set to explode and take all of us with it only moments before. Even though I was as dumbfounded as Don was about the Quentin bulletin, it was something we could better come to grips with on our own, once we'd had time to cool off.

Don tried to get back to his original agenda. "So anyway, Oliver, what I wanted to discuss with you—"

Oliver cut him off as he put an arm around Don's shoulder and began walking him away. "I'd like to talk with you for a moment, Don, alone."

He ushered Don away to his trailer, and left me to the craft service table. It was my turn to swill Evian and try to calm down. I guess Oliver had no problem talking to the two of us together when everything was hunky-dory, but once there was a confrontation to be had, Oliver was strictly a divide-and-conquer man. Boy, and people thought *I* was manipulative. I was clearly out of my league with this guy.

"So, how did it go?" I asked Don when he finally came out of the trailer.

He seemed remarkably cool. "Actually, he was great about the whole thing," he said.

"Yeah, once he'd lit you up like a pinball machine and gotten you so confused and agitated that you completely lost your game plan."

"You think he did that on purpose?"

"Jesus, Murphy," I rolled my eyes. "So what did he say about Woody?"

"Well, he told me that when he met with him, he could see 'the violence in his eyes.' He told me that Woody's father had been a professional hit man, and that Woody had that same violence in his genes. Maybe it was all bullshit, I don't know, but he sounded sincere. Anyway, Oliver is the guy who got the best performance out of Tom Cruise he's ever given in his life," said Don. "Maybe he can do the same thing for Woody."

The other big task at hand was casting the female lead, the role of Mallory Knox. Oliver originally asked for a meeting with an actress he thought would be perfect, so I called her agent and set up a meeting between the two. In the meeting, Oliver asked the girl to dance, since the ability to do so was key to Mallory's role in the movie. The girl refused.

Her agent called me the next day. "So, I hear from my client that her meeting with Oliver went great," he said.

"You did?"

"Yeah, she said he asked her to do something she didn't want to do, and she refused. Oliver really loved it when she stood up to him."

Oh, yeah, he just lies awake at night pining for stuff like that to happen. Were we talking about the same Oliver Stone?

"Well, I wasn't there, so I really couldn't say." I didn't want to be the one to tell him that Oliver detested the chick and couldn't get her out of his office fast enough.

And so the search commenced. Oliver began to audition a variety of actresses, but nobody caught his fancy until Juliette Lewis, the young girl who'd given such a stand-out performance in *Cape Fear*, came in to meet with him. He told us that she grabbed him by the collar and said, "If you think that any of these other actresses could physically kill you, like I could, then hire them." Oliver cast her on the spot.

All over town, word was out that Oliver was going to do *NBK* as his next film, and actors were now circling the project like sharks around chum. After all, Oliver was the kind of guy who could deliver an Oscar-laden movie; a strong performance in one of his films could either make or resuscitate a career in an instant. Tom Sizemore, a young actor who had worked for Oliver on *Born on the Fourth of July* and gone on to give a bunch of solid supporting performances in the intervening years, jumped him one night at the Monkey Bar and made him promise to let him come in and audition for the role of Mickey. Oliver didn't think he was right for Mickey, but he saw an edge in Tom (not a tough thing to spot) that made him perfect for Jack Scagnetti, *NBK*'s violent, crazy cop.

For the role of Wayne Gayle, Oliver toyed for about five minutes with casting Geraldo Rivera himself. Then I think he came down off whatever he was on and changed his mind. But he wanted an actor who could deliver Geraldo's absurd, over-the-top intensity. In recent years, Robert Downey Jr. had been doing more dramatic, respectable roles like the one he delivered in *Chaplin*. But, looking at his past filmography, there was no doubt that he was capable of going over the top and out–Geraldoing Geraldo in his ridiculousness, and giving the role a strong comic bite. Since the two had been wanting to work together for a while, Oliver called him and offered him the role. Downey accepted.

Which left only the key roles of prison warden Dwight McClusky and Mallory's parents to cast. For the warden, Oliver decided that he could get Tommy Lee Jones to scrub off his Yale polish and get back to his Texas roots, and Tommy Lee liked the challenge of playing a farcical, comic character for a change. For Mallory's dad, Oliver came up with a brilliant inspiration. Carrying the sitcom motif even one step further, he would cast Rodney Dangerfield. And to complement him, he gave the role of Mallory's mother to sitcom veteran and Howard Stern regular, Edie McLurg.

Oliver finished shooting *Heaven and Earth* soon afterward. Normally a director would take months in the editing room to complete the picture before he embarked on another one. But Oliver decided that he wanted to shoot *NBK* back to back with *Heaven and Earth*, so as soon as that film had completed principal photography, we commenced preproduction on *NBK*. As soon as *NBK* had been shot, he'd come back to Los Angeles and finish editing them both at the same time.

So all systems were "go." We were ready to begin figuring out just how and where we'd shoot the film. I went in for a meeting with Clayton, who was extremely nice, but had a disturbing bit of news for me.

"We're going on a location scout," he said. "And Oliver doesn't want anybody else along—he wants it to be just him and a few critical crew members."

I went flying back to the office and told Don, who called Oliver immediately.

"This isn't what we agreed to at all," he said. "You promised that we could be along, every step of the way."

"I don't know what Clayton was talking about," Oliver said. "That's not true. I want you along on the location scout."

Well, I didn't know if this was Clayton's attempt to keep us out of the picture, or a bit of Oliver's shenanigans to try and pit Clayton and us against each other, but it didn't matter. We were in there.

Since I had more physical production experience than Don, it was decided that I should go and Don would stay in L.A. to handle our other business. (Believe it or not, in addition to *NBK*, we *did* have other business. Since we now had a lot more credibility as the producers of the next Oliver Stone film, we were hastily trying to take advantage of that fact.)

I packed my bags.

There's a picture of me that exists somewhere, taken by Don on the day he deposited me at the private airport in Burbank, where the Warner Brothers jet was due to shuttle Oliver, Clayton, a few other crew members, and me to Chicago for the first leg of our location scout. The photo is of me, standing in front of the jet, the first of the crew to arrive. At the time, I remember feeling incredibly puffed up and thrilled with anticipation. It was only when I got back ten days later, and saw the photo developed, that I realized how pathetically small and completely ill-prepared I looked at that moment in the face of what I was about to encounter.

As the first one on the plane, I got to jump around on its plush leather sofas, pick through an assortment of bins and cabinets that stocked every type of food, liquor, or luxury that a member of the Hollywood elite could expect on such a journey. Then one by one, the rest of the crew began to arrive, and I was introduced to the people whose lives would become inseparable from mine over the course of the next two years.

The first was production designer Victor Kempster. Victor had started in the Stone organization as an art director and had worked his way up through the ranks to production designer. He was impeccably well dressed and well spoken, Bennington educated, and possessed of a Dick Powell dry wit that helped him to navigate the turbulent waters of Stone with grace if not ease. At the moment, he was carrying a stack of folders with photographs that his location scouts had put together for him so Oliver could review them during the flight and narrow down the places we were likely to find what we were looking for.

Next came Clayton. And on his heels, cinematographer Bob Richardson. Bob was the resident genius, superb at his craft (he had won an Oscar for his work on *JFK*) and on the set, intuitively collaborative with Oliver to an almost uncanny degree. In large part, Bob was responsible for the cinematic vocabulary that Oliver had been able to establish in his films over the years. He was also something of a cantankerous sonofabitch. He didn't like the script for *NBK*, and he made no bones about it. In fact, initially he'd refused Oliver's request that he shoot the film. But when Oliver agreed to let Bob go wild and use whatever film stocks, rear-screen projections, video, and other visual damage he wanted to inflict, Bob acquiesced.

Then Oliver arrived. The first thing he said to me, as the plane took off, was "Get out of my seat, Jane." The second thing he said, in a somewhat more hushed tone, was "On this trip, you're going to become privy to some secrets in my personal life, and I have to be able to count on your discretion." I nodded to him, and told him that he could, although I had no clue exactly what he was talking about. Well, I was sure I'd find out.

When we landed in Chicago, I assumed that we would be chauffeured to our hotel, shower, rest, unpack and eat, and get ready to work the next day. Clearly, I had no notion of the Oliver Stone modus operandi. When Oliver is going to direct a movie, he becomes obsessed with it; every waking moment is devoted to its exploration, to its examination, to its evisceration. We were met at the airport by Al Cohen of the Chicago Film Commission, loaded into a van, and off we went to the Cook County Courthouse, where we walked immediately into the trial of a man named Raymond Sojak, a formerly mild-mannered accountant who stood accused of murdering his wife and children with a kitchen knife. As we walked into the courtroom, everyone turned to gawk in awkward silence. Suddenly, there was Oliver Stone—yes, *the* Oliver Stone—sitting in the back of the room. In the midst of a celebrated crime, an even bigger celebrity had walked into the room. It was a pretty scary notion to me, that in the end, the drama of the event was more important to everyone in the room than any notion of justice. But after all, wasn't that the movie we were making?

Oliver was bored quickly. Soon we left to interview the senior district attorney. Then we were off to look at prisons. Neighborhoods. Potential locations. Finally we arrived at our hotel and, I thought, some hope of rest. But it was not to be. After a quick shower, we were to join Oliver for dinner.

"You're the resident punk here, Jane," said Oliver. "Can't you scare up some entertainment for the evening?"

And so I became nightlife tour guide. I got on the phone as fast as I could, and into the night I led the tireless Mr. Stone to lesbian strip clubs, gay techno-dance parties, and punk-rock bars until the wee hours of the morning. At one point, we found ourselves in this basement club called The Smart Bar. We were all completely loaded by this time; Victor grabbed me and we started dancing, he in an extremely suave imitation of Fred Astaire, and me as his stumbling, uncoordinated Ginger Rogers.

Oliver spotted a painting on the wall, a giant image of baby Buddhas that he fell in love with immediately.

"Buy it for me, Jane," he slurred. He could barely stand up.

"What?"

"I want to buy it, and I'm not leaving here until I do!" he said. In my inebriated state, I had to scream over the earsplitting house music of the place until I finally found the guy who was in charge. At first he thought I was just some full-of-shit drunk, but then I pointed over to Oliver, who was still managing to stand by holding himself up at the bar.

"Oh," he said. Well, he didn't own the place, so he couldn't sell it to us, but he gave me the number of the guy who did, so I could call him about it. This seemed to satisfy Oliver, so we left. (And eventually, he *did* buy the picture.)

I think we wound up back at the hotel at 3:00 A.M., which gave me some sort of vague delusion that the next morning, we'd be allowed to sleep in. No such luck. At 8:00, bright and early, we packed ourselves into the van to travel out to Stateville Prison, one of the many prisons we would visit in hopes of being able to shoot there. Suddenly there appeared a very pretty, very muscular female Chinese martial artist in the van with us. I had no clue why she was there, but everyone else on the crew seemed to know her. I wasn't feeling up to asking questions at that particular moment; lack of sleep and a wicked hangover had completely managed to suppress any innate curiosity I had left.

Oliver seemed to suffer from no such malady. In fact, as time went on, Don would claim that Oliver had made some sort of pact with the devil, whereby he needed no sleep and whatever combination of substances he abused his body with had nary a residual effect. Oliver took his position in the front of the van's passenger seat, reached into his bag, and pulled out a tape. And at top volume, throughout the van, blasted the most ear-screeching, high-decibel, angry punk-rock music you could imagine. Music nobody wants to hear at 8:00 A.M., especially with the pernicious reminder of the previous evening's excesses pressing against our collective brainpans. All eyes turned to Oliver.

"Where the hell did you get that?" someone asked.

"It's the tape Jane made for me," said Oliver.

Suddenly I became the victim of death-wishing gazes from the entire crew. I was sitting in the back of the van with Victor Kempster. "Oh, shit, Victor, I gotta confess, I only put a lot of that stuff on there because I thought Oliver would hate it."

"Why would you do something like that?" he asked.

"It's kind of a long story, but mostly, it was because when he asked me to make those tapes, I had reason to believe he'd hate everything I put on there. So I liked the idea of torturing him, thinking that as he sat there listening, he'd be slapping his knee and saying, 'Okay, so this is what the kids are listening to. . . .' "

"And once again, he's found a way of turning it around and torturing us with it. Why did you think he was going to hate it all, if he'd asked you to make them in the first place?"

"Because I got this call from his music supervisor, Budd Carr . . ."

Victor raised a hand. "Say no more," he said.

Almost down to the last person, Oliver manages to surround himself, film after film, with the same group of incredibly smart, talented, and resilient people. One of the reasons for this is Oliver's innate insecurity—he needs to be around people he feels he can trust. Also, I don't think he wants to have to learn to push a new set of buttons every time he goes onto a set. And having seen him in action with Dave Veloz, I knew that these people were probably used to having their minds fucked with and their confidence undermined on a day-to-day basis. He might get your best work out of you; but when it was all finished, you had to have the confidence, the intelligence, and the self-esteem to put yourself back together and tell yourself it'd all be okay again—at least, until the next time.

But there was one guy in Oliver's organization I wasn't so sure about. Budd Carr. When Oliver originally asked me to make up the tapes for him, he'd also called Budd to tell him what I was doing. Budd called me immediately, to give me some "friendly advice."

"Oliver will never go for any music that is 'edgy' or 'out there,'" he said. "I gave him Led Zeppelin's *Black Dog* for *Heaven and Earth*, and he couldn't stand it. Said it was too wild."

It made me wonder if Oliver was simply having me on, and was going to default to yet another dreadful sixties sound track in the end.

"Well, what kind of music do you see for *NBK?*" I asked.

"I was thinking—you know, wouldn't it be great—maybe we could get Bob Seger to do all the music for the movie?"

After I picked myself up off the floor, I began to panic. *This guy was the music supervisor?*

Having learned long ago never to show your hand openly before you know exactly what you're up against, I kept my agenda to myself and swallowed my initial horror.

"Yeah, that *would* be neat," I said through lips that forced themselves into a smile.

I went running to Don. "What should I do?" I didn't know if I should pull back—give Oliver more melodic, accessible music that he might relate to more easily. But that would really compromise what I wanted to do.

"What exactly is it that you want to do, Jane?" he asked.

"Well, when Quentin wrote *NBK*, he was looking back to films like *Badlands* and *Bonnie and Clyde*, and bringing them back to life after everyone had forgotten them in the wake of all the *Star Wars* and *ETs*," I said. "I kind of wanted to do the same thing with music—people remember Peter Frampton and Journey as the big bands of the seventies, but now every garage band that can plug in an amplifier is citing people like The MC5 and Patti Smith as their big influences, even though almost nobody bought their records at the time."

"Then if that's your idea, I think you should go with your gut," said Don.

So I decided I would. And if this whole exercise was going to be for nothing anyway, at least I'd give myself a cheap thrill. If Oliver simply wanted to know what the "kids" were listening to, I'd give it to him. In between the music I really liked—Patsy Cline, Flipper, Bauhaus, The Modern Lovers, Iggy Pop, X-Ray Spex, old Sid Barrett Pink Floyd, My Bloody Valentine, original Stax/Volt recordings, the New York Dolls, Joy Division, Thirteenth-Floor Elevator, The Ramones, Jane's Addiction, and, of course, the admittedly narcissistic coda of the Cowboy Junkies doing "Sweet Jane"—I'd bury the unlistenable. Captain Beefheart. Throbbing Gristle. John Cage's musical experiments. I had the fleeting hope that all this atonal junk sandwiched in the middle would serve to make my sincere choices seem more appealing, if only as a relief.

But at the time, there was no way I imagined that the sonofabitch was going to inflict these tapes on all of us, over and over again throughout the duration of the trip, for ten days without interruption. Even *I* don't want to listen to that shit at 8:00 A.M. But Oliver seemed to be involved in an artistic process that I can only describe as "penetrating" the music. Whereas I'd had a lifetime of drinking in dingy clubs to learn to love the likes of Cabaret Voltaire and Wire, Oliver was trying to take it all in with one gulp. A brave effort; I was just wishing I didn't have to be there when it happened.

The only bright spot on that particular morning, as we made our way to the prison in the midst of all this earsplitting noise, came from Bob Richardson, someone whose artistic sensibilities Oliver probably respected more than anybody else's.

"I like this stuff," he said, despite its acknowledged ill-timed appearance. "You should use it in the movie, Oliver."

Stateville Prison is located in Joliet, Illinois. Although nearby Joliet Prison itself conjures up vivid images of chain gangs and lifetime offenders, in reality it's just a clearing facility for prisoners before they're sent off to the prison where they'll do their time. And the hard cases—the ones that are in for gang violence and murder and God knows what else—are sent to Stateville. Surrounded by lush green fields and pale, swaying willow trees, it hardly seems menacing until you get close and notice the barbed wire and armed-guard towers surrounding the place. Its perimeter wall is the longest of any prison in the country, running 8 feet below the ground to prevent prisoners from tunnelling out. Its most famous inmate was Richard Speck, notorious for murdering eight nurses in the mid-sixties.

Upon arrival, we were escorted into the offices of the warden, Salvatore "Tony" Godinez, who represented the new breed of prison warden, those with master's degrees and supposedly progressive ideas about rehabilitation. Tony admitted to me, however, that his master's thesis had been against capital punishment. After one week at Stateville, he'd thrown those grandiose theories out the window; his only complaint was that it took much too long for a death sentence to be carried out, due to the court systems. I think "It's like punishing a dog for wetting on the carpet years after he's done it" was the analogy he used.

One of the first things they showed us was the execution room, where six inmates had been put to death since 1990. The way that they carried out executions at Stateville was by lethal injection; three bottles with individual switches were hooked up to an IV that went into the condemned prisoner's arm. That way, three different people could throw the switch, and nobody would know who had actually given the lethal dose. There was an adjoining room with a glass window where the witnesses stood, with a floor that slanted toward a drain. We were told by the guards that this was because inevitably the witnesses would throw up, and it made

Jane shows off her new creation, Don.

The madman corrupts
the Mormon, David Veloz.

The Challenger—car of doom.

Juliette gets ready for her ass-whippin' scene.

Rodney Dangerfield, Juliette Lewis, Sean Stone (Oliver's son), and Edie McLurg as the family from hell.

Cast and crew try to push Oliver out of moving Challenger.

Oliver becomes honorary brave and develops massive headache.

Don and Clayton express their love for one another.

Woody and Juliette fret over next scene's
similarity to Oliver's real life.

Oliver having way too
much fun in the desert
during location scout.

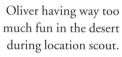

Don, Juliette, and a great big rock.

Oliver mistakenly signals in the
final air assault from *Platoon*.

Tom Sizemore sends his love.

Don performs mystic
dance to bless prison
roundhouse before riot.

The boys light up a cigarette after a nasty day at the prison.

Oliver right at home in the prison.

Oliver and Don each try to find their lawyers to get them out of their contracts.

Richard Rutowski prepares for recurring cameo as
prisoner with bad mustache.

Dr. Chris Renna sports distinctive birthmark.

Bob "the Billy Goat" Richardson contemplates both his right ear and his next shot.

Production designer Victor Kempster and his stand-by ambulance prepare for Oliver meeting.

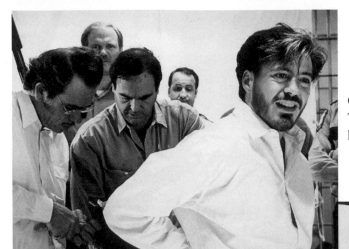

Oliver takes Tommy Lee Jones's lunch order.

Tommy Lee Jones and Tom Sizemore try to convince Oliver to let their characters survive for the sequel.

Woody prepares to shave his head, concerned that the positive ions of the electric razor are adversely affecting his health.

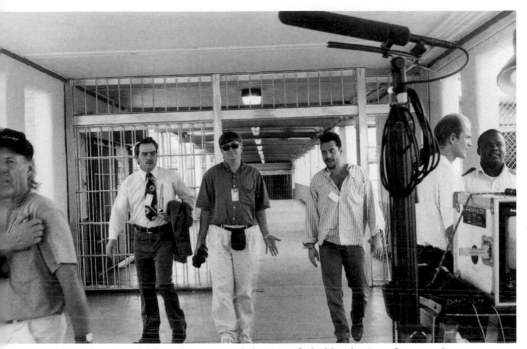

Don in prison with movie stars and the since-forbidden-by-Jane fanny pack.

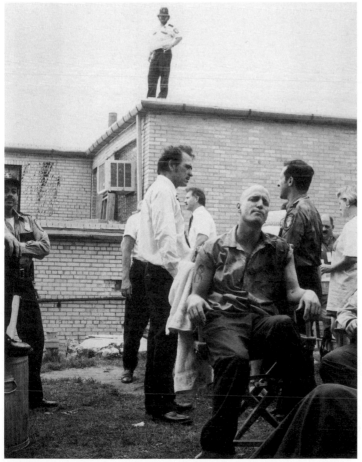

Woody and Tommy Lee take a break, unaware of the sniper above.

Tempers flare as the special forces stand by.

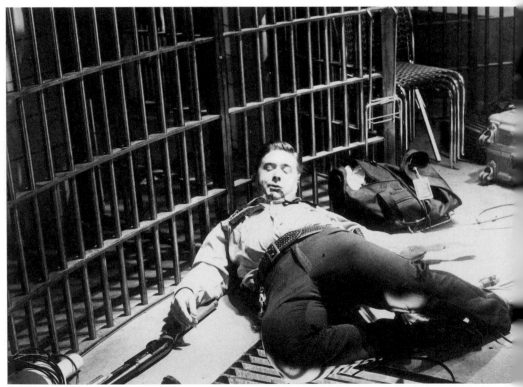

Don as dead guard.

The prisoners start to riot when Clayton tells them the lunch menu.

Real prison guards join in the carnage.

Oliver frightens Donita Sparks by singing "Shitlist" to her.

Don, Jr. and Downey, Jr. prepare for action.

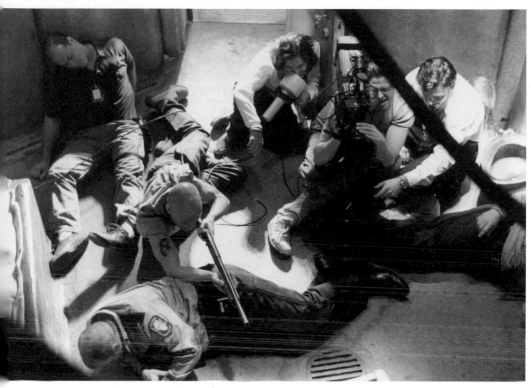

Woody rescues Juliette from the atrocious prop toilet in the corner.

The revised poster "towers" over Sunset. It was all worth it.

HOTEL EXCELSIOR
Venezia Lido

Dear Jane

Hi, you look great with blonde hair. When we sat next to each other at lunch, you wore these great shorts and your leggs looked so sexy, I couldnt keep my eyes off of them. ~~Were~~ (were you wearing them for me?) My number is 213 560-2147 Maybe we should talk.

Q xoxo

Lungomare Marconi, 41 - 30126 Venezia Lido, Italia - Tel. (041) 5260201 - Telex 410023 - Telefax (041) 5267276

An original composition from the Academy Award–winning writer, Quentin Tarantino.

it easier to hose down the mess. Maybe they were just having fun with us, I don't know.

One of the reasons we'd come to Stateville was because the prison had been hospitable to film crews before. Both *Weeds* and *Bad Boys* had been shot there; however, both of those films utilized a wing of the prison that was no longer in use, which they had filled with extras from outside the prison. Since that time, that wing had been torn down. Oliver was attracted to the architecture of the prison. One of its wings was circular, with a guard tower in the middle. This "roundhouse" was the last of its kind in the United States, and modeled on a seventeenth-century French prison design. Known as "F" house, it was the hard-core wing, where you pretty much had to have earned double life sentences to get in. Each wing, as we were to learn, had its own character. "B" wing was the longest Auburn-style prison in the country: the typical corridor-style you see in most prison movies. It had two separate sides, and "B" West housed the lifers, who were in there with no hope of parole. Although they probably controlled most of the activity within the prison, they were the least likely to cause problems amongst themselves. "B" East was where the "punks" were housed, as the guards described them, the newcomers—the gang members—who were more likely to scrap and get into it with each other. If we were going to shoot there, Tony told us that there was little chance that anyone would be hurt—looking at me specifically when he said so. The biggest danger we faced, he said, was that one of the prisoners would convince a crew member that they had been imprisoned unjustly, and somehow we'd aid in an escape, as had happened on *Weeds*. (A prisoner had bonded with a crew person, complaining about being raped and abused continuously. The crew member smuggled him out on top of a truck in a brilliant escape. The brilliance ended as the inmate was caught two days later, driving 100 miles per hour down a South Dakota highway.)

Tony's assurances that we would be "safe" came into serious question upon entrance into his office, when he'd whipped out several bags of homemade weapons that had been confiscated over the years, constructed with everything from bedslats to plastic utensils. Well, he ran the joint, and seemed to be proud that as he escorted us through the halls, the prisoners would greet him by name, and want to talk to him. If he was confident . . .

And on that note, he led us into "F" house, or the "roundhouse" as it was called, where we anticipated shooting most of our footage. As Oliver and Bob began scouting the place for possible angles and potential shots, I stood there looking like some freak who came from another planet. Although there are female guards at Stateville, the presence of a woman in a maximum-security unit is always going to be conspicuous. I could've landed there from Mars and the reaction would have been the same. Suddenly I was surrounded by guys who wanted to know what my function was on the film; there are no secrets in prison, word travels fast, and they knew exactly why we were there.

"I'm a producer," I said.

Instantly my hands were being stuffed with small scraps of paper from the inmates, who wanted to give me their prison numbers and exhort promises from me that we'd use them in the movie. Since we were contemplating using active wings of the institution, Tony had told us we'd have to use the inmates who lived there. There was no place we could evacuate 450 guys while we shot, especially since Stateville's capacity was 1,500 inmates, and it currently housed some 2,800. And we'd be paying the inmates to appear in the film. The money they'd receive would be used as credit in what I can only describe as the most pathetic 7-Eleven store you've ever seen. Mostly, they wanted to be in the film to alleviate the boredom of prison life.

Oliver stood in the middle of the huge structure, looking around at all the black faces that were staring at him with suspicion and amusement. The whole place was a dirty, grimy, cockroach-infested hellhole.

"I love it," said Oliver. "Let's shoot here."

I called Don that night after another exhausting evening of debauchery, during which Oliver virtually passed out in the cab on the way home. Every time we went by another Chicago landmark, he'd start babbling, "I like it—let's shoot there. Victor, take a note."

"So how's it going?" I asked Don.

"I think I finally tied up the rights to *Elektra Assassin* with Marvel," he said, referring to one of his favorite Frank Miller comics he'd been chasing for a while.

"That's great, Murphy. Congratulations," I said.

"It's going to be one king hell bastard of a deal to get through a studio—

they want all kinds of injunctive relief and stuff—but I think if I do a big tap dance, we may be able to set it up," he said. "So how about you?"

"I spent my day traipsing through every prison in Illinois. I think we're going to be spending a great deal of time in a place called Stateville."

"What's it like?"

"Well, the place virtually screams 'tetanus shot,' but it'll look really cool on film."

"Speaking of prison, The Alien got busted again today."

"What for this time?" I asked.

"He was doing his usual trick, where he goes through the Von's Market with a basket full of shopping bags and fills them up, then leaves them by the entrance and picks them up after he's walked through the cashier's lane."

"Oh, man, grocery stores really are going to be his Waterloo," I said.

"Well, he's got a good attorney this time, and if the guy can drag it out, more than likely the guys that busted him at the Von's in '93 are gonna be smoking dope in Arizona in '94, and they ain't gonna fly them back to prosecute you for stealing a bag of Oreos."

"Now that I've been to these places, I don't think he'd last very long inside, Don. I'd tell you to wish him my best . . ."

"Yeah, yeah, but he still thinks you don't know," said Don. "More importantly, I hope you're taking care of yourself. You sound loaded."

"You don't think I could handle this guy sober, do you?"

"Oh, I'm not worried about you. When it comes right down to it, you're probably crazier than Oliver."

He meant it as a compliment . . . I think.

After Oliver had his fill of Chicago (at one point, he fell asleep in the front of the van as we were scouting rural neighborhoods; nobody wanted to wake him up, and Victor noted, "It's like dragging John Barrymore's corpse around Farmville, Illinois"), we moved on to the Southwest, where I think Oliver's heart really lay. He has a sort of '60s glamorization of Indian/desert spirituality that he wanted to integrate into the film, whether it belonged there or not.

When we arrived in Santa Fe, we were greeted at the airport by Richard Rutowski and Elizabeth Stone. We all piled into the van that Richard had waiting for us—he seemed to be a sort of self-appointed desert czar, and was going to be driving us on our journey through the Southwest. (I finally had asked Azita what Richard's job was exactly; "What do you call the guy who holds the tequila and gets the girls?" was her response.)

Almost immediately, Oliver and Elizabeth started bickering. Elizabeth had seated herself in the back of the van with Victor, while Oliver once again rode shotgun. You could tell that Oliver had his ears peeled for every word she was saying.

"What? What was that?"

"It was nothing," Elizabeth said.

Bob Richardson started laughing. "Oliver can't imagine Elizabeth could be having a conversation that wasn't about him." Bob was the only one who could get away with baiting Oliver like that, and he did so frequently, especially when he knew Oliver was pissed off, which he clearly was. Elizabeth was ordered to change places with me as the van rolled out, so Oliver could hear whatever she said.

Things only got worse as the day progressed. It seemed that Oliver and Elizabeth had recently had their Telluride home redecorated by a friend of Oliver's mother, Jacqueline—a guy with the ridiculous name of Anthony Pompeii. As a favor to Anthony, Oliver had agreed to let the home be featured in *Architectural Digest,* and Elizabeth had given an interview.

"How could you *say* shit like that?" Oliver grumbled. I don't think I ever read the article, but Elizabeth had given some kind of quote that in Oliver's mind boiled down to the fact that the Mexican decor now matched the Mexican household staff, something that didn't exactly fit with Oliver's image of himself as a man of the people. The argument continued through dinner, where for the sake of peace and harmony, we all did our best to assure Oliver that it did not damage his reputation.

"Jesus, Oliver, you're a guy with three Oscars and a decade's worth of hit movies. It shouldn't be a surprise to anyone that you've got some dough at this point," I offered.

Everyone looked at me like I'd just spit in their food or something. I guess it wasn't what Oliver was looking to hear.

But even though the hostility in the troupe was now palpable, I had to admit that having Elizabeth along was a relief for me. At some point during the Chicago trip, I'd realized that the Chinese martial artist was no member of the crew—she was one of Oliver's many girlfriends. I supposed this was the "secret" about his personal life that Oliver had warned me about on the plane. So I kind of felt for Elizabeth, as someone who was trying to hold on to a shaky marriage. But all during the Chicago leg of the trip, I felt like I'd kept everyone in the boys' club from doing what they'd normally do if a woman hadn't been along for the ride. I was glad to finally be sharing that burden with someone else.

The next day, things went from bad to worse. It started when Oliver got out of the van to relieve himself (something he did frequently and freely, in a sort of territorial pissing kind of way).

"This will be a great place for my Indian scene," he said, standing on a Santa Fe hillside.

"What Indian scene?" I said in a panic, far enough away not to see anything I didn't want to, but close enough to hear what he said, which was clearly meant for my ears. "There *is* no Indian scene in the script."

"Oh, Jane, you know I always have to have an Indian scene in my movies," Oliver said, as he zipped up and returned to the van.

I started wondering if we hadn't sold ourselves to the devil. Meanwhile, Elizabeth was standing on a nearby snowbank with Victor, covering the countryside in a horrible, screeching caterwaul:

"I hate this movie! It isn't me! It isn't *meditative!*" she screamed.

What the fuck had I gotten myself into?

We drove to Taos, where we stopped at a Taos church. Elizabeth got out of the car, ran into the gift shop, and started buying souvenirs. Oliver went into the old Catholic/Indian church and began pacing the nave, the apse, looking at its candles and icons as if assessing the appropriateness of the interior decor.

"This is great!" he said gleefully.

I couldn't take it anymore. I might have wandered significantly from the church in recent years, but the idea of having this ancient church overrun by legions of rude crew people brandishing C-stands and big 10Ks lights was just too much. That, combined with the bizarre vision that seemed to be overtaking the project was more than I could endure.

Clayton found me crying in the van and asked me what was wrong.

"I don't care where we shoot, Clayton—just not here."

"Don't worry," he said. "It won't happen."

"How can you be sure?" I said. "He loves the place."

Clayton winked. "When we check it out, it's just not going to be available."

I smiled and took a deep breath. Even if he might be insecure and paranoid, Clayton suddenly didn't seem like such a bad guy after all.

I was prepared for the next day to become even more tense; but as we climbed into the van early that morning, Rutowski whipped out the mushrooms.

Now, I'd never done mushrooms before in my life; although I was no stranger to drugs, all my acidhead friends had always told me I had the *wrong* personality for psychedelics, so I'd always steered clear of them. But hell, we were in the desert, and there's nothing worse than being a straight person in a van full of drug-addled lunatics. However, not wanting to have a repeat of my experience of the Keith Richards evening, I took only the tiniest bit until I could tell how it would affect me.

It wasn't enough to make me start having visions or anything, it just made the desert seem incredibly expansive, a world without walls, and everything anyone said seemed hysterically, convulsively funny.

Rutowski started driving aimlessly around the vicinity of Taos, up into the snow-covered mountains, trying to find some house he claimed he used to own. "I had to sell it fourteen years ago, but I still have an option to buy it back if I want to. It's in a great place. I'd like to get it back and fix it up."

Why we were going to this particular place at this moment made absolutely no sense, but we were so fucked out of our skulls that nobody raised that question. Richard drove around and around until he finally hurled the van up on a snowbank near a house. "This is the place," he said. "I know the owners. I'm going to go talk to them."

He got out of the van and knocked on the door while we all watched. An Indian woman answered the door, and Richard began talking to her as we looked on through the windows of the van.

"Hi, I have an option to buy this place if I want. . . ." Victor mocked as we watched the woman looking at Richard in puzzlement. She clearly had no idea who he was or what he was talking about.

"And I have some wallpaper samples I'd like to check out. . . ." Victor went on.

Rutowski looked like he was trying to get the woman to let him come in, but she was having none of it.

"You wouldn't mind if I brought in a few carpet swatches?" Victor said, as she closed the door in Rutowski's face. "Maybe a few paint chips?"

Richard climbed back in the van. By this point, we were all peeing ourselves with laughter, but he didn't seem to notice.

"I think she must be house-sitting," he said. "She didn't even seem to know the owners."

Richard pulled the van out of the snowbank and sent us off again down the mountain.

"It's a great place, don't you think?" he said. "I'd love to get someone to redecorate it."

Victor leaned over the seat and into Richard's ear.

"Might I suggest Anthony Pompeii?"

We somehow managed to make our way into the middle of the New Mexico desert. By that time, Clayton—the only one who was even moderately straight—was begging to drive the van. But Oliver wouldn't hear of it, mostly I think just to antagonize Clayton.

"That's Richard's job," he said.

But by the time the Navajo police had been tailing us for about five miles, Oliver's paranoia took over, and he flipped out.

"You're going too slow!" he screamed at Rutowski as we rolled across the Arizona desert, 100 miles from almost anything anyone would consider civilization. "He knows we've got drugs in the van."

"I'm doing sixty-five—that's the speed limit, Oliver."

"That's what's making him suspicious!" Oliver hissed. Without waiting for Rutowski to respond, Oliver threw his foot over the median hump and jammed his foot on the accelerator. The sudden burst of speed made the van swerve across the highway. As Rutowski struggled to retain control, it occurred to me that he'd easily consumed ten times as many mushrooms as I had, and was in no condition to be operating a motor vehicle. If I could just stop laughing, maybe there'd be something I could do to keep us from getting either arrested or killed. Then again, maybe not.

Rutowski slowed the van down to an arid crawl as we cruised into Shiprock, a Navajo town a couple of hundred miles from nowhere near the Arizona/New Mexico border. At least I think it was Shiprock; at that point, nobody could really read a map. We were all laughing so hard and so fucking high and paranoid we couldn't function, when suddenly up ahead we saw a police roadblock.

Oliver lost it.

"It's for us!" he screamed.

The only available alternative, besides stopping for a police roadblock we couldn't possibly hope to fool into thinking we were straight, was the parking lot of a Kentucky Fried Chicken to the right.

"Pull in here!" I screamed.

A frantic Rutowski pulled in.

"What are you doing?" Oliver shrieked. "They'll get suspicious."

"No, they can't possibly be looking for us," I said, although I was by no means sure. But the alternative seemed to portend disaster, and it was the best I could think of at the moment.

Oliver reached around and grabbed me by the scruff of the neck, dragging me out of the van and into the KFC.

"Order me something so they won't be suspicious while I take a leak." He deposited me at the counter.

I was left standing in front of a KFC menu and a somewhat perplexed Indian counter clerk as I tried to remember just how, exactly, one ordered and paid for fast food.

I struggled desperately to maintain as I ordered a Pepsi and paid for it arduously. It took an eternity. When I returned to the parking lot, I looked to the field next door and saw Oliver running back and forth with his suede bomber jacket spread wide to catch the wind. Oh, good, I thought. That'll throw the cops off.

"Fly lone eagle, ride the snake," said a slightly cynical Victor Kempster, who clearly had grown accustomed to the frequently repeated motifs in Oliver's obsessively limited repertoire over the years.

I fell over laughing and spilled the Pepsi across the pavement. As I struggled to compose myself, I made a note of two key facts: (a) mushrooms were not a very ladylike drug and did not particularly bring out the best in me, and (b) I had stepped through the looking glass into a very weird place where the ordinary laws of the space-time continuum didn't seem to apply.

By the time we packed ourselves back into the van, the roadblock had disappeared, leaving us with the suspicion that it had all been a group hallucination. But whatever weird world I'd stepped into, with Oliver Stone and his whole mad ensemble, it didn't seem like I was getting out anytime soon. I was now along for the *NBK* ride firmly and irrevocably.

Chapter 6

How Much Can I Pay You to Let Me Quit?

I arrived back in Los Angeles and walked into the office, bags in hand, to find the place stacked with moving boxes. Don was busy packing up everything we owned, helped by a kid who'd been working on the Roman Coppola film across the hall, a twenty-one-year-old Brit named Justin. I must've looked like I was ready to drop because even Don noticed.

"Are you okay?" he asked.

"If you can call exhausted, depleted, and completely anxiety ridden 'okay,' then I suppose I am."

"Did you have a good time, anyway?" Justin asked.

"There's no way you can have a good time around that man. You can't believe what it's like, being with him every single moment of the day. He's a maniac. I feel like I've been jacked on speed for the past ten days. I need a vacation."

"Well, you can't have one," Don said. "We gotta move."

In the midst of all the location-scout madness, I'd forgotten that when I got back, we were due to move into the *NBK* production offices, where we would be in close proximity to Oliver every day. Don was absolutely rejoicing about the whole thing. Having just spent ten uninterrupted hellacious days with Oliver, I was something less than enthusiastic about the prospect.

"We also get to hire an assistant to start working for us, so we'll have someone more reliable than The Alien to occasionally answer the phones," Don said. "Justin's been helping me out here because he wants the job."

Ordinarily, I would have given a lot more thought to taking on someone who would become integral to our lives on a day-to-day basis, worried as to how well the person could handle Don's intense and aggressive nature. However, Justin had been hanging out with us long enough to know what he was getting into.

"You did all this work so I don't have to?" I looked at all the boxes they'd packed up.

"Yeah," said Justin.

"You're hired."

And so we set forth from our shabby little Culver City offices and carted our belongings over to Oliver's big new space on Second Avenue in Santa Monica, as he'd recently vacated his old digs in the Schwarzenegger Building. Although Oliver would no longer have the fun of accosting his landlord Arnold in the hallway to tell him that the windows in his office needed washing, he was now in need of a lot more space. *NBK* was going into preproduction, *Heaven and Earth* needed editing suites, and he also wanted his production company, Ixtlan, to be in close proximity. Oliver just loved the idea of being Production Emperor and having all that activity going on at once around him. The notion gave me a headache.

When we arrived, we found Clayton had ensconced himself in a lovely office with a porch and a beautiful view of Santa Monica Bay. He was sitting behind a desk he'd appropriated for himself—the one Michael Douglas had used in *Wall Street*.

"We're kind of short on space here," said Clayton, "so I think you two may have to share the same office."

He escorted us around an almost-vacant floor to the very back of the building, to a tiny little office near the editing bays.

"You've got to be kidding me," Don said. "Short on space? The place is completely empty."

"It's going to be filling up real soon as we gear up for production and the rest of the crew comes on," said Clayton.

Having gotten to know Clayton a little bit on the location scout, I pulled him aside and tried to defuse what any idiot could see to be an oncoming confrontation with Don.

"Listen, Clayton," I said. "I've been locked up in a room with that guy for the past two years. I was really looking forward to being able to hear myself think again. Can you help me out here?"

Clayton smiled. "I'll see what I can do."

And so, for the first time in our careers, Don and I had separate offices. They were small, they looked out on an alleyway that ran between our building and the one next door, but they were better than anything we'd ever had before. I was happy.

But Don was not quite so ecstatic. "What kind of a cheap power play was that? The accountant, the production coordinator, even one of the fucking Ixtlan P.A.s have their own office. What's he gonna do, make Justin sit in the can?"

"Look, Murphy, it's our first day here," I said. "I don't want to get in a fight over this whole thing. We'll put Justin in the cubicle outside, move all our files and shelves and computer shit over here, and appropriate as much space as we can. Then if Clayton doesn't like it, he'll have to come to us and make an issue of it, rather than the other way around."

"I still don't like it," Don said. "He's sitting in an office looking like Donald Trump, and we're stuck in here next to the room where they store the sodas. We're the fucking producers, for Christ's sake!"

It was easy to see why we made Clayton nervous. He had risen through the ranks of production as Alex Ho's protégé, and had never even finished high school. At the same moment he gets his big break and Oliver promotes him into a producer's spot (mostly, rumor had it, just to piss Alex Ho off), suddenly he's third man on the tier because Oliver is embracing these two upper-middle-class degree-clutching college kids.

I didn't want Clayton to feel threatened by us, and in reality he never should have been. The roles we served on the film were completely different. People always ask what producers do, and the answer is that there are different kinds of producers. From the outset, Don and I had concentrated on establishing ourselves as "creative producers," the people who find the books and scripts and writers and directors, and are responsible for the deal making, the development, and the creative supervision of a movie. These are ultimately the real power brokers of the business; the Joel Silvers, the Jerry Bruckhimers, the Scott Rudins. They have the contacts with the studio execs, the agents, the writers and directors, and stars that can bring a picture together in the first place. However, once you're ready to shoot, creative producers rarely want to look after the nuts-and-bolts stuff; Scott Rudin isn't going to get on the phone and make sure the location permits are secured and you aren't getting ripped off in your equipment rentals. Thus, they rely on line producers to take care of all the grunt work. Like Clayton, most line producers work their way up the ranks by working on sets and act as something like a shop foreman of the film. There's rarely a distinction made in the credits, but there's a big, big difference. No agent or studio exec in town would return someone like Clayton's call unless he was calling at the behest of someone like Oliver Stone. Don and I had been struggling to build those relationships on our own, and as the people we went to school with started climbing the ranks at the various studios and agencies, we were doing a pretty good job. It was definitely a blue-collar–versus–white-collar world. While we were tickled to death to be working with Oliver Stone, our careers weren't vested in him. Clayton's most certainly was.

As we moved into the new offices and began all the preparatory work it would take to shoot NBK, Don and I were faced with a dilemma. As producers on a movie, we'd usually be responsible for hiring all the key crew and dealing directly with the studio about the major details of its execution. But buying into Oliver Stone meant that you got the package complete: His crew was comprised of the people he'd been working with for over a decade. And on a studio level, his dealings were handled by Arnon Milchan's company, New Regency. Arnon was (and is) one of the biggest power brokers in Hollywood. Oliver's overall deal was with New Regency, and Arnon contributed 50 percent of the budget to NBK. In fact, he had been responsible for funding about one-third of all Warner Brothers films. When Arnon spoke, the halls of Warner Brothers trembled. Gracious and respectful though Arnon was, he needed us like he needed a hole in the head.

Which left us with a big problem: How did we, as fledgling producers, fit our way into the Oliver Stone organization? In Oliver's mind, we were cast as a set of hip, modern toys, there to feed his insatiable appetite for whatever could connect him to the "youth" market. This was a role I could jump into with gusto—I began chasing him around the halls of the office (for Oliver rarely makes himself accessible, unless there's something he wants to talk to *you* about) in order to bombard him with some new ideas I had for the movie.

Sample conversation:

ME: Oliver!

OLIVER (walking away): Not now, Jane, I'm busy.

ME (chasing him): You've got the transportation coordinator looking for a Cadillac for Mickey and Mallory to drive. I don't think they'd drive a Cadillac.

OLIVER: I can't think about that now, Jane, we'll have to talk about it later.

ME (waving big, shiny book): Look at these muscle cars, Oliver. How about a '70 'Cuda with a 426 hemi? That'd be the dream car of a couple of psychotic Midwestern hillbillies. I know from experience. That basically describes my entire family.

OLIVER (stops—ooh, bright shiny pictures): Let me see. (Scrutinizes the book intensely, deep in thought.)

ME (now's my chance): You don't run from the law in a Cadillac, Oliver. That's the car that Elvis worshipers and James Dean wannabes drive. Mickey Knox would want something with a big motor, something wedge-shaped and angry and aggressive looking. Probably a Mopar, a late '60s or early '70s E-body. A 'Cuda or a Challenger, with headers and glass packs and a full race cam that he installed himself . . .

OLIVER (snapping the book shut and handing it back to me): I'll have to think about it. (He walks away.)

The same exchange will occur a few more times, with the same result—but each time he'll get a little bit more exasperated. He begins referring to me as "Miss Opinion," but I figure constant reassertion of my position is a better way to get his attention than whacking him over the head. He never says yes, but eventually I hear the transportation coordinator scouring the city for a '70 Challenger convertible. I smile inside. Sometimes I win, sometimes I lose. Then I go and pick my next battle.

But Don didn't have it so easy. A born deal-maker, he felt completely shut out. Somehow, over the course of time and experience, Don and I had switched the roles we'd prepared for in school—although my degree was in motion-picture business, my realm had become the creative side. And whereas Don had trained as a writer and director, he felt more comfortable negotiating contracts, overseeing business matters, and putting deals together. Thus, when Clayton was always trying to keep Don out of the flow of information, it frustrated him to no end.

"How do we even know if he knows what he's doing?" Don sputtered with rage one day when he'd discovered he hadn't been copied on the circulation of a new budget or something.

"We don't. But it's not like we have any choice in the matter. Look, he has a shitty job—he's Oliver's lapdog, and he has to take the daily abuse of the old man's mood swings, his temper tantrums, frustrations, and all the constant button pushing and mind fucking that drives you crazy."

"But he's never *done* this before," Don said. "And when he took a step up the ladder, so did every other self-important hanger-on in the organization. None of them know what they're doing. And if Clayton is the only one with Oliver from moment to moment, he's the only one who knows what Oliver is planning. His inexperience is giving the Warners people and New Regency hemorrhoids. They always knew that in the past, Alex Ho knew what he was doing. What if Clayton fucks up? We're into huge cost overruns, and then we become the producers of a movie that went outrageously over budget."

There was no denying the truth in Don's argument, though what exactly he was arguing *for* I don't think even he knew. All he knew was that he was pissed off and bored, and the focus of all his hostility became Clayton Townsend.

What Clayton didn't know—but I knew only too well—was that an idle and anxious Don is a dangerous Don. It was only a matter of time before they hit outright confrontation. I think Clayton was in over his head and didn't want anyone to catch him slipping up, hence the secrecy—I don't think he was looking for a fight with Don. But he wasn't quite seasoned enough to hold it at bay, so it pretty much amounted to the same thing.

We'd been there about a week before they came to loggerheads. Thinking nothing of it, Don had put a card to his mother for Mothers' Day in the outgoing mail. By mid-morning, Clayton stopped by Don's office, carrying the card in his hand.

"All of the mail that goes out of here has to be *NBK* related," he said. "You can't send out anything personal."

Don puffed up like a blimp. "You mean this is how you spend your time, going through the mail to look for a letter that might cost us the grand total of thirty cents?"

"That's not the point."

"So you think it's your job to decide what I can and cannot do?"

"I guess I do."

I grabbed the card. "Sorry, Clayton, we didn't know," I said. He walked away while Don seethed.

"Now I'm *really* worried," Don said. "If this is what this guy thinks it means to be a line producer, we're all gonna get to the set and nothing will be there. We'll be spending our time eating doughnuts and picking our butts while we wait for the cameras to show up."

"Could you use some other imagery please, Don?"

"One of these days, he's gonna do something that's gonna *really* piss me off."

"And God help the poor miserable bastard when he does," I muttered to myself as I walked back into my office.

"One of these days" turned out to be the next day. Justin requested a book of parking validations so that any of our guests could park in the lot for free. He was told that any parking validations had to be authorized by the production coordinator and justified as relevant to the movie.

Well, Don just went ballistic. "I'm a producer on this movie, and he wants me to justify myself to the production coordinator???!" There was no way I could have even slowed his trajectory as he went storming into Clayton's office, slamming the door. Everyone on the floor stood there in trepidation as the walls began to shake with all the screaming and blustering that was going on inside. But when it came to outright confrontation, Clayton was way, way out of his league. Finally, Don emerged with a book of parking stickers.

"I know it's a prime operative of business that people always hire other people to work for them who are stupider than they are so they'll always feel superior, but someone should have told Oliver he didn't have to go quite that far," Don said.

Fortunately, it wasn't long before Clayton made a huge tactical goof, and Don saw an opportunity to fit himself into the organization by putting his unique talents to use. Clayton had clearly not been thinking straight when he gave a copy of an early draft of the script to a product-placement company, one of the many that arranges for companies to donate their products in exchange for appearance on film. They had run away screaming in horror at the sight of all the violence, blood, incest, sex, and torture in the film—no respectable, publicly held company, concerned with its image, was going to want its product associated with such a project.

Don stepped up in a production meeting one day. "Um, do you mind if *I* take over product placement?" he said.

You could almost hear Clayton breathe a sigh of relief; he thought this would be a harmless place for Don to concentrate his efforts, certain that he could make no headway in this arena, and at least it would get him out of his hair.

What he didn't realize was that Don Murphy's gift for scamming is unparalleled in this world. Don takes absolute delight in it. Nothing, he insists, is as pleasure-giving, as enjoyable, as much fun if you have to pay for it; true satisfaction can be derived only from that which is free. While he never went quite as far as The Alien did on that front, it did fuel him with an enthusiasm for his new task that bordered on religious zeal. He told a whole new cast of product-placement people that they couldn't see the script because Oliver was very protective of his material, but instead gave them a whitewashed synopsis and kept repeating his mantra: "Forty-million-dollar Oliver Stone/Warner Brothers film. Did I mention Oliver Stone?"

Well, it became Don's dream come true. Truckloads of products began wheeling up to the door, much to the amazement of Clayton and everyone else, especially Oliver, who, despite his millions, is as cheap as they come and as enamored of free stuff as Don.

Oliver would taunt Clayton constantly. "Did you see what Don Murphy got me?" Clayton began investigating the appearance of all this stuff, trying to nail Don for personally absconding with cartloads of this crap. Which of course he did, but only after it had appeared liberally in the film. Camcorders. Cameras. Cell phones. Clothes. Suntan lotion. Gym equipment. Athletic gear. And of course, cases and cases of Coca-Cola, Don's beverage of choice. All the product-placement people were delighted with the diligence with which Don Murphy worked to display their products over the course of the film. In fact, he built up such a great relationship with the Coca-Cola product-placement people that they agreed to provide all sorts of signage for the opening café scene, and one of their famous "Polar Bear" commercials to be broadcast during the live interview between Wayne Gayle and Mickey in prison. I wondered what the fallout would be when they finally saw the final picture, but I figured I'd worry about that when the time came.

For the moment, I had other things to worry about. Azita came in one day and plunked a script down on my desk. "It's Oliver's rewrite of *NBK*," she said. "Could you please sign this form, acknowledging that this numbered copy of the script was issued to you?"

Nothing like a little paranoia to start the morning with. I looked at the title page, and noticed that this new draft was attributed to Richard Rutowski *and* Oliver. Also, it listed Rutowski as an associate producer on the film. Well, I suppose you had to pay him for doing *something*. After all, there was no budget line item for "guy who carries the tequila and gets the girls."

As I sat down and began reading the script, I noticed that Oliver was hovering around my office, trying inconspicuously to look at the reactions on my face as I read through it. Well, he should have worn something a bit less sartorial that day if he didn't want me to notice him. A while back, he'd posed for one of those "Gap" ads, and they'd given him a bunch of free shirts. The colors he'd chosen had all been these intensely bright, eyeball-punishing lime greens and yellows. ("His shrink must've told him to wear bright colors to cheer him up," Don mused.) On this particular day, he'd chosen yellow, and he looked like a canary flying past my door every five minutes.

I'd known for a long time that Hollywood's Rule #1 was that nobody ever gave you their script in order to hear your "honest" opinion, no matter what their protestations to the contrary. What they want to hear is how much you like it; and if you don't, you can damn well keep it to yourself. If I thought Oliver with all his Oscars would be any exception to the rule, I was dead wrong. It was only then that it began to dawn on me how hypersensitive and insecure he was about his work, and he was as anxious for me to read it and give it my approval as a grade-schooler on his first spelling test.

While it's a good script, it's very different from the original Quentin draft. And yes, there *is* an Indian scene, which I think Oliver lifted directly from *The Doors*. The songs I'd given him were written into the new script as a virtual score, and much of Dave Veloz's first third of the script—all of the Mickey and Mallory history and relationship stuff—had been left intact.

But as Oliver writes with a director's mind as to how a film will be shot, it read more like a blueprint for Something Bigger than Quentin's entertaining, readable little piece. But it was hard to see what that "something bigger" was.

After I finished the script, Oliver caught me on his next sweep by my office.

"Did you finish it?" he asked.

"Yeah."

He turned to Justin, who was sitting in his cubicle. "Um, Duncan . . . Quentin . . . get me some water." (From then on, Justin's name became "Duncan," and Don refused to call him by anything else.)

"Well, what do you think?" he said.

"I like it. I like it a lot," I said.

"Do you have any criticisms? Is there anything you don't like?"

"I'd like some time to think about it," I said. "You know, digest it. But overall, I think it's really good."

I could see he was deeply relieved. This made him happy. "Well, get me your notes as soon as you can," said Oliver. "Feel free to make any suggestions you think would make it better." Then he was out of my office before Justin even had time to come back with the water. I was biting my lip, because there were several things in this new version I had serious reservations about, but I wanted the opportunity to choose my words carefully and present my thoughts to him after I'd had time to think it over. I didn't want to be cut out of the moviemaking process for all the wrong reasons before I even knew what Oliver, as a director, was trying to get at.

Now that we were firmly ensconced as part of the "family," we also found that our grace period with Oliver was coming to an end. Which basically meant that we were now subject to all the tirades, the mind fucking, and the belligerence with which Oliver treated everyone he worked with. He was particularly fond of winding Don up. We'd be ready to walk into a meeting with someone, and just before it started, Oliver would say, "By the way, Don, my attorney called—he's really pissed off at you." Then he'd walk into the room, introduce himself to whomever he was supposed to meet, and watch Don sit there close to apoplexy as he waited for the meeting to be over so he could call Bob Marshall and find out what he'd done now.

My personal Waterloo with Oliver came on a second location scout to New Mexico. We'd now decided that we wanted to shoot a large portion of the film there, and so we went back with a much larger segment of the crew—including assistant directors, lighting and art department people— so everyone could assess their needs in the situation. I'd written up my notes on the new script, careful to present my criticisms as tactfully and as positively as possible, and yet be true to what I felt. I gave them to Oliver so he could read them on the plane to Santa Fe. Unfortunately, I'd also made a huge error in judgment. I'd also given the script to Justin, figuring that as a twenty-one-year-old film geek, he'd be the only member of the target audience for the film who was likely to read the thing before it got made. (People between the ages of eighteen to twenty-four buy 80 percent of all the movie tickets sold in the country, which is one of the reasons why so few films get made for more mature audiences—once you hit thirty, the studio statisticians pretty much figure you're never going to leave the house again.)

I thought Justin's criticisms were pretty interesting and mild by most standards, but Oliver didn't take it that way. I could see he was sore at me by the time we got off the plane, but I had no idea why. He wanted me to accompany him to dinner that night with an up-and-coming female singer/songwriter whom Budd Carr had suggested to be the "musical voice" of Mallory in the film. While I'm sure she's a nice person, I couldn't stand her music, so I declined the invitation. It seemed better to try to derail these things from the start, or they'd take on a life of their own before you could do anything to stop them.

By the time we arrived at the Santa Fe Prison the next morning things reached a boiling point. It turned out that Oliver was angry over the fact that I'd even *shown* the script to Justin in the first place, and wanted me to fire him for being such an idiot.

"I always knew he was stupid, just from looking at him," said Oliver.

"You've got to be kidding me," I said. "It's valuable feedback, Oliver. If anyone is going to go to the theater to see this film, it's not the geezer brigade you've got crowded into these vans, it's my twenty-one-year-old slacker assistant."

"Everyone else loves the script. He must be a moron."

Oh, that did it. "So everyone you've show the script to loves it, Oliver? Well, maybe that's because you surround yourself with sycophants and yes-men who depend on you for their livelihoods; they have no taste in the first place and don't want to jeopardize their positions by telling you what they really feel in the second."

I remember standing in that prison yard, the site of the worst prison riot in U.S. history, known as "The Devil's Butcher Shop," as Oliver and I stood there yelling at each other at top volume for a good twenty minutes. Everyone else was standing around in embarrassed silence. Nobody—and I mean *nobody*—ever spoke to Oliver like that. But unlike Don, who's used to getting angry on a regular basis, I rarely find myself in that kind of high emotional temperature. And once I did, there was no mechanism for shutting off my mouth. By the time the argument devolved into the truly childish "Oh, yeah? Well, same to you, but more" level, Oliver decided he'd had enough and stormed off in a huff.

But from then on, I was persona non grata. Oliver made me sit in the van like an errant schoolchild while everyone else got out and talked about the logistics of shooting. And I thought about something I'd once read in William Goldman's book, *Adventures in the Screen Trade*. He noted that once you became famous and powerful in Hollywood, you had to get used to the fact that *nobody in your world would ever tell you the truth again.* Well, I justified my temper tantrum by telling myself that my allegiance was to the film and not to Oliver Stone personally, and if given a choice between speaking my mind and having him think me a great gal, there was no question which side I'd come down on. But I also had to wonder at what a lonely and weird world Oliver must be living in; for everything he had, all of his success, he didn't seem like a very happy man.

There was one other person who was less than happy with Oliver's new draft of the script. Quentin Tarantino himself. He got wind that he'd been rewritten, and he tripped. He called Oliver, and said, "I've talked to actors who've read both your script and mine, and they say mine is better." Quite diplomatically, Oliver responded that he'd led a different life than Quentin, and his moviemaking was an attempt to come to terms with the real violence he'd experienced in his life. Of course he was going to make a different movie than Quentin would have. Quentin interpreted this as condescension, and Oliver claimed that Quentin later called Steve Buscemi and Tim Roth and told them not to be in *NBK*, or he'd never cast them again. They both turned down roles in the film.

Where Don and I saw it as business as usual, I think Oliver was truly hurt, as he'd gone to great lengths to try to make Quentin an ally, if not a friend. While Quentin was clearly still angry at me and Don for not giving him his way, it never occurred to anyone that he thought the words in his script were inscribed on stone tablets. After all, no matter how good a script seems when you read it, it's a document you will ultimately use as a blueprint for when you get on location and the cameras begin to roll. The filmmaking process is a collaborative one, with everyone—directors, actors, camera people, technical experts, and any one of the other hundreds of people who pass through a film crew—ultimately contributing to the final product over the months (or years) it will take to shoot and edit a film. As a director, Quentin knew this.

"One day he's gonna pay," said Don, who felt protective of Oliver in the situation.

"I think you've made that vow every day since this whole nightmare began," I reminded him.

"Yeah, well, I just want to make sure I don't forget."

Fat chance that.

By this time, both Don and I were thoroughly confused, feeling out of our depths and in need of some good advice. The only source we felt we could really trust—certainly on the level we were rapidly being drop-kicked into—came from Thom Mount, who had somehow become a kind of self-appointed godfather through all of this. He took us out to dinner at Dominick's, the legendary restaurant which has since disappeared into Hollywood ephemera, but at the time it was a place where the Hollywood power brokers liked to relax undisturbed within its dark, windowless booths.

Thom gave us the lay of the land. "Get what you can out of your experience with Oliver, but don't become dependent on him." He told us we should always be pursuing our own goals, because even though Mount considered Oliver a friend, he knew all too well that the moment Oliver thought we needed him, he'd eat us alive.

"And don't take this as a sign that you've 'made it' in Hollywood, either, or you'll wind up like many young producers do, with a film in the theaters and nothing to follow it up with," said Mount.

We appreciated his candor and honesty in the situation, because we didn't really know anyone we could go to with his experience and knowledge of the film business. Don and I found ourselves going back to him again and again as time went on whenever we needed someone with a longer view of things to temper our tendency toward overenthusiasm and our penchant for making beginner mistakes.

So while we were sorting through all the preproduction mess, we were also trying to take Mount's advice to heart. We began scouring the town for other projects that we could set up while the iron was hot. We were still unknown commodities amongst the people who held the purse strings of Hollywood; and since Oliver was always encouraging us to bring him new stuff, we decided to use the opportunity to lend ourselves credibility. Despite the presence of Ixtlan, his in-house development company which usually made the films that Oliver produced, we sort of became an unpaid farm team.

I should have been suspicious when Don gave me a script with no title page on it one day, with the recommendation that he loved it and I should read it, as the extremely talented director Keith Gordon (*Midnight Clear, The Chocolate War*) was interested in directing it. I took the script home, and could get through only seventeen pages before putting it down. As I later discovered, it was titled *The Brave*. It told the story of an impoverished twenty-one-year-old alcoholic itinerant man of mixed race and impaired mental ability who lived with his wife and two children in a shantytown. Realizing he's never going to be able to get the people he loves out of this desperate situation, he agrees to sell himself to be killed in a snuff film. He goes to meet the sleazy snuff filmmaker, who rhapsodizes in elaborate detail about how he'll be tortured and killed. (This was the point at which I bailed on reading it and chose to skim the rest.) He gives the young man $100 and a document which reputedly says he'll pay the man's widow $35,000 after his death—but the young man can't read, so he doesn't realize that there are just "X's" all over the page. The young man then goes home to spend the last two days of his life with his wife and children, and we see the squalor and hopelessness of his situation before he goes off to his death, leaving the meaningless document for his wife to find.

Without question, it's the most disturbing thing I've ever read. I had nightmares all night and spent the rest of the next day convincing myself that nothing like this could ever happen. I told Don I didn't think I could work on the project. But Don was so enthusiastic about it, and I really liked and believed in Keith (whom I was trying to interest in directing one of my passion projects, Jim Thompson's novel *Savage Night*), so I said it was okay if he gave it to Oliver.

"You better sit down, then," said Don, "because there's one thing I didn't tell you. The project is controlled by Aziz Gazal."

I nearly lost control of my motor functions. "Are you *insane?*" I screamed. "Aziz fucked over both of us and everyone else we knew when we were at USC. More than once. He's crazy. There's no *way* I'm going into business with him!"

But Don assured me, based upon representations from our mutual school friend Michael Zoumas, that Aziz had become more reasonable lately. After his wife Becky had recently developed breast cancer, she had really gotten her life together; she had left Aziz and moved to Idlewild, where she had become a teacher. Aziz had sobered in the process; Don had even met him for breakfast without telling me, and was personally attesting to Aziz's newfound sense of reason. My better instincts were still warning me to be doubtful of Aziz's trustworthiness in the situation, not to mention his sanity. But I reluctantly okayed passing the script along to Oliver.

Oliver loved it. Which left us in the dodgy position of having to negotiate a deal with Aziz. Who immediately turned into the old Aziz again. He became convinced that we were trying to steal the project from him and insisted on coming in to meet with Oliver personally. I rolled my eyes and did Don the courtesy of not uttering the words "I told you so." We set up the meeting, but almost immediately, Aziz was calling Oliver's office directly behind our backs, saying he wanted to meet with Oliver alone. I began shooting Don looks of death when I passed him in the hallway.

Finally, after much agony and with great concern on my part, the sitdown with Oliver was arranged. Don began the meeting by talking about how great the script was, written by our old USC pal Paul McCudden, and Oliver expressed to Aziz how much he liked the honesty and uniqueness of the script. He also let him know that his interest was based on Keith Gordon's commitment to it, as Keith had directed an episode of the *Wild Palms* miniseries for Oliver. It was probably the best episode of that show.

Out of nowhere, Aziz started babbling that he, Aziz, was the only man with the passion and vision to direct the film; even the author of the original book, Gregory McDonald, believed he was the only one who could do it. My head was reeling; how did I get suckered into this?

With his uncanny ability to put his finger exactly where someone is most sensitive, Oliver interrupted Aziz: "What exactly is your ethnic derivation, anyway?"

Aziz started to shake and twitch; he answered that he was part Israeli, part Palestinian (something Don and I both knew him to be very touchy about). Before Aziz could recover his composure, Oliver stood up, shook his hand, thanked him for his time, and bolted for the door.

Two days later, a letter arrived from Aziz to Oliver, saying that if Oliver would support Aziz as a director, he'd give Oliver *The Brave* to produce. Several days later, we learned that Aziz had sold the project to both Jodie Foster's company and Touchstone on the same day. Thankfully, Oliver never mentioned the incident again.

In the midst of all Don's shenanigans, I had been busying myself in the editing room with Oliver's new chief editor, Hank Corwin. Oliver's regular editor, Joe Hutshings, hadn't been available during the *NBK* time frame, which irked Oliver to no end, but with Bob Richardson's encouragement he had decided to give Hank a chance. Hank came primarily from a commercial and music-video background, and with the exception of cutting together a few of the more expressionistic segments on *JFK*, he had little in the way of a film-editing background. As Bob shot a lot of commercials, the two had collaborated successfully for years. Oliver thought Hank's unique eye would be perfectly suited for what he wanted to achieve on *NBK*.

We'd scheduled a test shoot in Los Angeles prior to our departure for location, and for the shoot Bob wanted to try out every bit of visual chicanery he could think of. Hank began to edit together snippets of found film to music for the opening credits—scenes of the Las Vegas strip, horses running across the desert, auto crashes, dead animals, rotting fruit, blazing firestorms—to music like Patti Smith's "Rock 'n' Roll Nigger." We planned to take it onto the stage and project it all on a background screen as we put Woody and Juliette in the Challenger and bounced the car around in imitation of the cheap way they used to do traveling-car shots in '50s B movies. For the background plates, I began scrambling around, contributing bits of wrapping paper and Tibetan prayer scarves and pieces of music that we could stitch together into the mélange that would ultimately start to define the hyperkinetic, channel-surfing style of *NBK*.

When we finally arrived on the set at the Warner Hollywood studios for the test, I don't think anyone had any clue what it was all going to add up to, least of all Oliver. Suddenly we had music blaring, giant fans blowing fake snow over Woody and Juliette as Bob Richardson pumped devastatingly hot, shifting colors of light onto them and they jumped around in the car with the projections flying behind them. It was mad. Nobody had ever seen anything like it.

Don and I were dazzled. "Man, is this what the whole movie is going to look like?" Don said.

I couldn't really speak at the moment; my teeth were covered in black stain, and I had lipstick smeared all around my lips, my eyebrows drawn up like flames across my brow. Oliver had decided that the world of Mickey and Mallory was infested with demons, and I was going to be the female demon. While I'd never been anxious to get in front of a camera, I kind of liked the idea that in Oliver's mind, I was a creature from hell.

Richard Hornung, the costume designer, put a black leather jacket on me—backward—so it looked like bondage gear. Then Bob Richardson set me down on a stool, underneath a set of extremely hot par can lights that blazed down from above and nearly set my hair on fire, as he got ready for the shot.

"I have an idea," said special-effects guy Matt Sweeney. "What if we take this compressed air and blow it in her face? It'll distort all her features and make her look really weird."

Like I could have looked any weirder. "Great!" said Oliver. "Let's do it."

And so my screen debut began. The cameras started to roll, and with all that compressed air shooting directly into my face, my lips were practically blown around to the side of my head as Bob commenced strobing the lights. I think Oliver was calling out directions in the background, but I couldn't even hear him for the rushing wind in my ears. I couldn't breathe, or I was hyperventilating—I don't know which—but I was ready to pass out by the time Oliver yelled "Cut!"

I almost fell off the chair. Oliver was laughing with glee. "That was great," he said. "Where's Phil?" He called for stunt coordinator Phil Nielson. "Do we have a weapon for her?"

I was just beginning to catch my breath as Richard Hornung took the black leather jacket off me. I reached up to feel if my hair was still there; I could see smoke rising, but Bob hadn't managed to ignite me yet. I was wearing a tight brown suede vest but no shirt. Oliver came over, grabbed the shoulders of the vest, and pulled them down onto my arms as Phil handed me a long saber. Before I'd regained the presence of mind to protest, the cameras were rolling again, the air was in my face, the lights were strobing, and I had this big, long saber in my hand.

I couldn't breathe. I could barely see. But I could still yell. I began waving the sword and screaming at the top of my lungs.

"Oliver!" I shrieked. "I'll get you!"

He jumped back from the monitor a few feet as if he had, indeed, seen a demon.

I'm sure that over the course of my life, there will be something else that gives me as much satisfaction as I got from scaring the holy living shit out of Oliver Stone.

It just hasn't happened yet.

Chapter 7

It's All a Matter of Priorities—Mine!

"What do you want me to do with all this beer, lady?"

I didn't know what beer he was talking about, but I didn't need to ask. It was obviously one of Don's product-placement scams, which meant we weren't looking for a place to store a couple of bottles—there would be cases and cases of the stuff rolling in at any moment. And there was no room left. Our conference rooms, our Xerox rooms, our supply rooms and spare offices were all filled with crap the likes of which you couldn't imagine. Cameras and tennis racquets, basketballs and audiotapes, cowboy boots and (of course) Coca-Cola. We were days away from shooting, and I was on my way to the conference room where the obligatory giant gang bang of a preproduction meeting was soon to begin—a tedious obligatory get-together between all the department heads, where the script would be gone through in meticulous detail and everyone would have their chance to voice their needs and concerns. The last thing on my mind was Don's fucking beer.

"Put it wherever you can," I said.

I walked into the conference room and took my seat at the head of the long table, surrounded by 40 or 50 crew members, where Oliver, Clayton, Don, and our first assistant director—a giant New Yorker named Herb Gaines—were getting ready to start. In the movie business, as first A.D., Herb's job was simply to have a loud voice and make sure that whatever needed to be done on a set got done, and fast. It's probably the highest-pressure job on a set, and was a position that was usually reserved for big, loud guys whom nobody would want to mess with. Herb was a nice guy. I had met him a couple of times, and since it was going to be his job to keep everyone on the crew in line, he presided over the meeting.

Unfortunately, this put him at the front of the line of fire. Almost instantly, he began taking shit from Oliver. "What are you talking about? Haven't you read the script? You're going to ruin my movie!"

Herb seemed to take it all in stride, which was exactly what we needed from him, because what we were entering into was shaping up to be a production nightmare. As a big-budget Warner Brothers movie, we had the luxury of doing something lower-budget films do not: shooting in chronological order. For reasons of economy, most lower-budget films (and certainly the ones Don and I had previously been associated with) shoot out of sequence, so that all scenes which take place in a particular location are filmed back to back, regardless of where they appear in the final film. However, Oliver felt that performances on a film like this were greatly aided by the ability to let the actors progress their characters as time went on, and he was certainly right on that point. As Mickey and Mallory developed from slightly demented trailer-park trash to full-blown serial killers whose very presence instigates a prison riot, the mania of the atmosphere needed to be allowed to bloom.

Hank had been working now for a couple of months on editing together all the rear-screen projection plates that we'd use during the shoot, fragments of images that would give the movie not only an experimental feel, but also a sort of schizophrenic quality that reflected the mind-set of the characters. The projection plates were a pain in the ass to execute. It would take forever to set up the equipment and shoot the scenes with those giant screens in the background, and then sync them up with the main camera. But they were probably the most successful stylistic tool we had to reflect the frame of mind of the characters and reveal the sensory overload of the world that the movie was trying to communicate.

All of this wouldn't have been possible five years ago, when editing a film meant physically chopping it up and splicing it together in order to get the continuity you wanted. But with the advent of the new, computerized, nonlinear editing systems like Lightworks and Avid, the choices were myriad and instant. In theory, it should have made the editing of a film go faster, but in practice, it never did. The more choices you had, the more you wanted to explore. In the end, it would take us twelve weeks to shoot the film and a year to edit it.

The need for dragging around a huge crew and all our equipment for hundreds of miles each day presented a logistical ordeal, particularly for Dusty Saunders, the transportation coordinator. We had to cart our giant crew and all its accoutrements hundreds of miles each day across the desert for the next six weeks to shoot on some lonely stretch of road that Oliver had fallen in love with, before we moved on to Chicago, where we'd go back and forth between Stateville Prison, some local neighborhoods, and a stage. At one point during the meeting, I passed a scrap of paper back to him with a giant hole in the middle, with the words "Dusty's ulcer" written on it. He flashed me an agonized smirk.

And so, after much wailing and gnashing of teeth, we finally arrived in New Mexico. Don had gone on ahead with Oliver and a stripped-down crew to shoot some video sequences with Robert Downey Jr. in northern New Mexico, where Robert did some intros for the *American Maniacs* show as the sleazy Wayne Gayle. During the course of the shoot, we'd need to broadcast these segments over television in various scenes, so it was critical to have them before we set out on the road. When Downey was cast originally, he wanted to spend a couple of days with a tabloid journalist to get the feel of things. Geraldo got hacked off when he didn't get the role himself, so Don contacted the person he believed to be the king of television tabloid sleaze: the Australian Steve Dunleavy. Downey spent some time with him and, to everyone's surprise, when he showed up on the set, he was sporting a new Australian accent. Oliver, who loves to improvise in these situations, decided to go with it. Wayne Gayle became an Australian.

Meanwhile, I lagged a couple of days behind and traveled with Woody and Juliette and the bulk of the crew to Albuquerque, where our Southwest production headquarters was located, and we were building the stages we would ultimately return to. The first real location where we would assemble the entire cast and crew would be Winslow, Arizona, where we had built the diner set out of an abandoned roadhouse. In the meantime, our havoc-and-mayhem coordinator, Dale Dye, a former marine who had put all the actors through boot camp at Oliver's behest on *Platoon*, was trying to make convincing marksmen out of Woody and Juliette.

Together with Dale, Phil Nielson, Woody, Juliette, and our prop man Chuck Stewart, I climbed into a van and we traveled to a nearby military base, where we could fire guns (with blanks, of course) and not terrorize anyone. I had only recently met Woody and Juliette, and they both seemed pretty down to earth and accessible. Woody was into yoga and health food, Juliette into dancing and partying. The first sign that the two were not the most completely compatible people came during the van ride when Woody, in the back, asked that the air conditioning be turned off because he responded negatively to positive ions. Juliette, meanwhile, was lighting up a cigarette in the front.

When we got to the base, the firearms came out of a giant case, surrounded by all sorts of precautions by Chuck Stewart and Phil Nielson. (Brandon Lee had recently been killed out of negligence on the set of *The Crow*, and everybody was being careful not to make the same type of mistake.) Woody was pretty proficient with a gun; Dale would stand about twenty yards in front of him, screaming instructions—"Drop and fire three! Run to your left! Roll and fire two!"—while the actor followed his commands. Juliette seemed less than enthusiastic; her rubbery body held the guns without conviction, firing haphazardly. Oliver had been riding her hard recently about the lack of energy she'd been putting into her physical training (he wanted her to be muscular and toned for the role), and I think it was in large part due to a natural rebelliousness that she just wouldn't put her heart into the exercise. Exasperated, Dale Dye made *me* do it. I'd never held a gun before in my life, and hope that I never will again. I must've looked like a complete retard, struggling to remember everything he said about looking down the site at your target and clicking off rounds as I rolled through the dry grass and tumbleweeds of the military base. If he was hoping I'd inspire Juliette, it probably only made her laugh. But maybe he wanted to make her feel proficient in comparison— who knows. Oh, what a producer won't do.

Having packed our bags that morning, we got back to the hotel in Albuquerque, and sat around until the private planes that would shuttle us to Winslow were ready to leave. Somehow, instead of including Woody and Juliette on the direct private flights that would take about an hour and a half to get to Winslow, Clayton's staff had booked them on commercial flights that would take them from Albuquerque via Phoenix to Flagstaff, thence to be driven to Winslow by car, which would take a total of about four-and-a-half hours. When Woody and Juliette heard about it, they started yelling at *me*. I began calling the production office, telling them to change things, but because of weird bureaucratic chains of command, they wouldn't change anything until Clayton or his production manager, Leanne Stonebreaker, okayed it. I was trying frantically to call the two on their cell phones in the middle of the desert; they had already arrived in Winslow, and were tough to reach. When I finally got hold of Leanne, she said there was nothing she could do about it—that was that. I rolled my eyes, knowing that God himself probably couldn't keep Woody and Juliette from stepping on those planes, and that would inevitably leave crew people behind. (Each plane carried only eight people.) I finally reached Clayton, who started scrambling for excuses, but the upshot was that we had to charter another plane instantly. Don Murphy's predictions were coming true. Woody and Juliette got my seat and Phil Nielson's on the next departing flight, which meant that Phil and I were left there at the hotel to drink beers and wait for the next flight.

As Phil and I were sitting around sharing a Cobb salad and shrimp cocktail in the hotel restaurant while waiting for our ride to the airport, a bellboy came up to our table. "Are you Jane Hamsher?" he asked.

Well, that was weird—I was supposed to be gone by now. Who would have known I was still here, besides Clayton? By that time, I'm sure he had no desire to talk to me.

"There's an urgent message for you from a man named Al Cohen." I took the slip of paper from him in complete perplexity.

"Who the hell is Al Cohen?" I muttered.

It was Phil who finally tumbled to it. "Wasn't he the guy from the Chicago Film Commission who always drove us around when we went there?"

Sure enough. I went to a pay phone and dialed the number in Chicago.

"I hate to bother you, Jane," he said. "But remember when you were location-scouting with Oliver and you used to play all those L7 songs in the van? Well, the lead singer of the band, Donita Sparks, is a good friend of mine. I'd been talking to her about how much you liked her music, and she started complaining about how some guy named Budd Carr was treating her. She's really pissed off, and she doesn't want her music to be used in the movie. I told her you were really cool, and that before she made any decision, she should talk to you. So she's sitting by her phone right now, waiting for your call."

Oh, this was just *great*. Donita Sparks was my hero; she wrote tough, angry, funny rock-'n'-roll songs from a female perspective with a vigor that nobody else could match. I'd sent Oliver a copy of her "Bricks Are Heavy" album in Thailand because I worshiped the ground she walked on. The very next day, we were set to shoot the diner scene, which we'd choreographed for weeks to her song "Shitlist." And Budd Carr had sat there in the production gang-bang meeting not a week before and assured everyone that the rights to the song were cleared.

Now this.

Well, there's nothing like knowing you're going to be yelled at by your personal idol the first time you talk with her. But the situation demanded it. I called Donita.

"So this guy, Budd Carr, calls me up yesterday and says that he want to use 'Shitlist' in your movie," said Donita, who I could hear dragging on a cigarette as she spoke. "I told him we don't let anyone use our music without reading the script, and he told me that it was a privilege for my music to even be considered for an Oliver Stone film. And that if I didn't give him a yes by the end of today, he'd use something else. If I said no, he threatened to tell Oliver I said he was a sexist pig, which I never did."

Oh shit, did I start talking fast. I gushed with genuine enthusiasm for her music and tried to communicate to her what it meant to me to be able to use it. Still, she wanted to read the script before she'd give her approval. Since time was critical (we couldn't shoot a scene to music we wouldn't be able to use, especially if the main character was singing the words to the song during the scene), I paged Oliver at the Winslow airport and explained the situation to him. Budd had been with him for years, and he wasn't about to take Donita's word over Budd's; still, we were set to shoot tomorrow. He didn't want the script out of the office, having had bad luck in the past when it got into the wrong journalistic hands, and he didn't want to have to start defending himself to the press before he'd had the chance to make his movie. Could they come into my office and read it, I suggested? Oliver okayed it.

I called Donita back and told her that if she and the band wanted to come down to my office, my assistant, Duncan, would treat them like queens, and they could review the material at their leisure.

I guess she recognized that I was sincere and in a jam, so she acquiesced. Later that day, the whole band trooped down to my office, read the script, and gave their approval. I took major shit from Oliver, who believed Budd when he did indeed tell him that Donita had called him a sexist pig. I took even more shit from Budd, who told me I should have called him instead of Oliver when the whole thing went down. I wanted to call him a lazy, incompetent liar who shouldn't have represented days ago that everything was copacetic when he hadn't even started to get the clearances he needed, but I held my tongue and tried to explain I was only doing the best I could under the circumstances. My only comfort lay in the fact that once the smoke had cleared, Oliver probably chewed Budd out much worse than he did me.

Winslow, Arizona, is at the asshole end of the world. You can go there and find out for yourself, or you can take my word for it. I don't care. But believe me when I say that our motel accommodations made any Motel 6 look like the St. Regis, and they were the best in town. But by that time, everyone was so juiced up with enthusiasm about the movie we were about to start that nobody was complaining—at least not to my ears.

By the time I got to Winslow, the rest of the crew had already arrived. It was the first time I'd seen Don in days. I told him about the chaos I'd encountered in Albuquerque, which confirmed his suspicions that Clayton's preplanning had been something less than proficient. It made him laugh.

"So, how did the preshoot go?" I asked.

"It was great. We were out there in the middle of nowhere, and Downey was hysterical. He's a really good guy. We had a great time. And best of all, no Clayton."

"Will you stop riding that one? It's only going to bring us both a lot of grief."

He thought about it for a minute. "No," he said.

That night, we were invited to dinner at the Chinese restaurant in the motel across the street, the only half-decent place to eat in town. With us were Oliver, Woody, and a guy we met for the first time, introduced to us by Oliver as "my good friend, Dr. Christian Renna." While Woody and I struggled to communicate to the waitress exactly how we wanted our vegetables cooked (steamed), and argued about the virtues of macrobiotics over "Fit for Life" (me the former, he the latter), Don was wondering how you said "burger" in Chinese. I noticed that Oliver seemed to pay Dr. Renna a lot more respect than he did most people, including his stars. I thought the guy must only be visiting for a few days or something. But no, it turned out that he was the set "doctor."

. Which was really weird. Most sets have a medic on hand in case something goes really wrong, especially if there are a lot of stunts involved in a shoot, but rarely is there a full-fledged doctor around. What I learned, over the course of time, was that Renna was Oliver's personal physician who resided in Texas, and was into longevity programs. Oliver accepted his word as gospel. On the set, Clayton later told me that Renna was an osteopath, and since he was licensed only in Texas and California, he technically had about as much right to be writing prescriptions in Arizona as either of us did. Clayton referred to Renna as "Dr. Quack." Nonetheless, Renna was a repository of pharmaceuticals for the crew. Got a hangover? Dr. Renna was there with a B_{12} shot and a Vicodan. I began calling him "Dr. Feelgood." His wife, Melinda, was also there—she would ultimately play the news broadcaster in the see-through blouse who spoke with Downey during the prison riot. Most bizarre of all, he also had his three young (and very innocent) daughters, aged nine to sixteen, in tow for most of the shoot. Given the irresponsible, gypsy nature of set life in general, it struck me as a weird thing for a parent to do, particularly on this movie.

But as time would bear out, we were hardly venturing into the normal.

On our first day of principal photography, we all traipsed out to the diner that Woody and Juliette (mostly Juliette) would destroy during the opening sequence of the movie—and I first became exposed to rules of the Oliver Stone directing technique. First, you take the actors and you put them on the set. Then you remove anyone except for the director and the first A.D. The actors run through their paces; in addition to being taunted and pushed mercilessly by Oliver, they are also encouraged to improvise and bring new elements to their characters. Then the rest of the crew comes out, Bob Richardson does his lighting thing, and we shoot. All the while, Oliver is yelling at everyone in attendance: "You're not moving fast enough. Go, go, go! We're wasting time here!"

All of this keeps the tension level on the set at a peak. But it seemed to work. As the cameras began to roll and Juliette started to dance, I looked through Oliver's monitor. It looked great; it invited you into the scene, and yet had a sense of menace. Then "Shitlist" came blaring over the sound system, and Juliette began to beat the crap out of the hillbilly who had interrupted her dance reverie. If she'd shown any wishy-washiness on the shooting range, it was not in evidence here. As Donita's song blared loud and angry, Juliette pounded the shit out of the poor guy. She managed to work up so much visceral, physical anger that everyone was shocked to see it coming out of a ninety-pound girl. She took the script as a departure point and started building her character from there.

"All I wanted to do was dance, Mickey!" she shouted as the script supervisor looked down to her pages and saw nothing of the kind written there. "Why couldn't they just leave me alone? Huh? All I wanted to do was dance!"

She began throwing the hillbilly through the windows, smashing him on the floor, covering him with ketchup and mustard and jumping up and down on his back as she screamed uncontrollably. "How sexy am I now, huh? HOW SEXY AM I NOW!"

As Oliver yelled, "Cut!" a hushed silence fell over the room. And then suddenly, out of nowhere, all the women on the crew (the few of us that existed) began to clap and cheer. Juliette had somehow managed to tap into something that was inside us all, consciously or not. It stunned me. I know it stunned Oliver. Whatever limitations he'd been trying to over-come in his ability to portray women on-screen, he seemed to have made a breakthrough that even he did not understand.

I was even happier when Oliver took me by the arm and ushered me outside.

"If you have any thoughts or suggestions during the film, Jane, I want you to feel free to let me know."

Gee, this was great. Was he finally coming to trust me? Was he identify-ing me with whatever magic was coming out on screen? I didn't know. At the time, it just seemed like I was living in a wonderful world, and all my dreams were coming true.

I had often wondered how Don would function on a set. He was infi-nitely more social than I was—I couldn't give a flying fuck about bonding with the crew, but Don really wanted to be liked by everyone. Yet, I had a function there—a creative dialogue with Oliver—that he did not. All he had was a war with Clayton Townsend; and over the course of twelve weeks if that's all he had to do, it would spell trouble for everyone in the vicinity.

But on the first day, I found that Don had found a tool to preoccupy himself with—the cell phone he'd got out of the product-placement deal.

Whenever I didn't know where to locate Don, I'd simply have to walk outside to find him pacing about, wherever reception was the clearest. He'd be calling Los Angeles, having Duncan conference him in to agents and studio execs around town as he tried to set up other projects for us.

"No, no, it's a great deal. You'll love it. Here's the sketch. . . ." he'd be saying whenever I found him out on some lonely dune or stretch of desert, his weapon (the phone) clutched tightly to his ear.

In Winslow, I also got a taste of what it was like when Hollywood invaded rural America. At night, women would arrive in black '73 Cutlasses, pounding on my motel-room door, asking, "Is Woody there?" As Woody informed me, "Every week, forty million people watch *Cheers*. That's more people than have ever seen *Gone With the Wind*."

Woody tried hard to retain vestiges of a normal life. In his off time, he would orchestrate pickup games of basketball at the local high school with people who lived in the area. I'd usually be there, working out with weights or something, and saw the lines that would start forming around the building as word spread through the neighborhood that Woody Harrelson was in the building.

One day Don tried playing ball with Woody. He came out wheezing and breathing hard after about ten minutes.

"Basketball," he gasped, "I love it."

"Hey, pizza boy. Maybe you should make friends with a vegetable or two," I said. "And a little regular exercise wouldn't kill you."

The words "fuck you, bitch" didn't quite come out of his mouth, but you could feel them hanging in the air.

In Winslow we discovered we had another big problem: namely, that Oliver wanted to blare the music he'd chosen for each scene at top volume while he shot, and nobody had bothered to tell the sound people. Budd

Carr had provided a digital audiotape of "Shitlist" for the diner scene, which they had no problem rigging up, but little other music had been provided. Oliver wanted Juliette dancing on the hood of the Challenger to "Sweet Jane," and there was no DAT copy to be found. Finally, I located a CD copy of it from the most unlikely of places—Clayton, who liked it and had it in his car. But there was no CD player on the set. I finally scrounged a portable player off Kevin, the cable guy, and we hastily patched together a system that could play it. Still, as the day went on, things got more and more complicated, as the Jack Scagnetti/prostitute scene was shot. I had a copy of my Barry Adamson record and Alban Berg's opera *Wozzeck* on hand, but now we had to find two CD players and jury-rig a system where the Barry Adamson could be playing during the beginning of a scene, then time the *Wozzeck* cue so it came in precisely at the moment when Scagnetti turned and tried to kill the girl.

Fortunately, the sound man—David MacMillan—was the best in the business, and a really great guy. There's little in the way of sound that he can't improvise, and almost nothing can get to him—even Oliver Stone's rantings and ravings. As much of a pain in the ass as it was to execute, I noticed that Oliver's decision to blare the music over and over again as each scene was shot became an incredibly effective directing tool. It established a mood on the set that affected everybody, both actors and crew, so it was easy to keep the energy up and everyone in the emotional signature he wanted for the scene. Everyone might get sick to death of hearing these songs played over and over—I sure did—but it became an aural extension of the iron Oliver Stone will.

From this relatively easy stage work, we moved on to the gas-station scene, where Mallory seduces and then kills a young gas-station attendant, played by Balthazar Getty. We went into split day/night shoots, which meant that everyone showed up roughly at noon and we shot until the sun came up. Without a doubt, it's everyone's least-favorite shooting schedule; you never really get your sleep adjusted, and after a few days of this everyone is bone tired.

For the scene, Victor had outfitted the old gas station with $25,000 worth of neon. It was a garish Route 66 nightmare, awash in grease and soda-pop cans—and to my eye, a thing of hideous beauty.

As the crew arrived, an even bigger eyesore pulled up to the gas station:

a 16-wheeler bearing the neon-colored logo of a cow's skull and the insignia "Abilene Boots."

The driver announced to all that he'd just driven here from Alabama for the express purpose of having the truck appear in the scene.

"What the hell is this all about? I didn't order any boot truck," said a perplexed Victor Kempster.

Don ran up waving his hands. "Don't worry, I'll take care of it." He hustled the driver off.

I found him stuffing the guy with sandwiches at the craft service table.

"Murphy, what are you up to?" I said.

"Look, it's okay," he said. "It's just for one of our product-placement deals."

"You told them they could have their truck in the movie?"

"Well no, not exactly—not at first, anyway. See, to begin with, I figured they could give us just a couple of pairs of cowboy boots for each of us, we'd put some on the extras, and everything would be cool. Then they said, 'How about if you put our sign in the movie? Then we'd give you ten pairs.' And I said, 'Okay, great, I could do that.' But then they said that if we put the truck in, we could just go nuts."

"Uh-huh. And you agreed to this, Don, without checking with anyone."

"Well, I figured if we used it, great; and if we didn't, nothing lost."

"Don, that guy drove *all the way from Alabama.*"

"Look at him over there—he's happy." Don pointed to the driver chowing down at the craft service table. "He's eating sandwiches, having some soda, he gets to see the stars, be on a big movie set. I tell him the camera's pointed at the boot truck, how's he gonna know the difference?"

"Murphy, you've got the biggest balls I've ever seen." I was pretty certain that I was being hosed, and before the evening was over, the issue of the boot truck would be revisited. But at the moment, I had more important things to worry about.

Juliette was having trouble with the scene, and it was no surprise; it had never really made a lot of dramatic sense. Supposedly, this was Rutowski's contribution to the script. (By now Don had dubbed him "Pimpowski," and the amusing moniker had spread through the crew like wildfire, to the point where I don't think people remembered his real name.) I remember when I first read Oliver's version of the script, that this was the scene that gave me the most trouble. It just didn't follow that Mallory, a woman who was supposedly so much in love with Mickey that she'd kill for him, would just casually go out and fuck some gas-station attendant for fun. It was an icy, misogynistic scene, full of fear of women and their sexuality. (Rutowski probably *was* responsible for it.) Despite the fact that almost everyone had expressed concern over this scene, Oliver dug his heels in and held to it.

In order to make some sort of emotional sense of the scene, Oliver decided that Mallory was now trying to seduce the gas-station attendant because when she looked at him, she saw Mickey. In the end, I think they just wanted to shoot a scene where the girl kills a guy as he's going down on her, whether it fit or not. For the scene, Oliver had selected the Jane's Addiction song, "Ted Just Admit It." It was an extremely dramatic song about Ted Bundy that starts out with a slow dub and builds to a crescendo of violence, much as the scene did.

But the music was obviously at odds with what Juliette was trying to do. Juliette is a bit vain and headstrong, but essentially as insecure as any actress, and twenty years old to boot. To make matters worse, she was definitely caught up in awe of Oliver. Even as she wanted desperately to please him and make him happy, she wanted to express herself. On her side, she wanted her character to be something more than a gun-wielding slut; on his, he wanted to push her past a performance where she's simply sticking her fingers in her mouth. This struggle managed to inform the most compelling creative exercise on the set—perhaps because having the least to work with in the script, she and Oliver were largely creating her character as they went along. But Juliette had to work really hard to get over Oliver's progressive decimation of her self-esteem, and it was tough going. On his own, he's an imposing, intimidating sonofabitch. On the set, surrounded by an almost-completely-male crew who are loyal only to him, he's worse; add to that the level of "butt licks" (as Don calls them) whom he uses to communicate his wishes, and you'd better have some steel in your spine if you hoped to stand up to him.

Juliette refused to just "play" the scene. Over and over again, she'd opt out in the middle. Oliver was pissed off and pacing around. We were moving into the night, and we had many more scenes to shoot. When he's having trouble, Oliver starts sending everyone away. He screened off the set, so no one could see the actors except through the camera monitor that fed to himself (in the cocoon, a black canvas-draped contraption created to keep Kevin Costner from looking into his monitor on the set of *JFK*), and to David MacMillan, the sound mixer. When that still didn't work, he had the crew pick up and move around to the other side of the building, so they weren't even in the proximity.

Push 'em back to Los Angeles if you want, I thought to myself. If it was possible to cut out this scene completely, I would have been delighted. But unfortunately it was a pivotal scene that triggered a chain of events critical to the rest of the movie.

"I won't have it," said Victor Kempster as he approached the sound cart where everyone had congregated after having been banished while Oliver and Juliette battled it out. "The thing's an eyesore."

Victor had clearly tumbled to the fact that people were trying to wheel the ungodly boot truck into the scene. As can happen on sets late at night when no progress is being made, people get a little punchy, and as we took a turn for surreal, the boot truck was now the subject of crew conversation everywhere.

"I kind of like it," Herb Gaines said. My head snapped around in disbelief. People were *defending* the damned thing now?

"Yeah, it's not so bad, Vicky," Bob Richardson agreed.

Victor stormed off to find Don and thrash him, and I saw that the driver of the truck was still having a heck of a time at the craft service table hanging out with the extras. I knew why Victor hated the truck: It was polished within an inch of its life, and would be completely obtrusive in any shot that was composed around it. But why were people thinking about using it, when I knew Don wasn't even actively pushing the ugly, gleaming thing? We must be really bored.

Juliette's shrill, adolescent slumber-party-sounding cry of "Oliver!" rose up several times from the set, but no progress seemed to be forthcoming.

"It's not going to work—she's just not into it," Bob Richardson said to me.

And she wasn't. Every time we shot the scene, she was just sort of lying on the hood of the car in a lump until we brought in the music. Then she whipped out her gun and shot Balthazar Getty dead with enthusiasm.

"Why don't we use more of the music she likes, Bob?" I said, referring to an Aretha Franklin tape she had provided, but which Oliver was loath to use in anything but the very end of the scene. "As soon as we bring it up, she gets into it. Is it just an Oliver thing? Will he just not do it because that's what she wants?"

"I've tried to tell him that," Bob said. "You tell him. Maybe he'll listen to you."

Remembering what Oliver had told me at the diner about making suggestions, I decided to put in my two cents.

I approached the "cocoon," and I waited until the bustling sycophants had done their job reassuring Oliver that the scene was solid and he was a genius and it was only Juliette's lack of talent and immaturity that was keeping the scene from working. Oliver was sitting there alone, so I went up.

"Oliver, she seems to engage when you bring up her music in the scene. Maybe if we brought it in earlier, she'd be able to connect?"

Oliver didn't say anything. He just nodded, thought about it for a second, then said, "Okay." He turned back to his notes, his signal that I was done.

I went back to the sound cart. Shortly thereafter, David MacMillan was called by the second A.D. to the cocoon. A few minutes later, he returned.

"Jane, I'm really sorry," he said, "but Oliver wants me to take away the headphones from anyone but me and the sound crew."

I didn't know which part of this made me more furious and humiliated—the fact that he was punishing me by denying me the opportunity to even listen to what was going on, or the fact that he'd embarrassed David so badly by making him do this.

I gave David the headphones and did my best to make light of it for his sake, but deep down I was seething. So much for "welcome suggestions."

In the midst of battling with Oliver, or perhaps because of it, Juliette managed to finally come up with a level of pathos and wounded pride that invested the scene with *all* its meaning. It was a lesson for me in how a scene could virtually be rewritten by an actor (and under downright hostile conditions) who is struggling for some sort of consistency of character, beyond the stagy theatrics of the violence itself. I loved Juliette that night and wished her total happiness forever. Even as the shoot went on, and she spun out of control and had her vision of reality warped by the insanity that was brewing steadily both on and off the set, I'll always remember her as she held out at the gas station.

It was not long after that much of the nonessential crew decided to call it a night, when we only had one more shot left to take: a wide shot of Juliette driving the Challenger up to the gas station. Sunrise was in an hour, and I certainly could have gone back to the hotel myself, but I didn't—I'd never let Oliver think he'd gotten to me, so I was determined to stay there until the last awful minute when Herb Gaines called out, "It's a wrap." Meanwhile, Victor Kempster decided he'd done everything he could do, and he went back to the hotel.

He'd barely disappeared from the set when I heard Herb call out over the walkie-talkie, "Okay, bring in the boot truck."

"What boot truck?" Oliver asked.

"Don Murphy's boot truck," said Herb as the frightful thing fired up.

Don went scrambling up to the cocoon, talking fast. "See, Oliver, we have this product-placement deal with this boot company. And if we put the truck in the movie, they'll give us all free boots."

"Free boots?" Oliver's eyes lit up. "How come I didn't know about this, Clayton?"

Clayton jumped. "I didn't know about any deal. . . ."

"Alex Ho would have told me about a boot deal," said Oliver. "You mean I get free cowboy boots?"

"Two pair," Don said.

"We all do," said Herb.

So that was why everyone was on Don's side—he'd promised them all free boots.

"Let's get that boot truck in there!" Oliver called.

The shot was a tricky one, a crane shot that started on the road and rises as Juliette drives by in the Challenger, and finally stops on a wide shot of her pulling into the gas station. With roughly forty minutes to go before sunrise, it's decided that the boot truck will be driving in the other direction as she pulls in. Which requires resetting the two vehicles roughly a half-mile apart from each other, with two walkie-talkies cuing them. Clayton was starting to sweat—it's a tough shot to pull off, and if we didn't get it, our schedule was screwed, because it was a critical establishing shot. We'd have to come back, at tremendous expense.

"Do we have that coyote?" asks Oliver, referring to what coyote I didn't know. "Let's start the shot on the coyote in the road so that he walks out of frame as we rise up. Can we get him to do that?"

Suddenly a guy with a coyote on a leash walked up. "Sure we can," he said.

If you want to screw up a shot, especially one this complicated, put an unpredictable animal in it, standing under bright lights at 4:00 A.M. Clayton was wringing his hands.

"Cue the car!" Herb shouted in his loud, booming voice over the walkie-talkie. "Cue the boot truck!"

The coyote freaked and bolted.

Clayton was developing ulcers. I was tearing my hair out. I wanted to go home. The absurdity that can overtake a group of extremely exhausted people at four in the morning had definitely struck. The trainer went running through the desert brush to track down the coyote.

"Herb, maybe we should forget the boot truck . . ." I offered.

"No!" everyone shouted in unison.

"Don, go get the coyote," said Oliver.

Don took off after the trainer, who was coming up in the darkness with the coyote on the leash. Don took the leash from the trainer and paraded the coyote up to Oliver.

"See, Clayton, Don Murphy can get me free boots *and* a coyote!" Oliver said, just to get Clayton's goat. I could see it was working.

We finally got the shot off just before sunrise, with the entire crew focused obsessively on Don Murphy's fucking boot truck. Oliver had gotten his coyote in the shot and succeeded in stretching Clayton Townsend's nerves tight as a drum. But Don Murphy's luck had held out, validating his theory that "there's no need to tell anyone anything until the last minute." As he'll often say, "I hate these people who want to create all these problems by making issues of them before you absolutely have to." I don't know if it'll work for you; it doesn't seem to work for me. But it sure works for Don Murphy.

From the outset, we had wanted *NBK* to look and feel like nothing else cinema audiences had ever seen before, and what had bonded us with Oliver—a director whose work I have to admit I was not nearly as fond of as my partner—was his willingness to really step out and take a chance with this film. (Well, that and the fact that if we *didn't* go with him, we were completely boned.) That someone of his stature was willing to use his clout to fuck with the conservative studio mentality was something we could really get behind. It was something we had to keep reminding ourselves of as the shoot progressed; this guy may be a complete bastard at times, but he's putting it all on the line, and for that you get a certain amount of credit.

By the time we traveled into the middle of the New Mexico desert to shoot the "Mickey and Mallory fight in the desert" scene, the wild, reckless spirit that had inspired the film was starting to spread beyond the domain of celluloid and into the cast and crew itself. We spent the morning driving 200 miles into the northern New Mexico desert, around and around until Oliver found a place he liked. The temperament of the day was established quickly when Juliette and Woody were running through a scene at base camp, one in which their relationship in the movie was starting to dissolve, and they end up screaming at each other. Woody wound up throwing Juliette against the hood of a car and twisting her arm behind her in a half nelson.

"Knock it off, you fucking asshole! I'm just an actress, playing a part!"

It wasn't until then that the crew, Don, and I realized that they weren't rehearsing at all, but having a knock-down drag-out fight. They'd never really gelled much as pals—they lived totally different lifestyles—but until this moment, no real tension had erupted between the two. Great. It's 110 fucking degrees out here, and it's shaping up to be a swell day.

So in the midst of a dope-smoking, mushroom-chewing morning, we decided to rip the backseat out of the Challenger and stick Bob Richardson in it; we pulled the hood off the truck, and in went David MacMillan. We chose the film format by flipping a coin, and off went Woody and Juliette driving through the desert. It was a scene improvised around the real experience we'd had on our location scout, when we'd been eating mushrooms and were followed by the Navajo cop. It was weird to watch them reenact the alternating paranoia and hysteria of our own previous experience as the camera rolled. Where did reality stop, and the movie take over?

That thought continued to weigh on me as the day continued and things got weirder and weirder. On the first day of the shoot, Elizabeth

Stone strategically had filed for divorce from Oliver. It wound up as a joke on the Jay Leno show, much to Oliver's bitter consternation. The lawyers began battling it out, firing salvos back and forth as the Stones fought for control not only of their assets (Oliver was forever whining about how much money she was taking him for) but also their kids. By the time we hit the desert that day, his exasperation with Elizabeth had hit critical mass. And whenever anything is stirring around in Oliver's gut, it will ultimately wind up on the screen.

For the scene in which the fight between Mickey and Mallory finally erupts, Oliver chose a site two miles off the road, so we had to carry all our equipment out into the desert by hand. The most ridiculous thing we dragged out there was the cocoon and Oliver's giant monitor, carted across the sand as if it were Cleopatra herself being shouldered by a crew of slaves. Russell Means was with us that day, playing the role of the sage Indian out of Oliver's leftover '60s drug-induced spiritual hallucinations. Bob Richardson and Oliver decided to tie a high 8 video camera onto the horns of a ram and set him out through the desert chasing Woody, whom we costumed for the day in women's pink lace underwear. (A great shot that didn't make it into the final film, but can be seen on the director's cut.)

Then it was time for Oliver to vent his spleen.

Suddenly Woody and Juliette were up on top of a sand dune, screaming at each other.

"It's not some demon, Mal, it's me, your lover," said Woody.

"You ain't my lover, you ain't been loving me, huh, you been lovin' me real good." Juliette shoved him hard across the dune.

"Hey, it's the nineties. A man has to have choices," Woody said.

"Choices? You want choices? You want to fuck some other women?" Juliette pulled out her gun and shot at Woody's feet.

I turned to Victor Kempster. "Haven't I heard this argument before?" I said. Victor just smiled knowingly, as Victor is wont to do, but we both had. Suddenly Woody and Juliette had become Oliver and Elizabeth.

The crew was a little freaked out; this exchange was completely un-scripted, and nobody was quite sure, after the morning's events, whether Juliette would whip out her gun and shoot Woody's nuts off in the heat of the drama.

Suddenly, a call went up on the walkie-talkies, across the miles of desert, and shooting came to a halt.

"Don Murphy to the cocoon."

Huh?

Woody and Juliette were shuffling around, trying to stay in character at this very extreme moment while Oliver drew everything to a stop and talked to Don. What could he possibly need Don for at this moment?

I saw Don cross the desert as he trudged up to the cocoon. Oliver put his arm around Don's shoulder, and the two went walking off through the dunes.

Everyone was standing around, picking their noses for God knows what reason, when finally Don and Oliver came back, and shooting resumed.

Don made his way over to me.

"What was that all about?" I asked.

"Are you sure you want to know?" he said.

"Well, now that you say that, yes,"

"Oliver says that he doesn't know if he can have you on the set, because you're so negative."

Huh? "What the fuck is he talking about?"

"He says that you've never liked Woody."

"I think that was you, Don."

"I told him that, but I don't think he heard me."

I could never quite figure out why Oliver intermittently had such an ax to grind against me. Part of it was the erratic nature of his own personality, part of it was probably drug-induced, maybe I reminded him of his ex-wife or something. But he spent a lot of time griping about me and trying to disempower me, afraid that I was worming my way into the hearts and minds of his cast and crew in order to exert influence around him (which was not, by the way, untrue). Then, in the next moment, I would be his most trusted confidante. Whether it was true or not (because it made me feel better), I decided that he was riding me in correlation to how much creative influence I was having with him. Poor Don got earful after earful as shooting went on and beyond, through the release of the film, but it allowed him to act as sort of a pressure valve for Oliver on the set, who— when he had nothing better to do—could grouse about me.

Part of this was because we never came under the control of Caligula

Stone. Whereas there were wild bouts of bacchanalian revelry being conducted on a regular basis with Oliver as band leader, Don and I never participated. To a large extent, I think this always made him suspicious of us. It's not that we were puritanical; far from it. But I needed my head about me to concentrate on what I was doing on a day-to-day basis, and to stay in Oliver's face regarding my creative feelings no matter how dismissively or humiliatingly he treated me. And Don is on the whole happier playing Nintendo. Besides, there was something sad and desperate about the NBK goings-on. They looked more like pathetic attempts on the part of the truly lost and lonely to convince themselves that they were having a good time, when all they were trying to do was numb the pain and stress, and the people who were regulars at these events seemed to become progressively more and more unhappy as the shoot went on.

Juliette had started the shoot as a sweet, approachable girl. But as things progressed, she became so exhausted from what was being demanded of her on the set and the all-night partying that I'd find her utterly despondent and sobbing in the hotel elevators. Tom Sizemore, who was initially just ecstatic to be cast in such a prominent role, wound up in a fight with the captain of the plane that was shuttling him back to Los Angeles after he wrapped filming, and eventually was charged with air piracy. (The charges were later dropped.)

Although both Don and I tried to support everyone as we saw things getting nuttier and nuttier, it seemed best to concentrate our energies on keeping ourselves sane. For the moment, we were just glad that the filming in the desert would soon come to an end, and hoped that as we moved on to Chicago, life in the big city would make things easier.

Chapter 8

Hey, It's Not Really a Prison—We Get to Leave!

During the three-day break between the Southwest and Chicago, I flew back to Los Angeles to take care of some other business. Out from underneath my watchful eye, Don did exactly what I expected him to.

"Just tell me you didn't hit him," I said when Don called me.

"No, I wouldn't give Clayton the satisfaction of hitting him. Then he could go flying back to Oliver crying like a girly man."

"So what did you say?" I knew full well that Don's mouth was much more lethal than anything he could land with his fists, but much less likely to land him in jail.

"Well, on our last day in Albuquerque, Oliver wanted to have a send-off dinner at his favorite restaurant with all the regulars on hand—Clayton, me, Bob, Pimpowski, Dr. Feelgood, Dave Veloz, and Heineken Sue." (Dave had been on hand to see the Drug Zone scene being shot, one which he'd been responsible for penning; Heineken Sue was one of Oliver's girlfriends, dubbed so by Dale Dye, who noted, "The girl's got teeth on her that could open a Heineken.")

"And?" I said.

"So after dinner is over, Clayton's been sucking down a few grappas, and he decides that since you're not there to defend yourself, he's gonna launch a preliminary strike, and do some CYA." ("CYA" was the abbreviation for "cover your ass," something Clayton and his staff managed to do better than they did anything else.)

I wish I could say that Clayton's attack was another one of his stupid, spontaneous stabs that was unprovoked by the intended victim, but I knew that it was probably something I had stumbled into in L.A. While in the office one day, I saw one of Clayton's P.A.s watching dailies. Since Oliver was such an extreme control freak, and even the Warner Brothers brass were prohibited from seeing unedited dailies, this sort of crime was punishable by death. I didn't want to get into it, so I told Azita and made her deal with it. I knew Azita wouldn't burden Oliver with this kind of potentially enraging bullshit, but no doubt some idiot had mentioned it to Clayton.

"I guess Clayton decided Oliver was in the right mood to hear it from him before he heard it from anyone else, so he piped up and said, 'I guess Jane was in L.A. raising hell again today.' So I said, 'No, Oliver, what actually happened was that Clayton's penchant for hiring people stupider than himself backfired, and Jane fixed it. And now he's trying to shoot the messenger before there's even a message.' "

While Clayton knew that Oliver's loyalty to him was unquestionable, I don't think he was quite smart enough to see that Oliver had been orchestrating this train wreck between him and Don for a long time. I knew I should have scolded Don, but I couldn't keep the guilty relish out of my voice.

"And then?" I asked.

"You would've loved it," he said. "The entire table went flying for the bathroom as Clayton and I went at it. Clayton started to defend his guy, saying, 'He didn't do anything wrong,' and I said if he wasn't doing anything wrong, then why even bring it up?

"So in the midst of all this, I turn to Oliver, who was sitting there at the end of the table with a big shit-eating, gap-toothed grin on his face. He was loving all this chaos and madness. He wanted me and Clayton to hate each other, and he'd finally achieved his goal. It was mind-boggling. The great Academy Award winner had nothing better to do than fuck with sad old Clayton and little me."

In the end, I felt kind of sorry for Clayton. Don was truly indomitable, and would learn and grow and thrive, no matter what kind of bitter politics you managed to distract him with momentarily. But Clayton, on the other hand, was someone whose status in life depended entirely on the goodwill of Oliver Stone. There were signs everywhere that our budget was getting out of hand, that the advance planning Clayton and his staff were responsible for had been nothing short of piss-poor, and our firing (nay, scapegoating) of three production coordinators in a row had only served as further evidence of this.

That evening, Clayton went on to get mind-bendingly intoxicated at a rave, picking a fight with someone much smaller than Don, only to wind up dead drunk and rolling around on the floor. For Don, the scene at dinner was just another battle in the seemingly endless war we'd both been enduring for over a year now; but for Clayton, it must've been a real ego-bender. It's hard to be reminded just how much fealty you owe someone, especially when the thing you're responsible for delivering is spinning out of control. The specter of Oliver's loyalty suddenly disappearing as he refused to take sides in the Don/Clayton confrontation must have been devastating for him, compounded by the fact of knowing that as the numbers kept climbing, you just weren't able to keep the gaffes from happening, and one day there just wouldn't be enough CYA in the world to make up for all of them. Alex Ho had lasted because he was smart; Clayton's position was much more that of a loyal basset hound. And that kind of dramatic realization must have been a very painful and frightening thing.

As I rejoined the crew in Chicago, I found myself ensconced in a lovely suite at the Omni Ambassador East, not far from the shore of Lake Michigan. They were luxurious digs, full of swirling pink draperies and brocade armchairs. But these lush nighttime surroundings hardly made our stay any easier. The irony of living in such elegance served only to completely fracture my consciousness, because now, off and on for the next six weeks, our days would begin and end at Stateville Prison.

It had been one thing to be a part of a small band being personally escorted around the prison in the company of the warden, where all gates were immediately unlocked and every wing accessible. It was quite another to be a part of a crew of hundreds—and, needless to say, one of the only women.

Each day, a "call sheet," as it's known in the business, was distributed among the crew, usually pushed under your door in the wee hours of the morning when the assistant director staff finally got it together to figure out when everyone should show up for their "call." On a normal shoot, everyone's "call time" is relatively close together; actors report for makeup, the lighting guys start rigging their equipment for the day, and set dressers (who are probably working a day in advance of anyone else) are there just prior to shooting to make sure everything meets the director's approval. When you start shooting in a maximum-security prison, all those conventions are thrown out the window.

In the rear of Stateville Prison was a place known as the "sally port": two giant, forty-foot gates separated by a cyclone-fenced cage where everyone and everything is examined meticulously by the guards before being allowed entrance into the prison. Prior to our arrival at Stateville, everyone had been required to fill out sheets giving exhaustive personal histories, which the Stateville officials used to check any record of criminal past. Since the Chicago Teamster union was so strong, Dusty Saunders wasn't allowed to bring along his L.A. drivers, and we were forced to use the locals. Of the forty-some Chicago Teamsters we tried to get approved, all but a few were denied access for felony weapons violations. (And I think it finally took an act on the part of the governor's office for Pimpowski to get clearance; the place clearly made him nervous, and he was rarely on hand while we were there.) Fortunately, once we got all our crew trucks and trailers and other assorted junk inside, we didn't have much daily use for drivers. But each and every day, it took four hours for our crew and equipment to be searched and approved admittance. When everyone and everything is on the clock the minute they get into a crew van, the expense was astronomical. And once those giant gates opened to allow you admittance, they didn't open again on a mere whim. Once you were in, you were in until the day was over. Since a day inside a maximum-security prison is endless even for those who know they'll be getting out after sixteen or eighteen hours, it was unimaginable to me what it must be like for those who wouldn't see the outside world for years.

The first scene we were set to shoot took place in the roundhouse. When I arrived, Herb Gaines pulled me aside and said that for security reasons, he didn't want any women to go inside. Which immediately triggered this knee-jerk reaction I'm predisposed to, and there was nobody that was going to keep me from going into "F" house. Most of the crew were assembled outside of the facility, trying to figure out how they were going to shoot the first setup, where Bob Richardson wanted almost 360-degree freedom to go in with a hand-held camera on his back and shoot whatever happened, in this case a prison riot employing 450 of the institution's inmates. Which meant the presence of almost none of the crew members in the ward while the riot was going on. Let me tell you, nobody on the crew had any complaint on that front. Everyone was freaked out, not only by the security they'd had to pass through in order to get into the facility in the first place, but with the conditions they witnessed once they got in there. It was a hot, stinking hellhole with no ventilation, and every time they turned around, their equipment was being stolen and turned into zip guns or something. From the moment we arrived at Stateville, they were all eagerly counting the minutes until we'd be gone.

"Murphy, you're coming with me," I said as I grabbed his arm and pulled him into the roundhouse. I think I was expecting the entire place to be infected with B-movie prison agitation with the advent of the crew's presence or something, but there was nothing that was any different than the droning rap music and the air of diffident boredom that I had been greeted with every other time I'd stepped into the place. But if I thought they'd forgotten me during my six-month absence, I was mistaken. Cries of "Jane!" went up everywhere, as the inmates I'd met during the scout—Charles, Ali, Hollywood, and an inexplicable number of people called Mad Dog—huddled around me.

Usually, still cameras are not allowed within the prison, but the warden had allowed Don and me to bring them in because we were producers. And for reasons that are still unfathomable to me, every inmate begged to have his picture taken. It wasn't as if they wanted some sort of memento from the shoot, because they never wanted us or the stars to be in the photograph; it was always either by themselves or with their pals throwing gang signs. While not much of a photographer, I was only too happy to oblige. I was fascinated to see how much of the emotion, the lurking violence would be captured on film, not only in the still photographs, but also in the filming of the movie itself. And nobody, but *nobody*, was keeping me out of the roundhouse while that riot was going down.

And what a riot it turned out to be. Never in my life have I been witness to anything like it. Having lived through the joy of the L.A. riots where the worst fires on the second night were six blocks from my house, I had some basis for comparison. With the exception of a couple of stunt guys who were set to fall over railings, the only crew members allowed in the place besides me were the set photographer, Sidney Baldwin, and the boom guy, Steve Bowerman. We were all situated right above the only entrance to the building, where the central part of the riot was set to be filmed as Bob Richardson ran in with his camera. The central guard tower was backlit, and the place was filled with smoke, giving it an atmosphere somewhere out of Dante's inferno, or some Faustian nightmare.

As Herb yelled a barely audible "action," a team of storm troopers dressed in riot gear went tearing into the mob, who were equipped with rubber shovels, garbage-can lids, and whatever other implements our prop guys concocted to look lethal without actually being so. But authenticity required no props. What the prisoners didn't know—what even I didn't know at the time—was that one of the warden's stipulations was that the people who acted the part of the storm troopers had to be actual prison guards, so in case things got out of hand, they'd know how to handle it.

Well, to say things got out of hand is an understatement. No sooner did the prisoners recognize the guards and realize that this was their chance to really wail on them than the whole thing went wild. Don had fixed me up with an auto-advance camera from one of his product-placement deals, and I could barely grasp the things I was seeing through the lens as I stood not twelve feet over the riot scene, snapping off shot after shot. Then suddenly the sound of gunfire erupted.

Now on a movie set, when blanks are going to be fired during a scene, the A.D. will shout "fire in the hole" before you start shooting, to let everyone know what to expect. But the place was so big, and the possibility of communicating anything to 450 people in the huge, echo-filled chamber was so completely impossible, that I don't know if he ever called it out, but I sure didn't hear it. And even if everyone had, I'm pretty certain the prisoners had no idea what it meant—to them, gunfire in the facility means that a real riot has broken out.

The place went wild. Prisoners were jumping over railings, tearing into the guards and each other, their pent-up rage suddenly finding release as the cameras rolled. Guys who had nothing better to do than work out with weights in the prison yard all day had an outlet for all the aggression they'd been physically preparing themselves for over years of life in prison. Herb Gaines's pathetic yells of "Cut!" went unheeded and unheard. My camera kept snapping away, and I could see Bob Richardson in the midst of it all, capturing it on film. I was too overwhelmed to absorb what was going on.

And when I finally did start to think, it occurred to me that there were 450 rioting murderers out of control, blocking the only exit to the building, and I was the only woman in the place. I should have been terrified, and even now I don't know why I wasn't. There was something in the air that was so electric, so kinetic, so visceral and cinematic and real that I felt utterly and completely alive. Whatever the reason, no concern for my safety—or lack thereof—ever entered my mind.

Eventually, the bullhorns of the A.D.s yelling "Cut!" and the persuasiveness of the guards' batons managed to communicate to the inmates that it was time to stop, and the place quieted down. Great deliberation went on before it was decided that we would explain to the prisoners a little bit more about the details of what we were trying to do. Now that they knew the guards themselves were going to be present in the scene, the whole event would be a little less volatile. We'd go again, same scene, same action.

But not before one of the A.D.s came up to me and said, "Uh, Jane, we think maybe it would be best if you left for the next take."

"No way," I said.

I ran up to the third tier to see if I could get a better vantage point over the riot the next time, and standing there I saw none other than Raymond Sojak, the man whose trial we'd walked into at the Cook County Courthouse on our first Chicago location scout. Talking with him, I found he had no recollection of Oliver or any of us walking into his trial. Since he'd been in prison, he'd found Jesus and spent his time in religious activities. I don't think Oliver remembered him either, but he liked his look, and early on had cast him prominently in the lunchroom scene where Tommy Lee Jones stops a fight between the inmates with a pair of nose pliers. (Sojak is the balding, gray-haired white guy that the black inmate goes after with a fork.) It was weird to see the whole thing come full circle like that, but hey, this was *NBK*.

Because many of the cinematic flourishes of the film could not be accommodated in the limited circumstances of the prison shoot (things like the rear-screen projections, overhead shots, and cells with moving walls), we eventually had to move to a stage in Chicago in order to shoot Mickey and Mallory's scenes in prison. Oliver, who had been completely invigorated by shooting at Stateville, was bored as hell on stage and began to make everyone's life miserable. By that time, the crew was exhausted, primarily because our cost overruns were becoming the stuff of rampant gossip, and Clayton had apparently decided that the best way to perform CYA was to blame all our overruns on the crew's incompetence. Oliver bought into it and started to hate them one and all, blaming them for causing all this added expense and making their lives all the more unbearable.

Enter Don Murphy. Even as Don was driving everyone crazy on the set (for whenever he didn't have a phone in his hand or deals to cut, his penchant for being hyperanxiety boy and stirring up trouble was bound to manifest itself), he also saw that the crew needed some outlet after the intolerable hours and conditions they were forced to work under. He tried to convince Oliver that we needed to throw some sort of party to let everyone bond and blow off steam. But because Oliver was resenting them so much, and we were watching the budget so carefully, Oliver now had a great excuse to turn Don down.

But Oliver's and Clayton's reluctance to address the problem didn't make it go away, so Don went into action as the king of scams. Without a budget for a party, he began fast-talking the local club owners.

"Hi, I'm Don Murphy. I'm producing the Oliver Stone movie that's shooting in town, and I'd like to bring Oliver and a bunch of movie stars to your club on Saturday. You'll comp us? That's great. Hey, while you're at it, could we have some free drink tickets? Cool. Oh, by the way, some of our crew might come along, so you won't mind letting them in. . . ."

Chicago's Red Dog, Shelter, China Club, Ka-Boom—each week a different bash. Oliver, who loves to be the center of attention, could always be counted upon to show up, which meant the actors were in tow. We couldn't have cared less, but they were the bait, and at that point, our crew was in desperate need of some release.

Clayton fumed, angry not only that Don had upstaged him, but that the crew—many of whom muttered in anger against Clayton every time his back was turned—were being rewarded for their efforts.

"Why do they need this? We're paying them a lot of money for all the overtime, aren't we?" he said to Don.

"Yeah, Clayton, but they don't really have a choice, do they? They *have* to work overtime. It's not like they have the opportunity to pass up the cash and go back to the hotel."

I remember standing in the middle of one of these Chicago clubs one night, dressed in a black cocktail dress as the specter of a soaking-wet Don Murphy (who had been pouring full mugs of beer over his own head) charged me at full speed while a drunken mob of 100 or so crew members were waving their fists in the air and screaming, "Go, Don, go, Don!" Somehow, my all-business partner from Los Angeles had made the transition into "Don the Party Man." Don who never drank, who was now blindly intoxicated on (God help us all) tequila, was doing a Cossack dance in the middle of the club to the cheers of the crowd, and was spinning out of control, charging club patrons like a wild bull. We were no longer just making a film, the film was making us.

It was all wreaking hell on the actors, too. Life on the set became ever more troubled for them. On the day we were set to shoot the scene where Mallory beats up Jack Scagnetti in her prison cell, nobody could rouse Juliette. Don eventually had to have the hotel security people break down her door so we could get her to the set.

As the cameras began to roll, Tom Sizemore as Jack Scagnetti was supposed to walk up to her prison door, knock on it, and say, "Rise and shine, Knox." Which he did. But Juliette didn't move; she just lay there. "Rise and shine, Knox," Sizemore said again, but still, Juliette didn't stir.

Tom turned to Oliver. "She's asleep."

"What do you mean she's asleep? She's *supposed* to be asleep in the scene," Oliver said.

"No, I mean she's *really* asleep."

We cut the cameras. Sure enough, Juliette had passed out on the cot. We took her to her trailer and finally got her awake enough to perform. In her next scene, she was supposed to beat the crap out of Scagnetti—which she did with such force that she literally broke Sizemore's nose when she smashed it against her cell wall.

Chris Renna looked at it, thought it could use some attention, but there was no way Oliver was taking the time out. "She's awake now, we're not stopping, let's go!"

Tom was not the only one who suffered injuries on that day. After Scagnetti knocked, Mallory was supposed to charge the door head-on with such force that she knocks herself out. Which meant that Oliver wanted a shot from her point of view while she charged. Bob Richardson took a hand-held camera and charged the door, but he wasn't going fast enough or getting close enough for Oliver's satisfaction. "Closer! Closer! Faster!" Oliver screamed. Finally Bob hit the door so hard that he fractured his hand. So Oliver sent in the second-unit cameraman, who injured himself doing the same thing. Bob got angry and stopped speaking to Oliver for two days.

Oliver was becoming increasingly inaccessible. Every time I wanted to talk to him about something, he'd either walk away or threaten to have Dale Dye throw me off the stage. Finally I brought him something that seemed to sooth him for a while: a copy of Leonard Cohen's new record, *The Future*, that I'd picked up at a local record shop. But most of the time, when we weren't actually shooting, I'd find him pacing around the stage, muttering, "There's a demon on this set, Jane."

I did him the courtesy of not mentioning my suspicion that its name was Oliver Stone.

Around this time, Peter Gabriel gave a concert in Chicago. While I was much too tired to attend my own showers these days, Bob Downey went to the show and told him we were trying to use some of his music in the film (we'd chosen one of his tracks from the film *Birdy* as accompaniment to the Drug Zone scene, and since that time, Hank Corwin had cut the scene with the music as background score). He came down to the editing suites, and he liked what he saw. So Downey decided to have a big dinner with Gabriel in attendance, and invited Don and me.

Of all the actors on the shoot, Robert Downey was probably the one that Don and I became closest to, and the one we liked the most. He never cared what the political climate on the film was from day to day, who was in or out of Oliver's favor. He liked whom he liked, and that was that. He was forever throwing lavish dinners, where he'd invite everyone from the day players to the sound guys. He really just wanted everyone to be happy and had a genuine desire to be loved. In light of all the problems that he's encountered with the law recently, I'll say that there is no doubt that Robert loves to party, but I never saw him out of control or in such bad shape that he couldn't do his job. As he told me one time, "I'm a fifty/fifty man—If I can feel great fifty percent of the time, I'm willing to feel like shit for the other fifty."

I don't know why Oliver had his nose out of joint on that particular day, it could have been anything. But when he arrived at the restaurant and saw that Downey had invited Don and me to the dinner, he was instantly pissed off, and retreated to the restroom in a fit of pique. Pimpowski was left to arrange the seating arrangement at the long table to his master's liking.

"Move down," he said to me.

"No," I said. "I'm happy here."

He physically pulled the chair out from underneath me. So fierce was his loyalty to Oliver's wishes and his own delight in celebrity sycophancy that he scooted me down the table and prepared to arrange himself, Oliver, and Downey at the end of the table with Gabriel. Unfortunately, he didn't feel quite so free in ordering around the singer, who seemed to think that if I was moving down, he should, too. I wound up sitting next to Gabriel's seventeen-year-old daughter, with Peter sitting next to her, and Oliver across the table. I could have risen to the occasion and landed a very satisfying punch in Pimpowski's face at just that moment, but to do that would have been to cede the battle to General Stone, whose orchestration of such skirmishes was his way of maintaining control, of keeping your energies away from anything that could threaten his indomitable command of the situation.

I had decided that anytime I went head to head with Oliver now, it was over something that would finally wind up on the screen and matter in ten years, in fifty years, and not to do with the personalities engaged in the execution of the film. No more energy was wasted on incompetent production coordinators, stamps, and parking stickers. Which, I think, is part of the reason why he found me so frustrating to work with. Whenever he would dig at me, try to get at my raw nerves, no matter how soft the spot he hit, I would try to joke it off and return to business. "About the next scene . . ."

Oliver had almost no idea who Peter Gabriel was at that time; in between pounding down glasses of expensive wine and feeling up his model du jour, he demonstrated his knowledge of rock music to Mr. Gabriel and his teenage daughter by explaining to them that what he's always *really* wanted to do was fuck Grace Slick. Feeling somewhat responsible for the singer's late entry into the steadily escalating *NBK* debauchery, I tried to change the subject. I mentioned that we were looking for some African music to use in the prison scenes, as Oliver had chosen to make a political comment on the overwhelming African-American element of the prison population (85 percent) by calling the institution "Batongaville" in the film, evoking overtones of the South African system of jurisprudence. Peter said he had the perfect piece of music, which eventually turned out to be by Nusrat Fateh Ali Khan, and he agreed to send it to us. I told him we'd been really inspired by the work he'd done on the sound tracks for *Birdy* and *The Last Temptation of Christ*, which he mentioned he'd had five years to work on.

This woke Oliver up. "Huh?" he said.

"He says he had five years to do *The Last Temptation of Christ*," I repeated.

"You know, Christ lived to be ninety years old," said Oliver. Gabriel looked slightly confused, as if he hadn't heard him quite right. "His followers hid him and distorted the truth. Now *that's* the movie you should make," he said.

"Um, Oliver, he's a musician, not a filmmaker. . . ."

"I'd make the movie myself, only they'd call me a conspiracy nut," said Oliver, with great seriousness.

Just then, Woody Harrelson stuck his newly shaved bald head into the conversation. " 'Scuse me, Mr. Gabriel, but could you tell me, was your music influenced by the music of the Beatles?"

As I frantically signaled the waiter for more wine, I could only hope that enough alcohol would eventually be consumed over the course of the evening that the whole thing would seem a blur the next morning.

By day, I'd split my time between the stage and hanging out in the editing room with Hank Corwin, who was cutting together rough assemblies of the scenes we'd already shot. It was exciting to watch the whole thing coming together—it was bizarre, frenetic, and like nothing I'd ever seen. Oliver got wind of my hanging around there and thought I was exerting too much influence over Hank, so he banned me from the editing room altogether. Unfortunately for Oliver, he'd done such a good job of intimidating Hank and undermining any self-confidence he had by that time that Hank was easy to bully. So I kept up my visits.

"How's it looking?" Don asked one day as we were on the stage.

"Great. Strange. Everything we ever wanted it to be."

"Well, I had an interesting experience this morning."

"I hope it didn't involve any raised voices," I said.

"No, I went to pick up Sean to take him to the comic-book store." (Sean was Oliver's eight-year-old son, and Don had befriended him over the course of the shoot—they both had a love of comic books and action figures, in addition to sharing similar levels of emotional development.) "When I got to Oliver's room, he opened the door and was standing there in nothing but a pair of red-white-and-blue boxer shorts."

I snorted out a laugh. "He really has no sense of humor about himself, does he?" I said.

"No, you can safely say that Oliver Stone is not, and never will be, a funny guy—at least not intentionally."

As we left the Chicago stage and returned to Stateville, we found that during the two-week interim, conditions there had turned even uglier. Several prisoners had beaten up two of the guards, and the warden had put the place on lockdown, which meant that none of the prisoners could come out of their cells. Now whether it's true or not, rumor had it that about a third of the guards were in gangs themselves. Which might explain how, during the lockdown, one of the gangs had distributed bad drugs to another of the gangs. Eleven people had been hospitalized and two had died.

Meanwhile, one of the guards had written to a local paper, saying that the prop weapons we were using in the shooting of the film were endangering their lives. It caused a media sensation that went all the way up to the governor's office, and we were informed that we would no longer be able to use prop guns in shooting the film.

This was nothing short of DISASTER. We'd given the prison warden, the state officials, anyone who wanted it a copy of the script before we made any agreement. We'd been very clear that the end of the film was a prison riot, that we absolutely had to have fake weapons on hand in order to make it realistic. But because of the media pressure, the state was adamant. Immediately, Oliver had to get in there, invoking his Washington political connections in order to get us some help in the situation because if they stuck with the decision, we were doomed.

Blame was flying everywhere and started landing on the location super-visors, whom Oliver was cussing right and left for not having made provi-sions for such exigencies. Well, the location supervisors dragged out our contracts with the prison, and to everyone's astonishment, it included a clause which said we could not bring anything that even looked like a weapon into the prison.

"It's a pro-forma clause that the state always insists on," Clayton stam-mered when confronted with this situation. "They always wanted the right to rescind things if they wanted to. . . ." went the babble. But the prob-lem was still at hand. We had a prison riot to shoot before this whole thing was over, and what the hell were we supposed to shoot it with?

Somehow, Oliver's bigwig political connections got the governor's of-fice to agree that if they kept the prison on lockdown, and we shot only with extras from the outside with no chance that any prisoner could get near any fake weapon, that we could continue at Stateville. But for every fake weapon we had, one guard had to be hired to watch it at every moment. And every time a shell was discharged, we had to shut down and account for every casing before we could proceed. Now, when other people complain about production nightmares, I can only laugh.

I was afraid that our presence here had stirred things up to such a degree that the death and violence that had exploded during our absence was somehow our fault. So I pulled Tony the warden aside and asked him as much.

"No, it's just the summertime," he said. "Every time the place heats up, it gets like this." I remembered hearing in the past that a lot of big-city riots happen during heat waves, and given the scorching Illinois summertime temperatures, combined with the exhausting levels of humidity and the lack of ventilation at Stateville, it wasn't hard to believe.

But it was still tough to ignore the new atmosphere of the prison as we started shooting Mickey and Mallory's escape scene, which at one point led through this corridor that ran between "B" East and "B" West wing. I think it existed for some sort of maintenance access, but it was as close to hell on earth as any place I've ever been. It couldn't have been more than four feet wide; it ran the length of the Auburn corridor, with tiny holes that for reasons I never understood went into each prisoner's cell. Above the catwalk that ran across the bottom was an endless structure of raw lightbulbs and rusty pipes, dripping raw sewage down onto the catwalk.

Upon our first visit, Oliver had been enraptured by it (although he and I had been the only ones willing to traverse it all the way to the end). There wasn't much in the way of lighting or set decorating we could do, so we just sent our actors down with Bob Richardson following, camera mounted on his shoulder.

After one take, Downey couldn't handle it anymore. "This is criminal shit pouring down on our heads," he said, concerned because he'd heard that 80 percent of the inmates were HIV positive. He declared that it was a "wrap" for him that day and bolted. We took a few more shots with Woody, Juliette, and the other actors who were supposed to be in tow during the escape, in order to have something to cut together. The scene on film looks innocuous enough, but I still can't watch it without recollecting how well it reflected the horror of the conditions that existed in that place, and my skin begins to crawl.

If you look at the film now, by the time the riot starts to escalate, it looks like we'd managed to create an intensely crazy environment, but we didn't have to create anything. The prisoners were locked in their cells and were in a frenzy. At one point, we had to shoot a scene where Tommy Lee Jones walks down in front of the cells in "B" West with one of his guards as all hell is breaking loose—the prisoners are screaming, there's smoke and fire everywhere, and someone throws a carton of milk that lands on Tommy Lee's head. Well, that was no prop. One of the prisoners really *did* throw the milk; as it dribbled down his face, Tommy Lee, the consummate pro, just kept on with the scene. It was a great (if unexpected) touch that we ultimately put in the film.

But the noise made it almost impossible to shoot. Nobody could hear what Herb Gaines was calling out over the bullhorn, let alone any dialogue that the actors might be saying. So Don decided he'd use some of the friendships he'd built up with the prisoners in order to see if he could negotiate for some quiet.

At Stateville, all roads led to a guy named "Big Al," who rumor had it was second in command of one of the biggest gangs in the country. One didn't speak with Big Al directly (with the exception of Oliver, whom Big Al liked being able to approach at will). He had several "lieutenants," however, one of whom Don had befriended. Don wanted to know—was there any way he could use his influence to quiet the place down?

"How did it go with Fred, Murphy?" I asked when he returned.

"I think it went well, but it's not an association I particularly want to cultivate," he said.

"What do you mean?"

"Well, when I was trying to chat the guy up, he told me about how Big Al ruled the place with an iron hand. And if he took a liking to you, you were told by his lieutenants to show up at night—I think 'Smell nice and wear something frilly' was the expression he used. If you came, you'd be given enough drugs so you wouldn't feel a thing. But if you didn't, you'd be 'visited' by his lieutenants, who would show you the error of your ways—they'd break major bones, like hips and things. Then, when you were in the infirmary, they'd come and visit you and tell you that Big Al was sorry you'd declined his invitation, and maybe next time you'd rethink it."

"Oh, man, I hope The Alien never winds up in a place like this," I said.

"He'd be wearing Chanel No. 5 and sporting pink lingerie on a nightly basis," said Don.

Whatever Don managed to do seemed to work. On the next take, the place was almost completely quiet, with the exception of some guy on the top tier, who (we were told) was later reprimanded for his lack of willingness to fall in line.

This was the stuff they never taught you about in film school. But the strangest thing to happen in prison, by far, was the day that Claudia Schiffer showed up. Yes, *the* Claudia Schiffer. We were behind schedule, we were trying to improvise around our new limitations by bringing in hundreds of extras to replace the inmates we'd planned to use, the place was repellently hot, the prisoners had been in lockdown for two weeks, and the whole place felt ready to explode. When suddenly Claudia fucking Schiffer shows up with a camera crew.

"What's she doing here right now, Clayton?" I asked as production came to a standstill in "B" West.

"She's shooting a documentary on her life," he said, as if that answered anything.

I watched as Oliver stood there and gawked, acting like a goofy teenager for an hour while her video camera crew shot the two of them talking against a backdrop of the prisoners in their cells.

Later I asked Oliver what the whole thing was about.

"She was doing a documentary on her life," he said.

"Are you two friends or something?"

"I've never met her before in my life."

"Okay. So let me get this straight. She's shooting a documentary on her life, you've never met her before—does she just make a regular habit of going around to maximum-security prisons and visiting lifetime offenders or something?"

"Why, Jane, does that offend your feminist principles?" he goaded.

"No, Oliver, it's just shaking my grip on reality. We're standing here with a bunch of guys locked behind bars who will probably never see daylight again, and in walks the world's biggest supermodel. It's just too strange for words."

Every day we'd sit around for hours, bored out of our skulls as we waited for the next setup. Cockroaches crawling up our sleeves, all over our bodies, the heat never ending. And now we had hundreds of extras to contend with, since the prisoners were no longer allowed in the scenes. I needed some excitement, and I decided to do something I'd never done before on the shoot—invoke my first request for a producer's perk.

"Hey, Oliver," I said one day. "Remember how much Donita Sparks came through for us at the beginning of the shoot and let us use 'Shitlist' in the movie at the last minute?"

I'm not sure that he remembered the incident at all, focused as he was on trying to finish his picture.

"Well, we've kept up sort of a steady dialogue since the movie began, and I was thinking—she's from Chicago, anyway. What if we brought her out here to the set?" I think I started rambling down a list of why it would be great to have her support publicitywise, once the film came out, but I don't think he was listening. I think he just liked the idea of having a rock star come out and visit the set for his own amusement.

"Okay," he said.

I ran to the phone. "How would you like to come to Chicago, Donita?" I asked.

"Well, my sister lives there, and she's just had a baby. I guess it would be a great chance for me to get a free trip to visit my family."

It was all I could do to keep from yelling out loud. For the first time in a long time, something on the horizon looked like fun.

Before Donita's arrival, however, I was in for a major beating. I think it was around this time that I started adding up numbers, and I realized that our music budget was mounting into the stratosphere. When we'd started this whole thing, Budd Carr had budgeted for only about eight songs, which was the specific number Oliver had called out in the script. But as shooting progressed, and we started using music in *every* scene, and as those scenes were being shipped to the editing room and actually cut to the music we'd shot them to, it became evident that our music budget was wholly inadequate. I did some calculations, based on looking at cut scenes from the first quarter of the film. Some quick tabulations indicated that we had roughly thirty pieces of music for that section alone. Multiply that over the course of the film, give some really conservative estimates, and I came up with—over $2 million.

I wrote a memo to Oliver apprising him of this fact (a memo was the only way you could get Oliver to really pay attention to anything that required a detailed explanation), and letting him know that if we waited to start clearing all this music until we were in postproduction, we were going to have a horrendous task on our hands, not to mention outrageous cost overruns. Where most movies may have, at the outside, a record's worth of songs in them, we were probably going to have over 100 pieces of music. Since Budd Carr was responsible for clearing all the music, and he was in Los Angeles and had no involvement in what we were doing on a day-to-day basis, I wanted to alert Oliver to the potential crisis, and suggest some ways we could keep costs down.

And after our "Shitlist" near fiasco, I'd also started doing some quiet checking into what we'd cleared and what we hadn't. I learned that we had cut and shot four rear-screen projections for the opening title sequence to a particular song and edited the scene together, at tremendous cost, but had never contacted the rights holder about the track. (Ultimately the song turned out to be unclearable.) This despite the fact that the whole thing had been shot in L.A. before we ever left for location, and had been in the can now for nearly three months. To my mind, it was inexcusable.

But once again, Oliver interpreted this as a challenge not only to his own control, but to that of "his guys," as he referred to them, Clayton and Budd. Budd flew out to the set, and I was pulled into a room with the three of them. It was obvious that I was in for a gang rape.

"I've read your memo, Jane," Clayton said. Funny, I didn't give it to Clayton, and wanted to tell him so. But the minute I sat down, I had reconciled not to give anybody the opportunity to concentrate on my "attitude problem." I wanted to keep the issue focused on what I saw as the incompetence at hand.

"I've discussed things with Budd, and we've got things under control. There's no need for your help."

"Well, that's great, Clayton." I tried not to clench my teeth in the process. "I find that really reassuring. Just so long as everything's taken care of."

"You seem to have some personality problem with Budd," Oliver piped up.

"Why, not at all, Oliver. I think Budd's great," I said. "I just want everyone to be on the same page, to make sure. . . ."

"Budd fucked up," said Oliver. "But I took care of it. If he does it again, you tell me, and *I'll* handle it. You don't need to get involved."

"Gee, Oliver, I'm sorry, please accept my apologies," I said, knowing nothing would make him madder than refusing to play into his hand. "But about the potential budget overruns . . ."

"Don't worry about that," said Clayton. "We're taking care of it."

I was dismissed. Though on the whole glad to escape, I felt at the same time that the conversation would have been appropriately rounded off by Clayton Townsend's death.

I never got to see the look on the face of the Warner Brothers brass when they were handed the bill for the music, which eventually wound up just about where I'd projected it. Frankly, it cost so much more than it should have because of macho posturing, arrogance, and incompetence. But there are some things you just have to let slide. At the end of the day, we got to use the music we wanted. Even though we ran seriously over budget and it galled me as a producer to stand by and watch this parade of flaring imbecility, with a few minor exceptions, I'm proud of what we managed to do with the soundtrack. And as hellish as it was to work with such idiots at the time, I learned a lesson that perhaps will last me longest during my career in Hollywood: No matter how nice it is to always have someone muttering reassuring platitudes in your ears, you should never surround yourself with ninnies. Because in the end, they'll dig your grave, every time.

I wasn't the only one having to defend myself when voicing my concerns on the budgetary front; Don was having his own problems. At one point, Oliver started screaming that despite the fact that we were back on stage now, where virtually no transportation was needed, we were carrying thirty-eight Teamster drivers on full salary. He swiftly cast the blame on Teamster Captain Dusty Saunders.

Which was, quite frankly, patently ridiculous. Dusty had managed to pull off the Southwest portion of the shoot—when we were on the road every day for hundreds of miles—and bring it in on budget. However, once we got to Chicago, where we rarely had to move locations and virtually no transportation was needed, the deal that Clayton had negotiated with the Teamsters called for horrendous overstaffing that was driving our budget further over the top.

Clayton had come up the production ladder on the East Coast as a location manager, which—in East Coast unions—is a Teamster position. His mentor, who paved the way for the Chicago negotiations, was a big Teamster guy. Don began to get suspicious of the whole situation when he walked past the office of the local Teamster boss, Dickie De Angelo, while we were shooting on the stage.

"Good-bye, I'm leaving for the hotel," Clayton said to Dickie.

"No, you're not. Sit down," said Dickie, ordering Clayton into the room and shutting the door.

"Who works for whom?" asked a puzzled Don.

Don decided to schedule a meeting between Oliver and himself in order to bring the situation to a head. Lest Oliver try and turn it into a Don/Clayton thing, Don arranged for Dusty to be there to back him up. Considering what had just happened with me, he might have picked a better time, but the whole situation with Clayton had become a sore spot on his gums that Don just loved to prod.

The meeting took place in Oliver's trailer. Don told Oliver that he, like me, was worried about the financial feasibility of the rest of the shoot, and Dusty explained the situation to Oliver. This was something new to Oliver, who was used to getting all his budgetary information filtered through Clayton. Oliver said he would deal with it, thanked Dusty, and commented oddly, "Don't worry, you will work again."

Clayton went ballistic when he found out. He tried to have Dusty fired and was furious at Don for getting in his way. On the plus side, we managed to get some control over the situation, and cut the number of drivers down to a reasonable number needed to perform set functions, like picking people up at airports and running errands. But what followed— what finally sent Don over the edge—was certainly something Don and his big mouth were overwhelmingly responsible for. Still, there's no doubt that Clayton had a hand in busting him in the situation.

Three days after the Dusty meeting, Oliver pulled Don into a private meeting. When Don emerged, he was white as a ghost.

"What the hell happened in there?" I asked.

"I've never seen him like that," Don said. "No matter how pissed off he'd been with us, he's never unleashed that kind of fury before."

"What was he angry about?"

"He accused me of speaking on the phone with someone, saying that our budget was out of control."

"You probably did."

"Oh, I'm sure I did, although I told him I didn't. But he wasn't listening at that point. He told me I'd 'betrayed the family.' It was a scene straight out of *The Godfather*, with Oliver doing his best Brando impression. He told me I'd better change my attitude, or he'd banish me back to Little Italy."

"And you said—"

"I said nothing. I just can't give a shit about Oliver's opinion at this point, so I sat there and listened."

"Don't worry, he'll forget about it by tomorrow," I said. "He always does."

"I don't care. From now on, I don't give a shit about this movie anymore."

It was true. From that moment on, his enthusiasm for the whole project was nil. Emotionally, he was dried up; he could only look forward to *NBK* being over.

But I was still in the thick of it. Whereas Don had descended into a "fuck them all, I hope it's a disaster 'cos that's what they deserve" attitude, I continued the fight. Every day, chasing Oliver around the set, hoping to corral him for a few seconds to get him to render a verdict on something, even as he threatened to have me removed from the stage. Oliver was getting increasingly fried, drug addled, abusive, and worn out; the shoot was definitely taking its toll. And everyone knew that if you approached him at this point about anything, it was at your own peril.

One day he was particularly brutal and dismissive of me; I don't really remember over what. I walked away with all the dignity I could muster and made my way to Don.

"It's just so hard to stay in there," I said, looking for support.

"Give up," Don said.

"Huh?"

"Fuck him," he suggested glibly. "I don't know why you still even try. It's not worth it."

At first I started to cry, and then I got furious. Just because Don had gotten his butt kicked and was frustrated, I was supposed to abandon my objectives, too. To me, it reflected not only a total lack of awareness about what I was doing and what I was trying to accomplish, but it seemed a betrayal of the friendship that had supported us through some very tough times. It was childish beyond words, but I was not going to fight both Don and Oliver. It was nothing I had the energy to address at the moment; but once we got back to Los Angeles, you could be sure the topic would raise its head again.

"Miss Hamsher, there's a Miss Sparks waiting for you in the lobby," came the call from the Omni's receptionist one evening.

I went flying downstairs.

And there she was, so completely cool that I couldn't even believe it. I'd worried all day about what to wear, how I should look, what would be right—and here she was with nothing more than a striped T-shirt and torn blue jeans, with a backpack slung over her shoulder that carried only a notebook for writing lyrics. I'd overpack my own funeral. Her rock-'n'-roll whatever-the-fuck spirit put me to shame.

"Did you hold the limo?" I asked her.

"Sure did." We went peeling out and jumped into the black Lincoln Continental that had picked her up from the airport.

The one thing Donita wanted to do when she came to Chicago, aside from visit her sister and her newborn niece, was to see celebrities. Not in the kind of sycophantic suck-up way I was so annoyed with at the set on a day-to-day basis, but from the perspective of someone who appreciates the true kitsch factor involved. And on the day she arrived, the biggest starfest that was surely to be visited upon Chicago that year was in full swing—the opening of the Chicago Planet Hollywood.

As we walked in, we saw Oliver leaving with his entourage. "It's ridiculous in there," he said. "Arnold Schwarzenegger walking around with sandwich boards." He stormed away in disgust. We were thrilled. It was shaping up to be everything we had hoped for and more.

On the way in, I had to stop Donita from dropping her drawers and mooning the press, for fear the bouncers would toss us out before we even got started. But we made it inside and immediately began ordering double kamikazes (at Donita's suggestion) while we scouted the crowd. "Look, there's Roseanne! Cindy Crawford! Bruce Willis! Sharon Stone! Don Johnson!" There were monitors everywhere, displaying the activities on-stage outside, which had been erected in front of grandstands that accommodated thousands and thousands of the Chicago general public. At that particular moment, Jim Belushi was singing with the band. We were in heaven.

We found Don and handed him the disposable Kodak camera we'd purchased on the way over.

"Don, Donita wants her picture taken with celebrities," I told him. "And you're our cameraman."

Almost all the celebrities there were taking their turn onstage, singing with the band—Don Johnson jamming with Sharon Stone and Bruce Willis as the Chicago crowd cheered them on. Deep down, it was obvious that they were all frustrated rock stars. So we formed our plan.

I would walk up to them and say, "Hi, this is my friend Donita, she's a rock star, and she wants to have her picture taken with you."

"Sure," was almost always the reply from the slightly befuddled star.

"We want to make it a kind of sandwich thing," Donita would say, "so do you mind if Jane is in there, too?"

As Don snapped away, our increasingly intoxicated faces were captured on cheap Kodak stock by Don as we embraced Damon Wayans. Chris Tucker. Luke Perry. Bruce Willis. An assortment of Chicago Bulls stars we weren't even sure who they were. We tried for Don Johnson, but he looked over to his then-wife Melanie Griffith sitting in the corner, and whispered, "She's kind of sensitive about these things . . ." so we let him off the hook.

The next night, we decided to go to see X playing at the Central. We jumped into a cab and gave the driver directions to the club, noticing as we did that he had a tape deck in the car. We whipped out a copy of a Nymphs tape and asked him to put it on as we both eased back, lit up a joint, and enjoyed the long journey through Chicago, around the coast of Lake Michigan, getting high and feeling like nothing in the world could be better.

Eventually, Donita would write a song about that cab journey that would appear on her next album. It was called "Riding with a Movie Star." Well, we were far from movie stars. But at that moment, I guess we both felt like we were. It was true, this whole fucking *NBK* production thing had been hell, but at the moment it all felt very much worth it.

Donita returned to L.A., and Don and I managed to survive the last weeks of Chicago madness. We capped off the shoot by stalking Oliver on the last day to coax him into a photo shoot for the cover of *Film Threat* magazine. It was 11:00 P.M., we'd gone five hours over schedule shooting a scene we'd never use, but we knew if we didn't get some sort of shot now we'd never be able to regroup Oliver, Juliette, and Woody once we returned to Los Angeles.

For the shot, Woody and Juliette were supposed to hold Oliver hostage, pointing their guns at him. As architect of the whole thing, I began calling out instructions to the actors.

"Bite him! Kick him! Jump on top of him! Pistol-whip him!"

I looked around to see what was left of the crew looking at me.

"You're a little too enthusiastic about this, Jane," said someone.

Indeed.

Chapter 9

Are We Fucking Having Fun Yet? Hello!

By the time the shoot was over and we were back in Los Angeles, there was almost nobody in the office. Oliver himself had wisely taken off to Telluride to recover, and everyone else vacated to their own form of recoupment. Which left Don and me to fight with each other, since all the more likely targets had removed themselves from the vicinity.

Both of us were in terrible moods. I myself was exhausted and cross; Don still had his "fuck *NBK*" attitude, in addition to being physically and emotionally worn out. And when Don wants to vent his agitation, like Mr. Stone, he takes it out on whoever is around.

Up until that point, our assistant, Justin, had only had to work with Don during his ebullient preproduction stage, or long distance during the shoot. But now that Don was back in the office, and cranky to boot, Justin simply couldn't handle it when Don would grab any convenient excuse to justify his explosion. ("IS THAT MY PEN YOU'RE USING? WHAT THE FUCK ARE YOU DOING WITH MY PEN! THAT'S MY FAVOR- ITE PEN! YOU'RE ALWAYS UNDERMINING ME BY TAKING MY STUFF! I HATE THIS! I CAN'T WORK LIKE THIS!") Around the office, we had always fondly referred to these moods as Don's "lupus." (Don't ask me why, I can't remember.) The most likely time for lupus to strike was usually on Monday mornings, when all wise individuals tiptoed past his door until we figured out if he was infected with this peculiar malady before approaching him. By the time we got back from the *NBK* shoot, however, lupus was pretty much a daily occurrence.

The trouble was that the more Don yelled and fried his nerves, the more Justin screwed things up. It became a self-generating cycle. Finally Don put Justin on what he referred to as "palsy probation." "Don't assume anything," he told him. "Ask me first. No matter how stupid or inconsequential something seems, pretend you have palsy. Tell me about it first and ask me what to do." Well, Justin couldn't handle it. (Who could?) So when he got a job offer to work on another production, I heaved a sigh of relief, knowing that this particular source of contention would at least be removed from my life.

Into Justin's place we promoted Amy, a girl whom we'd hired to help Don on all his product-placement deals. Amy was in her early twenties, and I think "perky" was the best way to describe her. She'd been a child actress who had appeared on shows like *Little House on the Prairie*, and Don adored her. There was no way he was going to take his aggression out on Amy. Which left only me. Well, if Don was looking for a fight, I was a really great place to find one.

I don't even remember what precipitated the confrontation. I was still holding a grudge from the Chicago incident, where I felt that Don had let me down during the last leg of the shoot. Instantly, all the frustration and confusion we'd both fell victim to during the process of making *NBK* came out in full force. Suddenly we were at each others' throats. As I think I've mentioned before, I can be frequently annoyed, piqued, and bitchy, but it's hard to push me into full-on anger. But once I'm there, as Don describes it, "It's near apocalyptic."

"I can't handle you anymore." I grabbed my backpack and slammed my office door before I said anything that made it any worse. "I'm going home."

And so, for the first time in three years of partnership, I stopped coming in to work. Something was bothering me, something I couldn't put my finger on. In large part, it was Don's inability to manage his stress and his penchant for taking it out on me or anyone else who was within shouting distance. He did nothing on his own to try and deal with it and burn it off; he loaded up heavy on caffeine from the time he woke up in the morning, he was a complete stranger to exercise, and his diet was a prescription for heart attack and high blood pressure. Discussing these kinds of things with him was almost impossible, since he had virtually no idea what I was talking about. And any time Don gets into territory he's not comfortable in, and he thinks he's "losing" a point, the point becomes obscured, or changed, and things get flipped back on you, and it becomes impossible to resolve anything.

And so I went home. Nothing was happening on *NBK*, anyway, since everyone was on hiatus. It gave me some time to try and figure out why everything suddenly felt so wrong. Don, as usual, began calling me incessantly, so I called Karl our attorney and told him to have Don stop bugging me, or I told him I'd never come back. Don makes hollow threats on a daily basis, but he knew I never made a threat that I wasn't willing to follow through on, so he let me alone for a while.

I went to my doctor, who told me that aside from a slight case of exhaustion and unusually high levels of endorphins in my system (I'd been exercising like a fiend every morning since I'd been back, trying to reestablish my old routine and burn off whatever deep-seated anxiety I seemed to be harboring) he couldn't see anything immediately wrong with me. So I was left to assume that if I could figure a way for Don and me to continue pursuing our goals together in a way that was more harmonious and less stressful, I'd be okay.

Karl probably had an easier time negotiating between us and Rand Vossler than he did between me and Don, but he managed it. In the end, I came back to work, but only after we'd negotiated three conditions:

(1) No more Coca-Cola during working hours
(2) Don had to start some sort of exercise regimen, so he'd have some place to take out his aggressions other than the workplace
(3) We'd go for counseling, so we could have a reasonable dialogue about what was going on.

At first Don resisted, but when he realized I was dead serious, he relented. I came back to work, and Don immediately switched to caffeine-free diet Coke. It took a while for him to finally begin exercising, but when he did it had such a profound effect on his personality that people asked me if I'd put him on Prozac. (Don is now the most religious of exercisers, and never misses a session; in large part, this is due to the fact that when he goes to the gym, all the agents he needs to talk to are there, and he can get a lot of his business done while he's working out.) We chose a counselor named Adele to help us talk through the situation, and probably never has a therapist undertaken such a weird challenge.

For me, it was the first time I ever got to voice my feelings for more than two minutes without being challenged or interrupted by Don, compelled to raise my volume to hair-splitting decibels in order to be heard. And Don was forced to address my concerns. I'm sure part of his response came from the fact that he simply didn't want to go through the process again, but part of it was also because Don is as fearless about confronting his own faults as he is everyone else's. And once things had a chance to come out in the open, without devolving into our usual routine of name-calling and yelling, Don became pretty good at addressing my concerns. Oh, he still spewed the same mania as always, peppering his rants with abundant non sequiturs that only I could follow. But that, on the whole, is part of Don's charm, and if I didn't appreciate that I would have left him long ago.

Adele came to describe us as polar opposites on the Jungian personality scale, and explained that together we sort of made up one whole personality; me being the intuitive/intellectual side of the equation, and Don being the thinking/feeling extreme—basically the reason why we even got together in the first place, I guess. My Buddhist monk friend Kendall ascribed our differences to another cause—she said that I was a classic Leo, fiery and opinionated, whereas Don was the archetypal Taurus, stubborn and bullheaded and not fond of change. Right brain versus left brain dominance. The irresistible force meets the immovable object. Pick your own reason—it all amounts to the same thing.

And so we decided that I would be the one to continue working on *NBK*, Don's enthusiasm having long since abated, and even though he's much more persistent and doggedly determined about setting things up in the first place, he's not someone who has the energy for the long haul if his imagination isn't engaged. He, in turn, would focus his efforts in setting up other projects for us to have in the works once *NBK* was completed. During the editing phase, there wasn't much he could do anyway. But now he was beginning to understand that if I was going to get in there and fight every day, he needed to return the kind of unquestioning support he had always received from me.

'Cos things weren't getting any easier. While we were in Chicago and Oliver was on the set, there wasn't much he could do to keep me out of the editing room; but once we were back in L.A., and he was in the same office every day, I was officially banned from crossing what's known as the "DMZ," the area that separates the production offices from the editorial bays. (The editors had gotten really cute and hung fake barbed wire and a combat helmet next to the entrance. Ha ha ha.) So I really had little chance to see what was happening with the film until Oliver was ready to show his cut. At one point, I got to look at a tape of a rough three-hour assembly of all the scenes we'd shot, and although it was way too long and contained a lot of scenes that seemed horrendously digressive when placed in context, it still looked pretty good.

Still, contractually, we were obligated to deliver a film that was a good deal less than three hours long. (Because the amount of money a film makes at the box office is dependent, in part, on how many times an individual theater can show it in a day, films that are two hours or less in length make a lot more money than those that run for three hours. You have to be a pretty big Hollywood gorilla to get a three-hour movie through the studio system.) Besides, *NBK* was supposed to be a romp, a killers-on-the-run kind of movie. It wasn't *Schindler's List*. It needed cutting down to two hours. So it would be interesting to see what Oliver finally decided to excise before he showed it to everyone.

When Oliver finally finished his director's cut, he decided that he wasn't going to show it to a few select people first, get their opinions, and evaluate the film in light of them. No, he was going to show it to everyone at once. CAA's Mike Ovitz, Terry Semel, and Bob Daly saw it one day; and the next day, about eighty of us (including Oliver's personal CAA agents, his press people, Warners distribution and marketing people, production executives for both Warner Brothers and New Regency, editorial P.A.s, Bob and Victor, and, of course, Don and me) saw it for the first time.

"This is kinda weird, Murphy," I said, looking around at a packed theater full of the very people whose opinion of the film when they walked out of this theater would probably decide its fate. "Oliver must be really sure of what he's got."

"Well, you saw the rough assembly, you said it was good, so there's probably nothing to worry about except a few 'tweaks' here and there."

"I sure hope you're right," I said. "It just worries me that up until now, the only real feedback he's gotten is from a bunch of editors he's terrorized into mute submission."

"Yeah, well, it's not like he's exactly decked out with people who will give him an honest opinion in the first place," said Don.

If we were both worried about the implications of this event as we sat there waiting for the lights to go down, there was good reason for it. The first time you show a film to a studio, you'd better have it right; if you don't, you're screwed. At that critical moment, the powers that be will decide if they like it, if they think it's at all commercially viable—indeed, how much support they will ultimately put behind its release. The people sitting in the theater with us were not compassionate artistic collaborators who would forgive flaws and see a film's ultimate potential; they were businessmen, looking at the bottom line. And if they don't think there's anything they can do to make your film fly commercially, you're doomed.

But as the lights went down and the titles began to come up on the screen, all of these concerns evaporated. We pinched each other. Our pulses raced. Here it was for the first time, the fruit of all our efforts, the venture we'd poured the last two years of our life into, the thing that our friends and family would finally see that would prove we were not just a couple of self-deluding idiots, we had actually pulled off what we said we would. As the movie started, we could both barely breathe.

And it SUCKS. Suddenly, the thrill of anticipation has transformed itself into major heart palpitations. Where the HELL did this mess come from? The diner scene starts in the middle, with Juliette already fighting the hillbilly, then jump-cuts around back and forth so wildly that there's no way anyone could possibly understand what was going on. It looked like someone had put it through a Cuisinart since the last time I saw it. I knew Oliver needed to cut an hour out of the film, but this was out of hand.

During the shoot, as we looked at dailies and saw scenes coming to-gether, everyone agreed that the best stuff in the movie was the Mickey and Mallory stuff at the beginning. Well, that had all been cut out. Now everything was focused on Wayne Gayle and the *American Maniacs* se-quence; and, like most of Oliver's conversations, the whole thing was digressive and borderline incomprehensible.

If Don and I could barely stand to watch the movie in its present form, there was no way the middle-aged crowd sitting around us was going to respond to it. But to absolutely nobody's surprise, after the lights went on, everyone clapped enthusiastically, then stood in line waiting to tell Oliver what a masterpiece he had created. My legs were wobbling. Don was coughing and hacking and making all manner of disgusting noises he's prone to when nervous. I made a quick dash for the bathroom, leaving Don to give the obligatory blandishments to Oliver. On my way out, I saw the looks on the faces of the Warners people as they left the receiving line. They looked puzzled, confused, and barely able to contain their shock. Oh, Lord. Were we just massively screwed or what?

Don and I ran to the nearest bar and began pounding down drinks as fast as we could.

"Well, it's not *that* bad," Don said.

"It's fucking *awful*, Don, and you know it. I can't believe we went through all that for—*that*."

"Okay, so it's fucking awful. What are we going to do?"

The two of us are nothing if not proactive, but this one had us stumped. What do you do when your film blows, and nobody wants to tell the director? We foresaw a repeat of the Justin memo experience: "Everyone else loves it—you must be morons." Both Don and I knew we'd shot the footage to put together a great movie, but something as impressionistic as *NBK* required a strong creative vision, and somewhere along the line Oliver had lost not only his vision, but his mind. Victor Kempster had warned me, months before, that Oliver often lost his nerve during the editing process and pulled back, and here were the tangible results. A movie needed to be carved out of the available footage; in our case, there were literally thousands of possible movies that could be constructed from what we shot. Because of all the mixed formats we'd used and the non-linear story line we'd followed, its parameters defied the rules that ordinarily applied when putting a big studio film together in the editing room. We knew we had to at least make an attempt to get the old man to listen to us, but now having been publicly reassured by most of the free world that he'd just constructed a masterpiece, how much chance did we have of getting him to listen?

If Oliver insisted on releasing this version of the film (which, by contractual right, he could—Oliver is one of the only directors in Hollywood who has the privilege of the notorious "final cut," which means the studio can't go in and recut him no matter what he delivers if the film is of a preagreed-upon length and MPAA rating), we would just be majorly boned. There was no doubt about it—the studio would dump the film.

Well, we had to do *something*. We just weren't sure quite what. Where do you even begin in a situation like this? We went into the office the next day, and a reenergized Don began to do what Don does best—he got on the phone. He started lobbying people like Victor and Bob, people whom we felt had Oliver's ear that we could trust. Pretty much everyone admitted privately that the thing was garbage, but also acknowledged that there was footage to make a good movie out of, if only Oliver would listen. Well, I knew from experience that if I came right out and flew in his face about the whole matter, he'd immediately dismiss any kind of criticism we had to offer. The challenge was to constructively translate our concerns into "Oliverspeak," as I liked to call it, in order to sneak past his psychological battlements and get to him at a place where he would be receptive. With months of practice at being yelled at during the shoot, I was sort of an expert at this.

Ironically, even though he feared and frequently loathed me, Oliver allowed me a lot more latitude in this area than he did most people. Maybe it was because I wasn't a man, and it never boiled down to a testosterone contest between him and me. Or maybe it was because I was simply willing to take all the anger, humiliation, and constant abuse it took to stay in his face. Whatever the reason, I went home and did what I do best: drink a lot of coffee, jump around my apartment to really loud music into the night, drive myself berserk, and go sleepless until my ideas finally formulate and disgorge themselves onto a memo.

In the memo, I told Oliver that it looked like he'd lost faith in his own vision, and indeed he probably had. The horrific failure of *Heaven and Earth* only months before had shaken his creative confidence, and he'd removed all the elements he'd initially conceived with Dave Veloz: the Mickey and Mallory stuff, the things he was really driven to probe during his alteration of Quentin's original script and that now formed the emotional backbone of the characters and the story he was trying to tell. Now he was backing out of it, was trying to reinstate the story and sequence of events that Quentin had drawn in his original draft. Trouble was, it was too late for that. The tone of the performances and scenes were much too heavy for that kind of random, offhand, going-nowhere-fast structure and pace. It made for an ungodly blend of emotional textures.

Further, the style of the film had been allowed to completely overtake the material. I think Oliver was looking back to *JFK*, his last big success, and remembered with fondness the praise he got for the technical innovation he displayed in that film. Because it seemed like he was now trying to take it ten steps further in *NBK*. Well, it was stylish, you could certainly say that, but it was also completely unintelligible. Who the hell were these people Mickey and Mallory, and what in God's name were they doing? Hank Corwin's background in music videos and commercials was showing—it now looked like it had been thrown into a blender and cut in thirty-second blocks with no sense of overall pace to the story. Oliver himself had great editing sense, as he'd demonstrated in all his previous films. I reminded him of this in the memo and told him he needed to get back in the editing room himself and stay out on the limb he'd staked out for himself when he started the project, or *NBK* would always lack conviction and look like a great big mess. As I put the finishing touches on the memo, I knew there was no way Oliver was going to be happy with it, and that a whole lot of shit was probably going to come down on my head for having written it in the first place. But if it at least got him thinking, it was worth it. He'd kicked my ass before, plenty of times; once more wasn't going to kill me.

Oliver had been calling me, asking for my comments (he knew full well I'd have some—I always seem to), so I delivered the five-page memo to his house personally on a Sunday afternoon. Then I drove to Don's house to give him a copy, so he would be prepared for what we'd both probably have to answer to come Monday morning. When I got there, the door to his apartment was open, and Don was pacing around his living room on his cordless phone.

"No, I'm sure she didn't mean it like that," he said. "No, Oliver, I know she respects you. Yes . . . yes, I know . . . yes, she *is* opinionated." He looked at me and rolled his eyes. "Yes, yes, I realize that. . . ."

And on and on for the next fifteen minutes, as Oliver unloaded his spleen on Don yet again over something I had done. When he finally let him off the phone, Don was exhausted.

"So aside from the fact that he thinks I'm the Antichrist, which I got through inference, by the way, so you can save yourself the trouble of repeating it, what did he say?"

"Well, in between the ranting and raving, he basically said, 'I can't make the movie she wants me to make. I've got to do my own thing. . . . She wants to me to do this, she wants me to do that. I just can't work that way,' I just mostly listened and let him vent, trying to calm him down and convince him you weren't plotting his downfall."

By Monday morning, Oliver had calmed down considerably. He came into my office and made pretty much the same speech he gave Don, only at a much lower volume. "I can't make the movie you want me to make," he said.

"I respect that, Oliver, and ultimately you're the director. If you don't follow your own instincts, the whole thing won't work anyway."

Yet on the same day, he had Azita distribute the memo to the entire editorial staff. Less than flattered by the way I'd characterized his work, Hank Corwin stopped speaking to me. But by the end of the week, the Mickey and Mallory scenes had been cut back in, and many of the rambling segments from the *American Maniacs* show had been removed; the film-shredding editorial style that made the film so confusing to watch had been ejected in favor of building a more cohesive narrative that focused on character rather than gimmicks and stylistic flourishes. Also, the decision was made to go with an ending where Mickey and Mallory live, rather than the one which we shot in which they are killed, something Don had been lobbying for all along, so a small reshoot was scheduled.

It was a huge relief to both Don and me; and, relatively speaking, Oliver had inflicted minimal pain in the process. It's hard to know exactly what combination of influences turned Oliver around; in addition to annoying the pants off him, hopefully the memo opened him up to a bunch of stuff everyone was thinking but not voicing. Once he started asking around and broaching the subject, it probably made people feel a bit more comfortable about saying, "You know, now that you mention it . . ." We were just happy that the whole thing looked like it was back on track again, creatively. And we appreciated the fact that had Oliver not been so committed to challenging himself and scrutinizing his own art ruthlessly, he never would have entertained our comments or anyone else's (which is completely standard behavior for almost all directors of his status).

The next time Oliver showed us the film, it was starting to approach the version we finally released in the theater. However, we knew that we'd probably never be able to compensate for the fact that Warner Brothers' initial response to the film had been one of unrelenting disdain, and it was going to be damned near impossible to turn them around on it, no matter how Oliver recut the film. Had Oliver shown the original cut internally and shaped it before showing it to them, their reaction might have been completely different; it's difficult to know. We were just pretty sure that now we'd be facing an uphill battle when it came to putting the film out there before the public and getting the studio behind the effort. After all, Warner Brothers was the studio that was used to releasing films like *Batman*; they probably wouldn't have the slightest idea what to do with *NBK*. We figured that we were all going to have to get very creative about helping the film find its audience before the whole thing was over.

"Jane, your doctor is on line two," Amy said over the intercom one day.

I remember hanging up the phone after my conversation with him and thinking: How odd. I have cancer, and I don't feel a thing. So that was what was wrong all along. You think that when someone says words like that to you, you're going to have some kind of hysterical response. Being naturally prone to extreme emotional states, I was mildly surprised that I felt nothing   no fear or dread or anything. Huh, so I have breast cancer. Wow.

Don wasn't there at the moment, so I called my friend Kendall and asked her to meet me at my doctor's office, where I could find out exactly how bad it was. Luckily, Amy managed to drive me there in about ten minutes, which was exactly the amount of time it took for the shock to wear off and for me to come completely unglued. It was absurd. Breast cancer ran in my family. My mom and two of her sisters had had it, so the doctors began watching me closely for it when I was a teenager. I'd had a couple of biopsies in my life for suspicious lumps, but they always turned out to be benign. Well, not this time. But nobody got breast cancer at my age. It was the last thing I ever expected.

When I finally got the full download from the doctor, it actually wasn't that bad. Kendall held my hand as the doctor told me that I had what's known as "in situ" cancer, which means it's localized. It was a small, slow-growing lump and of a type that didn't spread, so there was no chance that it had traveled on to my lymph nodes and other parts of my body. They could remove it with a simple lumpectomy that would leave only a tiny scar.

"I want it out, and I want it out now," I told him. "And with as little hoopla as possible. Can you do it under local anesthesia?"

"Sure," he said. The lump was so small that they'd been able to spot it on an X ray only because of a telltale calcification growing near it. I could be in and out of the hospital in a couple of hours, and at work the next day.

"Why did this happen to me now?" I asked. "My mom didn't have cancer until she was in her late thirties."

He told me that cancer cells were growing in everyone's bodies all the time, and normally, people's immune systems could easily kill them off. But if for some reason the immune system was down, and the cancerous growth got to a certain size, the body couldn't kill it anymore. Some people, like me, had a genetic predisposition for this kind of thing. But he also told me that one of the biggest things that can wipe out your immune system was extreme stress.

"From the size of the lump, I'd say it started growing about two years ago," he said. "Was there any event, around that time, where there was some sort of emotional trauma, and you were under tremendous stress?"

I don't know at that point if I began laughing hysterically from the relief of it all, or from the knowledge that my worst nightmare had come true and it wasn't going to be that bad. However, Kendall was worried that I'd flipped out.

"Are you okay, honey?" she said, holding my hand even tighter.

"I'm fine." I was laughing so hard that I was crying again. "But can you imagine the look on Don Murphy's face when I tell him that Quentin Tarantino gave me cancer?"

Well, it was a joke, of course. Nobody but me was responsible for managing my stress level (or lack thereof) during the harrowing period of the lawsuit when it looked like there was no hope, and I'd stopped sleeping for months. But to Don, it was no joke. When I told him, he went rigid with a combination of anger, anxiety, and fear, even after I explained to him that I was going to be okay. In fact, I kind of felt like I was off the hook. It had been the thing I'd always feared the most, and now here it was, and it looked like I was going to be fine.

It was more than a little ironic; I'd always thought that hyper type-A Don would be the one to keel over from a heart attack one day, but whereas he let out all his anxiety and aggression daily, I internalized my stress and feelings, taking it out on myself. Honestly, I have to say that after the initial shock, it wasn't even the worst thing that happened to me that month.

Kendall stayed with me and took care of me, and Don was an absolute brick. However, he was still Don; when I begged out of a lunch meeting he'd set up for the day after my surgery, he grumbled only a little bit.

Although I'd meant the whole Quentin thing as a joke, it became cast in Don's mind as a dead-on, certifiable truth that Quentin had brought this on me. If there had ever been any chance that things could be repaired between the two, it ended right there. Quentin became the place into which Don channeled all his anger and fear that he felt about what was happening to me. And at that moment, he hatched a plan that he would work on diligently for the next two years, surely and steadily, as a way to pay Quentin back.

The whole incident forced us to do some reassessing on a personal level. We realized that we'd been putting too much emotional energy into this whole thing, with little thought of any life outside the business. Maybe some serious realignment of priorities was called for. Although we'd still work as diligently as we ever had, taking meetings and lunches and chasing down scripts and book rights and courting directors, we started taking a much more casual attitude toward everything. We'd win some, we'd lose some. That was inevitable. But if we were going to be successful, then we better goddamned well relax and live to enjoy it.

In fact, it was quite remarkable how life went on as usual. I didn't want any more disruption around me than the whole event had already caused, so I didn't tell anyone in the office. I didn't want anyone to treat me any differently. If I was going to get my butt kicked, I didn't want anyone holding back because they felt "sorry" for me. Which meant that there were still the same personalities at war, still the same battles to fight, still the same incompetence and imbecility to guard against, even now that the picture seemed to be back on track, and me with it.

The first thing on my mind at the moment was the soundtrack album. Originally, New Regency had negotiated a deal with Elektra Records to release the sound track. Despite everyone's trepidation over the dramatic content of the film, the one thing everyone seemed to agree upon—from Warner Brothers to New Regency and everyone else we'd shown the film to—was that the music was pretty remarkable and could potentially be a best-selling album. Never one to overlook the possibility of a buck on the horizon, Arnon Milchan invited Interscope Records' Jimmy Iovine to see the film. Together with his partner Ted Field, Jimmy had built up a company worth hundreds of millions of dollars in a few short years by signing acts like Dr. Dré and Snoop Doggy Dogg. Jimmy liked the film, he liked the music, and he wanted Interscope to release the soundtrack instead of Elektra. He began negotiating a deal with Arnon to do just that. Around the same time, he also invited Trent Reznor of Nine Inch Nails down to see the film, since Hank Corwin had liked one of his tracks and we'd cut brief parts of it into the Indian scene. Trent was also enthusiastic about the movie and the music, and decided he'd like to put the sound-track album out on his own sublabel that Interscope had given him. Arnon and Oliver agreed.

Not that anybody ever bothered to check with me. That would have afforded me a larger role in the situation, and Oliver at that point seemed to be worried that somehow I'd wind up with all the credit for the music in the movie or something, so he was being pretty sneaky about keeping me out of all of these negotiations. When I finally heard about what was going on, I wasn't displeased. At least Trent Reznor wasn't some idiot A&R guy at a record label who would have no idea about the music we'd used, and would try to jam some of his own label's unlistenable shit into the picture before they'd release the album. So, at the start, although "enthusiastic" is probably the wrong word to use, I was at least amiably acquiescing in the situation.

However, Budd Carr was giving me migraines. Hank Corwin was speaking to me again—mostly, I think, because he needed my help. Budd was coming back to him and saying that he couldn't clear a lot of the music that both of us had struggled to get into the picture. I called up one of the music publishers who supposedly had denied us permission to use a track, and found that no request had ever been made. They said they'd been contacted by us about other music, though, and would have no problem with granting us a clearance. It was memo time.

Oliver called me down to his office. I expected to be chewed out good and hard. Instead, he said he'd talked to Budd, accepted what I considered a lame excuse, but the track would be used. And then he really stunned me.

I'll never forget it. As he was dismissing me from the office, he looked down to his desk and began to speak somewhat haltingly.

"Jane, I want to thank you for all the effort you put into the music. It's really made a difference in the film."

It was the only time he ever acknowledged what I'd done. But it was enough.

However, this was not a happy little ending. Interscope wanted more of their music used in the film, and so suddenly some Dr. Dré and Snoop Doggy Dogg tracks made their way into the picture. Since rap music had been the incessant score to real life in Stateville, I'd always been trying to get Oliver to open up to using some of it, but his ears just couldn't adjust and he was steadily resistant. Well, neither of those two artists would have been my first choices for the prison music; I wanted to use less obvious groups like Spice and The Wu Tang Clan, but at least it was something. Then Trent insisted on throwing in a couple of other tracks of his own that sort of bugged me, but with 130 pieces of music now in the film, it wasn't a battle I had the energy to fight.

What did bother me in the extreme was when Trent's version of the soundtrack album finally showed up, I HATED it. I still do. There was so much range to the music we'd chosen for the film—everything from the Ramsey Lewis Trio to Steven Jesse Bernstein to Anton Webern—and none of the extensive variety was displayed in the tracks he'd picked. We'd already spent over a year working on carefully selecting every bit of music, piece by piece, moment by moment, before he showed up. And now I guess he thought he'd get really stylistic, and cut dialogue from the film into the music. Now, aside from the fact that they'd just done this with the *Reservoir Dogs* soundtrack album—which I was heartily trying to distance us from—the dialogue he used made no sense if you hadn't seen the movie, which really irritated me. I wanted the album to be able to stand on its own. If some really cool mixer had come in and used dialogue rhythmically to enhance the album and make it stylistically original, I would've been ecstatic. But this was a tedious, boring, and colorless way to approach anything. It irritated the hell out of me.

The final credits read: "Produced, Conceived, and Assembled by Trent Reznor. Executive Soundtrack Producer, Budd Carr. Soundtrack Album Director, Oliver Stone." All of Budd's assistants received credits, and zillions of people I never even heard of were thanked. My name appears nowhere on the album, except as the movie's producer. I guess it made me sore for a little bit, but since I think the album blows anyway, it didn't last long. And in the end, there's no song on the album called "Sweet Trent," "Sweet Oliver," or "Sweet Budd." There is, however, a beautiful track called "Sweet Jane" that got more radio airplay than any other from the album. And I smile every time I hear it.

Now that we were back in Los Angeles, it meant we were also back in Alien territory. He could frequently be sighted poking around the office, trying to retrieve all our data when our outdated computer crashed, which it did frequently and with impunity. He decided that the situation would be helped if he installed some new thingamajig, so he tore the whole system apart—and then disappeared.

"Don, when is the Alien going to rematerialize and put this whole thing back together so we can be functional again?" I asked.

"Well, there's sort of a problem," said Don. "He finally had his court case over the supermarket bust, and they prescribed therapy and medication, put an ankle bracelet around his leg, then put him under house arrest for thirty days."

"You mean I have to live with this mess for another *month?*" I shrieked.

"Oh, no. He went to court on that one a month ago. And all would have been good in the 'hood, but he had to be home at a certain time every day to answer the phone so they could make sure he was still there, or he got locked up again. The only time he could be away was for 'work' during the week—as if he had a job —and for two hours on the weekend to go see his psychiatrist."

"I fail to see what all this has to do with our computer."

"Well, he fucked everything up. He was one week away from being out from under house arrest, when he decided he needed some laser disks. So he goes into a store, puts fifteen or so under his jacket, the clerk sees him and says 'bustado,' and they throw him in jail."

"Oh, that's just *fabulous!* Now he's torn the damned computer apart, and nobody but him knows how to put it back together. So what's going to happen to him over the laser disks?"

"Well, luck was on his side—and it wasn't. When the DA realized he got busted before he'd even left the store with the laser disks, he said, 'I can't press charges.' But The Alien got busted on a Saturday and couldn't make bail until Monday, so he had to spend the weekend with the county. When they called his home and he was supposed to be under house arrest, his girlfriend had to tell them he was in jail. So he shows up before the hangin' judge again, who says, 'They might not be pressing charges, but I *know* you did it. If you're arrested for *anything* else for the next three years, I want to see you back in my courtroom within the next twenty-four hours.' Then he adds three more days to his house arrest for the laser disks and lets him go."

"And the upshot is . . ."

"His girlfriend is the one who made his bail, and she's making him stay home until his house arrest is over. You'll probably see him back here in a week or so."

"Well, I guess this effectively puts an end to my memo-writing career for a while," I said. "That should make Oliver happy. But I think you should have a little heart-to-heart with The Alien about Big Al."

"Good idea."

So when Amy came running into Don's office later that day in a panic, our first thought was that The Alien was in trouble again and needed bail money. But not this time—it turned out to be much, much more serious than either of us could have imagined.

"I just got a call from a friend at USC," she said. "Aziz Gazal just killed his family."

It seemed like somebody must have made it up—it would be the perfect joke about Aziz, except that it was true. Aziz had recently been fired from the stockroom by a new USC administration that had gotten wise to his scams. Then he had gone up to see his wife in Idyllwild; apparently he was angry that Kandijah, their daughter, the beautiful young girl I'd played with during *Lazarus*, who had just made the junior-high-school cheerleading squad, was going out with a boy Aziz didn't approve of. Nobody knows exactly what happened, the police would never talk about the details, but rumor had it that he chopped Becky and Kandijah up with an ax, then burned the place to the ground. In his last days, he'd been frustrated in his attempts to finally make *The Brave*, and had run around cursing Oliver, Jodie Foster, and everyone else who had expressed interest in the project whom he felt had never come through for him the way he wanted. The phone lines were flying with rumor and innuendo that he was on the loose and coming after everyone who'd ever done him wrong with a gun. It would be another month before we learned that Aziz wasn't coming after Oliver or anyone. After he'd killed Becky and Kandijah, he'd run up into the hills and shot himself in the head, where the police finally found his body.

It was chilling, it was unbelievable, and yet we finally had to face the fact that it was true. Like him or not, we couldn't ignore the fact that someone so close to our experience—who had shared our USC history, as well as our intense desire to make it in Hollywood—was capable of such a horrific act. I might like to separate myself from Aziz Gazal and claim that he was some sort of beast out of some other world, but that would be a lie. Aziz wanted what I wanted. When his world collapsed around him, it erupted in a violent tragedy that I don't even like to think about. The distance between Aziz, between Don and me and Oliver and everyone else who lived in a town that promised so much and came through for so few was perilously small. I thought back to the whole Rand/Quentin situation.

"Murphy, what would you have done if Rand and Quentin had taken *NBK* away from us, and we wound up feeling as broken and defeated as Aziz?" I asked.

"I dunno. Eddie Spaghetti and I used to joke about breaking their legs, but I like to think that was only talk."

Eddie Perez, or "Spaghetti," as Don called him, was a bodyguard and stuntman who was a good friend to both of us. While I'd never heard of Eddie actually hurting anyone, he was certainly capable of it physically.

"I wonder," I said. "I remember when we sat outside that courtroom, and I thought we'd lost. From then on I had to stop myself from ever thinking that failure was even a possibility, because once you started down that road, you don't know the lengths you'll go to in order to make sure it never happens."

"Don't I know it," said Don.

Whatever else could be said about our *NBK* experience, in the end we had succeeded. But at what price? We'd been marked and changed by our experiences in ways we didn't even understand. One thing was certain: There was no turning back. We'd never be able to be "normal" again. Going back to Seattle and flipping burgers for the rest of my life just wasn't an option anymore.

Chapter 10

Let Me Point It Out.
This Is My Ass. Kiss It.

I remember one time, at the beginning of my career with Don, when I'd
gotten into an auto accident. I was at a stop sign on a rainy day when the
car behind me went out of control and rear-ended me, crunching the
entire back end of my beloved '68 Firebird 400 convertible. There was
never any question that the guy who hit me was at fault, since I was at a
dead stop at the time, but his insurance company instantly began dicker-
ing with me about how much they'd pay, and the extent of the damage
that had been done.

The lowest estimate I'd gotten for the repairs was $1,100; still, the
insurance company only wanted to pay $900, arguing that some of the
damage hadn't been caused by the accident. While I can be as strident
and demanding and argumentative as anyone else, I guess there's just
something in my voice that tells people that eventually I'll give up, figuring $200 is not worth all that energy.

"Murphy, will you step in and handle this one?" I asked.

The poor bastard at the insurance company had no idea what he was in
for. Don began to harass him incessantly, unwilling to let him off the
phone whenever he got him until the guy was worn out and sick to death
of the whole incident. People can just tell that Don takes absolute delight
in this type of stuff, and I don't think auto-insurance people are used to
having to deal with the kind of people who actually enjoy being better at
their own bullshit than they are. Some $5,000 later, when every detail of
my car had been completely restored from front to back, they were calling
and begging me to settle and call Don off. It was one of the great eye-
openers of my life, watching a moribund bureaucracy crumble in submission in the wake of sheer, unbridled belligerence.

Well, now that we were entering the marketing phase of *NBK*, it was time to put Don's skills to use against something much more important than the state of my car. (As a side note, few things in life have that status.) Because we were about to do battle with the horrendous bureaucracy that existed within the Warners Marketing Department, and it was a sheer blessing that Don Murphy is a genius when it comes to confrontations that would overwhelm mere mortals.

Don has the best description of the Warner Brothers Marketing Department I've ever heard: "Everyone over there is Idi Amin Dada for life." Seemingly answerable to nothing and no one, they are capable of calling a halt to even the most simple and benign publicity activity on their own say-so. Early on, we had tried to enlist their help to get the publicity ball rolling during the shoot. We wanted to get the music/underground/alternative press behind *NBK* by inviting our journalist friends down to watch it being filmed, hoping that advance word-of-mouth would give it "cult" status by the time it was released. We were also sure our prison experiences would make for some remarkable stories. We felt that these journalists' publications would be the most successful venue we could have in reaching what we foresaw as *NBK*'s ultimate audience: kids who were into alternative music. Warners didn't seem to agree with us, and their response was to ban all press from the set.

Now, their anxiety on the press front was not without merit. In their defense, you never know what loony gibberish Oliver's going to come out with in the midst of an interview. Despite his omnipresence in the media, he has very little idea of how it actually works, or how to use it effectively, so he's always coming out with some incendiary half-baked comment that winds up getting him vilified. But that kind of stuff plays better in the edgier press anyway, rather than the *New York Times* or *Newsweek*.

And so early on, Don and I had to decide how to address our dilemma in the face of the Warner Brothers' edict. "What are we going to do if they won't allow any press on the set?" I asked. "It's really going to blow a lot of our plans."

"It's easy," said Don. "We just ignore them."

Oh boy. Well, I certainly wasn't against it. "That's only going to work if the old man is on our side," I said. "What do you think our chances are that Oliver will ignore Warners and do what we want?"

"Are you kidding? Oliver is the biggest press whore in the world," said Don. "He'll talk to *The Pennysaver* if he thinks he can get his name in print. Besides, I don't think he feels he's answerable to the Warner Brothers Marketing Department or anybody else when it comes to doing what he wants."

Don was right. Oliver was delighted; he told us that we were "reinventing him for a new generation." So during the shoot, we snuck a few of our journalist friends onto the set, from magazines like *Film Threat* and *The Village Voice.* Michael Singer, our unit publicist, would have kittens whenever he would suddenly see one of these people materialize on the set, knowing he would have the unenviable task of calling up Warner Brothers and telling them that, at our behest, Oliver was ignoring their demands. But I think in the end, even Warners had to agree that it resulted in some of the best advanced hype we managed to generate, even though they despised us for our arrogance in the process.

So by the time it came to plan for *NBK*'s theatrical release, the Warners marketing people held nothing for us but a barely containable polite disdain, since every time they'd vetoed our efforts, we'd gone ahead and done what we wanted anyway. But their feelings toward us were the least of our worries. We knew *NBK* had them scared shitless; they'd just had the corporate fiasco of Ice T's song, "Cop Killer," landing firmly in their laps as they faced their stockholders, and we also knew that they viewed this as another potential "Cop Killer."

But *NBK* was nothing of the sort. It exhorted no one to violence; at its heart, it was a satire, but a satire that would be appreciated most sincerely by a generation that had grown up on a diet of tabloid news, video games, and MTV. We felt that deep down, Warners wanted to try and crawl under an unenviable publicity rug by pretending that the film was something that it wasn't. And that was something that Don and I were completely unwilling to let happen.

We knew we were going to be in deep doo-doo by the time their marketing materials started appearing, but we had no idea how deep the doo-doo was until we saw the first trailer that they cut for the film. Oliver was still his ambivalent self when it came to showing us things before they were released, so our first chance to see the trailer for the film came on the day that it appeared in theaters. Mid-morning, Don and I walked down the

Third Street Promenade in Santa Monica to sit in a theater and watch it being thrown up on the screen for the first time—not only to see it for ourselves, but to see how it played to an audience.

"On the whole, I'd rather see *Forrest Gump*," Don said upon viewing that film's trailer right next to our own.

It was a debacle. Warners seemed to want to sell the movie on the back of Oliver Stone; the trouble was, that was their strategy for *Heaven and Earth*, and it had failed miserably: that film grossed only $2 million at the box office. Moreover, *NBK* was not a movie that would appeal to the traditional "Oliver Stone audience," whatever that was. The trailer started with a flag waving upside down, with images of *JFK* and *Platoon* taking center stage. Shots of *NBK* flashed by in an instant.

"Do they know that most of the people who will want to see *NBK* were in diapers when *Platoon* came out?" said Don.

I thought back to the looks on the faces of the Warners people when they first saw the film. My initial fears were coming true in living color. Unwilling to face the film for what it was, they were trying to pretend the whole thing would just go away.

When a studio is really excited about a picture, it will open it in theaters during peak times of the year when people flock to see films, like Christmas and summer and the big three-day holidays. They'll put a lot of money into advertising it, so that you can't turn on your TV or pass a bus stop without having the thing thrust into your face. They'll also put it in a large number of theaters, so when it starts showing, it's pretty much guaranteed to "open," meaning that it pulls in strong numbers (money) at the box office on its opening weekend.

However, if a studio thinks they've got a stinker on its hands, they don't want to throw good money after bad. You probably won't see a lot of expensive TV advertising, just enough to put the name out there so that when it comes out on video, they may have a chance to recoup some of their investment. They won't put it in a lot of theaters (they'll save the theaters that usually run their pictures for movies they think will bring in more money), and since not that many people will be aware of its existence in the first place, your film will open poorly, no matter how good it is. Theater owners won't want to "hold" the film, meaning that they won't want to keep it in their theaters week after week (which is when pictures really start to make the big money); they'll want to run other films that have more potential for bringing people in and buying all that overpriced popcorn. If Warners' sole strategy for getting people to see *NBK* was "Hey, come see another Oliver Stone film," it was a good indicator that they didn't have much faith in the movie and weren't going to do a whole lot to put it out there.

Up until that point, dealing with the press had always been my domain; but faced with this marketing crisis that threatened to kill the film before it even opened, Don got over his "fuck *NBK*" attitude and volunteered to help me on the publicity front. And so we began to double-team Oliver, trying to convince him that this trailer was crap and nobody who would want to see the movie would be drawn into a theater by it.

Suddenly, an even bigger problem materialized: the poster for *NBK*.

It was a beautiful, glossy cream-colored affair, with lovely pretentious silver-toned script and lofty text about Oliver Stone's forthcoming important commentary on the state of affairs in our culture. In the middle of the poster was a TV set with Woody's and Juliette's heads sticking out.

"It looks like 'Coming this fall from CBS'," I moaned in despair.

Don called up and began hammering anyone he could get on the phone from Warners. They all said that there was no changing the poster—it had already been printed, at great expense. Bob and Victor saw it when they came into the office shortly thereafter, and came flying down to us in a panic. "Have you seen the poster? Isn't there anything you can do? You're the producers!" Even Hank Corwin was crawling out from the DMZ, begging us to intercede.

We went to Oliver (who had approved the horrible thing in the first place, probably in a moment during the final mix when he wasn't paying much attention) and told him we thought it was a disaster. I wrote him another memo (The Alien had finally shown up again and reassembled our computer), attaching posters from *Reservoir Dogs* and *The Crow*, to demonstrate the kind of imagery an audience who would like this film would respond to, and to convince him that this wouldn't happen with the kind of sanitized poster the likes of which Warners had delivered. He didn't want to listen. But one Friday evening I cornered him as he was on his way out of the office.

"Oliver, you really need to reconsider this." I showed him another poster that the Warner Brothers art department had actually come up with. (The art department seemed more sensitive to what the film was about, despite the vetoes that came down from their high bosses in marketing.)

"You'll never get the kind of response you're looking for if we let them go forward with this frightful TV set thing. It's the kind of poster that would draw my mother into a theater, not 'the kids' you're hoping to appeal to."

"Stop bothering me about this, Jane. I'm sick of hearing it." He turned his back on me and walked away in disgust, cussing me under his breath.

But later that night, Azita called Don to say that Oliver had scheduled a meeting with Arnon for that Sunday, asked for a copy of the poster I'd shown him, and had an agenda to get the whole thing changed.

Monday morning, a slightly perplexed Warner Brothers Marketing Department was greeted with a phone call from Oliver Stone—he was changing his mind.

Warners sent over one of their ad people with more ideas, which seemed only to be riffs on their original theme. Only this time there were lots of TV sets, with faces of all the characters in them, stacked one on top of the other. Oliver pulled us into his office with the guy, and asked us what we thought.

"Well, they're lovely," I said as diplomatically as I knew how. "But I think they're for somebody else's movie, not ours."

The guy stuck an angry finger in my face. "You're lucky to have Warner Brothers marketing your movie—we've got the best damned marketing department in the world!" he shouted indignantly.

Later, Oliver took me to task yet again for being difficult. But shortly thereafter, he got on the phone with Rob Friedman, then president of Warners World Wide Marketing, who was trying to get Oliver to commit at that time to a heavy publicity campaign of interviews for the film. Oliver told him point-blank he wouldn't have to stick around and stump for the film if they had a decent poster. (Ultimately, he took off for Nepal for six weeks prior to the film's opening. The only interviews he did during that time were with our alternative- and music-press friends. I still remember the shock in my journalist friend Dave Jenison's voice when he told me that Oliver had called him from the high Himalayas to do an interview for his magazine, *Hypno*, that had a circulation of roughly 25,000, when he'd never been able to get the Warners people to give him the time of day. I thought about the guy who'd stuck his finger in my face so arrogantly that day. The words "eat me" jumped immediately to mind.)

In spite of our ardent efforts on the marketing front, it probably wouldn't have made a bit of difference had Warners not finally turned around on the film and decided they just might have a hit on their hands. And ironically, the thing that was responsible for their about-face was the strange concurrence of the Nicole Brown Simpson murder just as *NBK* was ready for release. It was also around that time that the "tracking studies," as they're known, began to show that there was an outrageously strong awareness of the film and want-to-see factor among young males in the 18–24 age range, who comprise the bulk of the people who go to movies, anyway. Well, it was no surprise to us. But Warners decided that with the media circus that had recently surrounded the Menendez brothers and Tonya Harding, to say nothing of the feeding frenzy that erupted when the white Bronco drove down the 405 Freeway, they suddenly had something on their hands that was utterly current and completely relevant to what the country was going through. Nancy Kirkpatrick, one of the Warners marketing people, even confessed to me that chairman Bob Daly could now travel the Bel Air cocktail-party circuit and brag about *NBK*, as it now related to something his peer group was fascinated with.

The poster was changed. We wound up with a black-and-white image of a bald Woody Harrelson, with the reflected image of Juliette Lewis in his red sunglasses. Not as stunning and graphic as we would have liked, but it certainly wasn't working against the film like we felt the original one had been.

Oliver ultimately came up with the brainstorm of cutting in snippets of O.J., Rodney King, Eric Menendez, and Tonya Harding into the ending coda of *NBK*, unwilling to leave it to chance that the public might not get his point after being hammered over the head with it for the past two hours. (He is not, and never will be, a subtle guy.) Though Don and I both felt it was a bit of overkill, we knew that he was in love with this idea and decided to save our breath, rather than try to beat it out of the final cut.

There were just too many fights that needed our energies these days, and we decided to save ourselves for places where we could make a difference.

One of those places was not with the ratings board. On that front, we were completely ineffectual. When the MPAA first viewed *NBK*, they decided its violence deserved an "NC–17" rating. Now, the MPAA claims not to be any sort of a censorship board—it is an organization that was put together by the studios in the 1960s so the industry could sort of "police" itself, rather than have the government step in and start deciding who could see what. Not a bad idea in theory. Ostensibly, the MPAA just views a film and gives it a rating. Its policy is to never criticize specific content or insist on the excision of certain scenes, which would make them a de facto censorship board. Which, we were to learn over time, is exactly what it is.

When a director signs an agreement with a studio to make a film, he or she becomes contractually obligated to deliver a film with a certain MPAA rating. The studio's concerns on this front are purely commercially motivated—a film's rating will determine how many people will be allowed to see it. More people, for instance, can get into a PG–13 movie than they can an R-rated movie, which ultimately affects the box-office numbers. (Since Blockbuster Video, the largest video distributor in the country, made it policy to refuse to carry NC–17 films, it virtually destroyed any studio's willingness to accept a film with that rating under any circumstances, as it severely cut into one of their biggest sources of revenue.) Well, nobody ever looked at the *NBK* script and deluded themselves into thinking it would be a PG–13, but we were obligated contractually to deliver an R.

When the MPAA came back after viewing the film for the first time, the members were mortified at its content. And despite all insistences to the contrary, they usually do come back and tell you specifically what they do and don't like. In fact, a memo that came to us from the Warners people outlines the head of the MPAA's attempts to explain just what it was they found so objectionable. They were deeply disturbed by the Rodney Dangerfield scene, for example, and thus we decided to go in and bleep a lot of Rodney's expletives, which kind of fit into the whole sitcom riff we were trying for, so it wasn't the most painful of compromises. But the worst problem we had was that the thing they were objecting to most strongly was the "tone." How the hell can you go back in and recut a film for "tone"?

In the end, we had to go back to the MPAA five times and make 150 cuts in the film in order to get the R that we were obligated to deliver. The trouble was, when you look closely at *NBK*, there are actually few acts of gruesome violence that you could point to specifically. While a lot of people are killed, no time is spent lingering on exploding heads or bodies being blown to bits. It resulted in only some five minutes of film being taken out in order to achieve our requisite rating, and devolved into a sort of ridiculous exercise in editing one bullet hit here instead of two. A few seconds of mayhem in the prison riot came out at another point, as well as the now-infamous shot where Downey gets a hole blown through his hand and you can see Tommy Lee Jones's face through the hole as he stands on the landing below him. (Ironically, to my mind, the excision of that particular shot made the sequence even more disturbing, it was replaced with a shot of Juliette simply shooting Downey's hand, and where one moment had been comic in tone, the new one seemed palpably painful to me.)

The whole thing angered me not only with the intense hypocrisy of the whole exercise, but also with the seemingly arbitrary nature of the process. There was nothing in our movie that was as brutal as the opening scene of *Basic Instinct*, where a naked Sharon Stone stabs her lover —who is tied up to the bed at the moment— to death with an ice pick. But as the MPAA people explained to us, what was "commonly acceptable" two years ago when that film came out was no longer felt to be in the cultural mainstream of what was appropriate. Which leaves filmmakers with virtually no guide to go with in creating their films, since they can only look at what's gone before them in order to judge what they can include and how far they can go in order to express their vision and still give the studio what it demands.

When I finally saw the final "theatrical release" version of *NBK*, as it's known, I wanted to cry. Although only five minutes had been cut out, it completely destroyed the whole pace and rhythm of the film. Well, Warners promised us that after we'd exhausted all the markets for the theatrical version, from pay TV to video and laser disk, that they would let us release an NC–17 version of the film, in order to be able to display (for our own satisfaction, if nothing else) the version we had originally crafted with such care. It wasn't much, but it was something.

As the countdown began for *NBK's* theatrical release, Warners was now committing big advertising dollars to the marketing campaign, and *NBK* was starting to saturate the media. The one thing we were dreading at this point was a press war with Quentin Tarantino. We'd sent the final shooting script to him when it came time to assign writing credits. He claimed he disliked it so much that he didn't even want a writing credit—he only wanted a "story by" credit. That was fine with us. He had had conversations with Oliver personally over the issue, because he wanted the right to publish his original screenplay in book form, a right which we held after purchasing the screenplay. (Ultimately we paid him a buyout price of $350,000, based on a contractual percentage of the final budget of the film; his quote to Roger Avary upon receiving his check was "You'd be surprised how quickly tears of sorrow can turn to tears of joy—I laughed out loud.") Oliver said that if Quentin refrained from comment, and from taking potshots at us in the press, that we would be happy to give him the book rights, but only after *NBK* had had its full release and people' wouldn't be confused by the two projects being out there simultaneously. Quentin agreed.

We thought we had avoided a direct confrontation, but just before the opening of *NBK*, we got a call from *Premiere* magazine, where editor Peter Biskind told us that Quentin had done an interview accusing us of "stealing" the script for *NBK*. We explained what had actually happened, point by point, but when the article appeared, our comments were reduced to "Hamsher and Murphy deny they fired Vossler."

To say the least, Don was frothing at the mouth. This kind of accusation was libelous and outrageous. Coming through on his promise to "help me with the publicity," Don had PR grande dame Marrion Billings, who represented Oliver, hold space in the following issue for a letter of response. He then composed a wild ten-page screed calling Quentin every name in the book, which was finally boiled down to the following:

> Writer Peter Biskind quotes Quentin Tarantino, who states that his script for NATURAL BORN KILLERS *"was stolen from me . . . this skulduggerous theft happened."*

*In reality no one can "steal" a script from anyone, since the author is
required to sign numerous chain-of-title documents attributing originality of authorship. Tarantino sat in a room with his attorney, knowing that my partner Jane Hamsher and I were paying him $10,000 out
of our own pocket, and signed over the script, ultimately realizing over
$350,000. Some theft. When the time came to look for directors, Quen-
tin not only okayed the search, but met some of them with us.*

*Despite what he says now, Quentin never had a problem with Oliver
directing NBK at first; rather, he had his agents call Oliver and ask
him to wait until our option was up so they could resell it for more
money. Oliver didn't, so now Quentin hates him.*

*As we told Biskind, we never "fired" [Rand] Vossler, three days later or
ever. He still receives a coproducer credit for his efforts on the film and
was handsomely paid. All steps taken regarding Vossler's involvement
with the film were with Quentin's approval.*

*Before Quentin is allowed to talk about stealing again, Biskind should
ask him about how he got Roger Avary to accept a "story by" credit on
PULP FICTION when he wrote one-third of the screenplay. Roger
also wrote the [unfilmed] bodybuilder scene in NBK that Quentin now
takes credit for in the article. Biskind should then ask why RESER-
VOIR DOGS plays like a scene-by-scene plagiarism of a 1987 Hong
Kong film called CITY ON FIRE, starring Quentin's idol, Chow Yun-
Fat. Or ask Quentin if he ever told Roger that he was going to appro-
priate the speech Roger wrote and use it when he "acts" in SLEEP
WITH ME.*

*There is an interesting Quentin Tarantino story to be told. It would be
the true story of a video geek from the South Bay who thought he could
act, watched far too many videos, worked them into scripts, and
claimed them as his own. After lying his way through his résumé, he
gets his foot in the door. He starts to believe his own press. He dismisses
most of the people who helped him get where he is going, disowning
friends like Vossler and firing his manager of 7 years. Now, with the
spotlight narrowing in on his lack of originality, everyone looks to see*

*what he's going to do next. So all you readers out there, write in to
Premiere; what film would you like Quentin to copy next? I vote that
he copy the old fairy tale* "The Emperor's New Clothes."

Don Murphy

Producer, NATURAL BORN KILLERS
Santa Monica, California

Don's role of avenging angel almost ended here because it was decided
(or one of us decided anyway, and the other one was forced to comply)
that carrying on a public vendetta against Quentin was really a pointless
waste of energy, particularly since *Reservoir Dogs* was a certifiable cult hit
and he was now cast as such a media darling that it was hard for us to find
fair representation in the pieces that were done on him. But despite my
admittedly less-than-ardent efforts to keep Don's vitriolic humor from
venting itself in the press, he got by me one last time.

I came around the corner to hear him on the phone one day, after the
Premiere letter appeared, clearly winding up an interview.

"Who was that?"

"Oh, just the *Village Voice*."

My eyes lit up. "I thought we agreed you're not supposed to talk to the
press without someone present," I said.

"Don't worry, I was fine. She loved me."

Loved him. Hmmmm. Don at times is almost as naïve as Oliver, and
doesn't realize when reporters are baiting him to get a response. I forgot
about the incident for the time being, but it came back to haunt me soon
enough.

One day I came in to see the fax machine buzzing. It was the *Village
Voice* article, written about the "artistic borrowing" Quentin had done on
Reservoir Dogs (in which Quentin, having invited the writer to his house
and cooked dinner for her, wound up coming off totally vindicated). And
there, as a huge pull quote, written in psychotic ransom-note lettering,
were the words:

"I would openly celebrate Quentin Tarantino's death."
—Don Murphy, Producer, *Natural Born Killers*

Once my pulse rate came down to normal levels, I resigned myself to the fact that he'd never be housebroken.

If you ever want a disorienting experience, open your first film to a media blitzkrieg. By the time opening week came around, Don and I were both nervous wrecks. Preliminary press reviews were coming in from across the country. "Oliver Stone is back, and this time he's delivered a film so raunchy, so rude, so exhilarating and blatantly provocative that he makes his own *JFK*, that paranoid rant-of-all-rants, look timid and wishy-washy by comparison," said Edward Guthmann in the *San Francisco Chronicle*. "It raises enough issues to keep the Op-Ed pages turning for weeks," said Jack Matthews in the *Los Angeles Times*. "The most radical film any major studio has released since *A Clockwork Orange*," said Steven Schiff in *The New Yorker*. "*Killers* touches a national nerve," said Chris Hewitt of Knight Ridder. Even Michael Medved, who deplored the film, had to admit that "*Natural Born Killers* may be many things gross, disgusting, pretentious, incoherent and excessive—but it is not for one moment dull."

Some critics were declaring it a masterpiece; others were vilifying it for its incendiary content, especially once the reviews got out of the big cities. "Oliver Stone's satire on violence backfires, descending into depths of its own slime," said the *Arizona Daily Star*. (I suppose we should've been prepared for a movie which attacks the media to receive direct salvos back from them, but I guess I was still harboring some naïve notion that film critics would see themselves outside of the tabloid journalism world we were indicting.) Some journalists picked up on all of Quentin's pissing and moaning about the injustice he felt had been done to his script, and ultimately, it probably hurt us at the box office. But the thing that really gored me was that all the reviews, both positive and negative, were so lazy in their critiques; hundreds of them came piling into the office, and they all looked like one review that someone had written up and everyone else had copied. "Oliver Stone is guilty of indulging in the violence he condemns the media for," ran the standard critical observation. What a stupid comment. Were they all just missing the point?

On Sunset Boulevard, a huge billboard of bald Woody Harrelson blazed down upon the Strip. Everywhere we went, we couldn't move without being bombarded by the images and the brewing controversy surrounding

NBK, although the movie hadn't even opened yet. Somehow this thing, which had originated in my dining room and had been such a hermetically conducted enterprise, was now open for the whole world to see. Which left Don and me facing much, much more controversy than either of us had ever anticipated. Or wanted.

Suddenly my mother was calling up and asking if she and forty-six of our closest lifelong family friends could get tickets to an advance press screening in Seattle. ("Uh Mom, maybe I haven't effectively communicated what this film is about. . . .") It was like our lives had suddenly blown wide open, and we were forced to see ourselves and everything we'd been doing for the past two years through the eyes of others, and that kind of bombardment instantly starts to distort how you see yourself. Although Don and I both enjoyed dealing with the press, we weren't prepared for how it felt to have all of this stuff flying back in our faces—it was not only disturbing, it was disorienting, and quite unreal. It made it hard to imagine why anyone in the world would want even fifteen minutes of fame, let alone any more. Your own notions about who you are and what you're all about evaporate as this monster you've created is reflected everywhere you go, and you start feeling completely subsidiary to its phenomenon.

I tried to explain it to my mom in terms she could understand. "What if you'd spent all this effort baking this great cherry pie, by yourself in the privacy of your own kitchen, then suddenly twenty million people show up and want a piece of it?" I don't know if it was an appropriate metaphor, but it was the best way I could describe to someone what it was like to have something so utterly personal, as *NBK* had become to me over the time we had spent making it, put on public display for everyone to tear into on a whim.

Since Oliver had pissed off to Nepal and refused to show up to a premiere, Warners had retaliated with the slightly creepy stunt of refusing to give us one. This irritated the hell out of Don; we'd been trying to get them to pop for a big party after the premiere for a while, and the marketing lords said they'd do it if Don could get one of the big bands from the soundtrack to play. Well, Don went to bat, and got Nine-Inch Nails to agree to play for the party; he also found a great warehouse space to have it in. It finally became evident that they were only trying to distract Don by making him chase himself; even after he delivered Nine-Inch Nails, they still refused to cover the expense of a party. It never occurred to us that they'd nix a premiere altogether. They also didn't want to have the standard "industry screenings," as they're known in the business, where studios typically show the film for people in the business prior to its opening as a courtesy to one another. (I think they expected really bad word-of-mouth to come out of such screenings, and wanted to avoid this destroying the public's desire to see the film on opening weekend.)

"This just sucks," Don said when he heard the news. "There are a lot of people who've been loyal to us over the course of this whole thing, and there's no way they're going to keep me from inviting them to a screening."

"What are you planning to do, steal a print of the film and show it in your den?" I said.

"No, though it's a thought. I don't care if Warners doesn't want to have a premiere or any screenings. The one thing they can't get out of is a cast and crew screening—and we're going to hijack it."

Don was referring to the obligatory screening that the studio gives to show the film to everyone who was part of its making, the "cast and crew." If they don't invite all of these people to a screening to show everyone involved how it finally turned out, they look like a bunch of ungrateful bastards. Warners tried to put it off as long as possible, but finally scheduled it two days before we were due to open.

The screening was set to take place at the Academy of Motion Picture Arts and Sciences (the same people who give out the Oscars). Our personal guest list grew to 200, then 300, then 400 people. Oliver, who despite previous announcements to the contrary had returned from Nepal for the screening, came flying into Don's office, furious because he had heard that Don was inviting legions of people. "It's only supposed to be cast and crew, Don!" he screamed.

"Oliver, I only invited, like, five people," Don said. "Somebody's confused." (If Oliver was ever likely to believe this gross lie, he didn't suffer under any delusions for long. During the screening, Don was completely busted when his own performance as the jovial, overacting prison guard who gets killed during the prison break flashed up on screen, and 400 of his close personal friends let out a giant collective cheer.)

On hand were everyone we'd ever known. The Alien and his girlfriend, Peter Rice, Michael Zoumas, Keith Gordon, Eddie Spaghetti, Justin, Karl Austen, Joe Rosenberg, Thom Mount and anyone else who'd had a hand in helping us to get to this point, the cast and crew, Oliver, and just about everybody Don ever met in Los Angeles. We were especially glad that Cathryn Jaymes showed up for the event, since she'd been pretty dispirited lately. Earlier in the year, Quentin had his agents call her up and tell her she was fired. When she finally got him on the phone, he told her, "You can't be upset. . . . Your job was to launch my career. Well, my career is launched, and your job is done. I don't need you anymore, anyway. What made you think I'd stay with you?" When she reminded him that he'd promised he would, he replied, "You can't hold me to that. Who do you think you are, the devil calling in a contract?"

The Academy Theater holds a couple of thousand people, but the NBK screening soon became the hottest ticket in town, and it was oversubscribed so quickly that Warners was forced to have an overflow screening at the Showcase Theater, which unfortunately was thirty minutes away in Hollywood. By the time the doors opened at 6:00, there was a line around the block. Once the theater was filled to capacity and beyond, they closed the doors and started turning everyone away, directing them to the Showcase. This had the unfortunate upshot of pissing off a lot of people like Leonard Cohen, who showed up shortly before the film was due to run, and were refused access by the Warners people, despite the fact that he had three songs in the film. (Pimpowski, in one of his few useful moments during the whole endeavor, managed to intervene on Leonard's behalf and got him into the screening.)

I don't remember much of the screening at all; my only recollection of the whole event was that my pantyhose were too tight. I vaguely recall looking around at all my friends as they stared at the screen, their mouths hanging open in shock, and thinking that despite all the bitching and moaning I'd done about NBK since the whole thing began, nothing could have prepared them for what they were seeing. They were all in sensory overload, and so was I, although for a completely different reason. I could only wonder at what would happen across the rest of the country in two days, as an unsuspecting public had NBK inflicted on them for the first time.

After the screening, in the face of Warners' refusal to pay for any sort of celebration, Don the Party Man reemerged. He got together with his friend Brent Bolthouse, a Hollywood nightclub entrepreneur who at the time was also running a restaurant called Babylon. He arranged with Brent to book the place for the evening. It was slightly embarrassing that everyone who had gone through so much personal hardship in the making of *NBK* had to pay for their own drinks, but it was either that or nothing. Don told Brent that if the turnout was low and the restaurant didn't make a profit for the evening, he'd slip him some money to make up the difference afterward.

Well, the whole thing turned into one big, wild party. The place was jammed; there was a line around the block to get in. My response was, of course, to get wildly drunk, slamming Manhattans with Eddie Spaghetti and Duran Duran's John Taylor. I don't think I saw Don during the entire evening. At one point, Tom Sizemore guzzled a bottle of champagne, then stumbled over to my table and announced to everyone in attendance that he and I "haven't had sex yet—but we will." I vaguely remember some model coming up to Oliver and asking him to sign a picture of her in some magazine ad. Later, she was waving the photo around proudly—it was signed "Eat me, Oliver Stone." He must've been as drunk as I was.

At one point, Don walked outside to see if there was anyone that we cared about waiting in line to get into the party. And there he was greeted by a strange spectacle—a large blond man from Warner Brothers' security force, who Don knew because he frequently used to throw The Alien out of Warner Brothers screenings when he tried to sneak in.

Which was bizarre—it wasn't a Warner Brothers party, it was our private party. "Why are you here?" asked a puzzled Don. "What's the concept? I'm confused."

"Warner Brothers sent me over in case something went wrong and one of the celebrities needed help."

Don thought about it for a moment. "Okay. Well, if you need a drink or anything, let me know."

The rest of the evening was a blur. The only thing I remember was waking up the next morning to find my body mysteriously covered in black charcoal scrawls. It wasn't until someone told me that REM's Michael Stipe had taken the charred end of a champagne cork and scrawled tattoos all over my arms at the end of the evening that I had any idea at all where they came from.

The day before the opening, the other shoe dropped on a controversy that we should have seen coming from the start. A member of the press, *Variety*'s Anita M. Busch, had been to the cast and crew screening, and had wondered what Coca-Cola felt about its polar-bear commercial appearing in the midst of the extremely violent and graphic *American Maniacs* sequence. Since the whole thing had been handled by Don and Coke's West Coast product-placement office, it turned out that the executives in Atlanta were pretty much unaware that they had ever granted such permission. They had an emergency screening of the film for the Coca-Cola board of directors, and collectively had a nervous collapse.

When the whole controversy started to break, however, all Don heard was that there was a reporter from *Variety* calling Oliver's office, wanting to know how we'd gotten permission to use the commercial in the first place. Don called one of our publicists in a lather—"If anyone's going to get credit for this, it's going to be me!" he said emphatically.

The next call he got came from Azita. "Don, I think you want to lie low on this one."

"How come? I'm the one who pulled it off!"

"Well, Coke is furious," she said. "They don't know how such a thing happened, and they've closed their Los Angeles product-placement office as a result, pulling all their people back to Atlanta so they can keep a closer watch on them. They're also demanding that we cut it out of the movie."

Don hung up the phone in silence.

"What, are you surprised?" I said. "The people who pump millions out of a few cents of carbonated sugar water every year, who essentially have nothing but a trademark and an image of being all-American and wholesome, are concerned about our insinuation that their advertising dollars are financing the production of violent, exploitive, socially debilitating TV shows that care only about ratings at all costs? Gee, who would have thought."

"Well, that's not the only place in the movie where we used their stuff," he said defensively. "Juliette's also holding a can of diet Coke in her hand when she visits Woody in prison."

"Yeah, and she's giving him a hand job with the other one," I said. "I don't think that's what they have in mind when they say, 'Things go better with Coke.' "

The subversiveness of the use of the Coke commercial had always thrilled me, as I'm sure it had Oliver, and I knew it had happened only because of a horrific gaffe when nobody was looking. However, the socio-political overtones of the appearance of a Coke commercial in our film had never entered Don's mind—he just wanted to scam some more free stuff.

He picked up the phone to call the publicist again. "Remember what I told you a few minutes ago? Well, forget it."

Friday, August 26, 1994. Don and I hook up with Peter Rice and go to Mann's Chinese Theater on Hollywood Boulevard to watch the 8:00 P.M. showing with a crowd who paid $7.50 to get in. Despite having watched the movie forty or fifty times by that point, it felt like a completely different experience when viewed through the eyes of people who were paying to get in. It wasn't just some film we'd made anymore—it was a *movie*. People were laughing, stomping, cheering, throwing things at the screen. And as the crowd emerged from the theater, they tended to be stunned and reaching for words. Like it or hate it, NBK seemed to elicit an ex-tremely thought-provoking response.

We came out of the theater to see Dave Veloz waiting to get into the 10:00 screening. Already, the midnight screening was sold out, and people were lining up for that one, too.

"Can you believe all this?" said Don.

"No way," said Dave, looking around at this mass of humanity pushing and shoving to get in to our movie. "I just can't."

Afterward, Peter, Don, and I went down to Farfalla Restaurant and met up with our friend Sue Berger of Penguin Books, who bought a bottle of champagne to celebrate.

"Congratulations," Peter said, as we all raised our glasses to toast NBK. "It looks like you opened."

"No," I said, "it looks like we *survived*."

The box-office figures for opening night around the country were phe-nomenal—$3.1 million. Every show at the major theaters in town were sold out for the evening. We won the night against *Forrest Gump*, which had still done a respectable $2.7 million, but we were the first film to knock it out of the number-one spot. Some theater owners across the country had been worried about potential acts of violence in their theaters, and in response Warner Brothers had provided them extra security. But it turned out that none was needed. Most people were walking out of the theaters overwhelmed and overstimulated, more numb than whipped into a mad frenzy. On Saturday night, we held at virtually the same figures as Friday, and Sunday we were still going strong—we wound up beating out the juggernaut *Forrest Gump* for the weekend.

We were number one.

On Monday morning, we were shaking our heads in disbelief as we looked at the numbers from across the country. It was the biggest opening weekend that any Oliver Stone film had ever had.

"Our first film, and we came out at the top of the heap," said Don.

"Now that it's all over, and we won, I can't even seem to remember any of the bad stuff anymore. Can you?"

"I wouldn't go that far," said Don. "But I know what you mean."

All we could think about was the fact that we felt great. The experience had been a killer, but we both knew that having our first film open to such a big splash had accelerated our careers at least ten years. More than anything else, we felt extremely grateful to everyone who helped us get there. We spent the morning writing thank-you notes to everyone in creation, even Rob Friedman and the Warner Brothers marketing people, for everything they'd done to help make the movie a success. Our classiest friends sent congratulatory flowers and champagne. But we also knew that a lot of the people we'd known since film school, and many others we had come up the ranks of the industry with, were almost certainly eating out their own livers at the film's success. Because, for some reason, in Hollywood Heinrich Hein's observation holds painfully true: "It is not enough that you succeed, but that everyone you know must fail."

Chapter 11

All the Oscars in the World Can't Fix That Forehead

Hello, Venice.

Because *NBK* is a success, Warners (at Oliver's insistence) agreed to pop for our tab to the film festival for the week, since the film was showing there. (It was a particularly gratifying moment for Don, who took immense pleasure when Nancy Kirkpatrick told me that Clayton had not been invited. When Clayton found out we were going, he decided to tag along, but it was on his own dime.) When we boarded the plane, we found our friends—director Jefery Levy and producer Dale Pollock, whose film *SFW* was also scheduled to be presented at the festival the only other occupants in the first-class cabin. We all proceeded to celebrate by swilling a lot of extremely expensive champagne, and eating beluga caviar (despite the fact that I don't particularly like it—it just seemed the most decadent thing we could do at the moment, and it doesn't taste that bad if you cover it up with enough onions and sour cream).

It was great to be traveling with friends; Jefery's wife, Pam, was a particularly close friend of mine. The two of us had only recently gotten completely shit-faced at a party up the street from the Sunset Strip, on an evening when Jefery was feeling especially dejected because he thought his distributor wasn't doing enough advertising for *SFW*. So Pam and I came up with the brainstorm that I should climb on top of the nearby Whiskey-a-Go-Go with a can of spray paint (as she, at the time, was sporting high heels, and I was wearing motorcycle boots) and do our own advertising. So up the ladder I went, and climbed up onto a billboard while the Whiskey staff were calling the police and screaming for me to get down. I wound up crawling across a catwalk on my hands and knees before finally arriving at the top of a billboard that sported an image of local celebrity wannabe Angelyne, swaying drunkenly 40 feet over Sunset Strip as I spray-painted the letters *SFW* across her ass. The police were arriving just as I got down, and Pam and I took off through the bushes and down an alley where Don had a getaway car ready. If you ever want to see it for yourself, the April 1995 issue of *Vanity Fair* published its annual Hollywood issue featuring an article on "Billy Wilder's Sunset Strip." And there, in all its glory and for all time, is the Angelyne billboard—with a big *SFW* still defacing her posterior.

When we arrived in Venice, Warners had us booked into the Excelsior, which looks like a Venetian version of a Vegas hotel. It was the most ludicrous and garish spectacle you could imagine—the sight of paparazzi chasing nubile starlets into the water had always seemed to be the stuff of bad Italian films, but here it was. Jefery and Dale were booked at a much more graceful and elegant old hotel down the street, the Des Bains, where Thomas Mann had written *Death in Venice*. I'd requested to be put up there, but the Warners staff told us that Oliver wanted us to be at the Excelsior, so we could be "close to him."

Well, the Excelsior seemed fine enough once I got off the canal boat that deposited us with our luggage. That was, until I walked into the lobby. And there, waving his arms around and calling attention to himself to anyone who would notice, was Quentin Tarantino.

With the success of *NBK*, I thought I'd gotten over all my ill feelings toward him, but seeing him in person for the first time since the whole mess began brought everything right back up. I ran to the Warner Brothers press office, begging them to change my hotel. A Quentin Tarantino encounter was just more than I could stand.

"Please, I'll go anywhere else—I'll sleep under a park bench, I don't care," I said.

"Sorry," they said. "Every hotel in town is booked up for the festival."

"Don't worry," said Don, who was just delighted to be in Venice and didn't want Quentin's presence there to spoil it for me. "We're here to celebrate and have a good time. You'll probably never see him."

Just then, across the crowded hotel lobby, I heard someone shout, "Look, it's Don Murphy and Jane Hamsher—with blonde hair!" (If I haven't mentioned it until now, I have a penchant for changing my hair color frequently.) I turned in horror to see Quentin Tarantino for the first time in two years, looking like the friendliest guy in the whole world.

"Alive and kicking," I said as I continued my uninterrupted trajectory to the front desk to pick up my key. "Famous last words, Murphy," I muttered between gritted teeth.

I don't know why I was more upset than Don to see Quentin there—maybe because Don relishes confrontations, he would've loved to have had one with Quentin at that point. You would have thought that after everything that happened, I'd be thick skinned and nothing would get to me. But I still felt as if Quentin had been my friend and had betrayed me for no other reason than blind greed. We'd survived nicely, thank you very much, but the creeping cynicism that such incidents engender about all things Hollywood was something I always had to keep in check, or it would take over my life.

I resolved to just get some sleep and forget about it. And by the next morning, when I woke up and walked onto my veranda and looked out at the ocean and the beautiful Venetian sky, I almost had. So I dressed and went downstairs to join Don, Jefery, and Dale for brunch at our appointed time, figuring that Don was right and any encounter with Quentin could probably easily be avoided in the madness of the film festival.

My room was on the top floor of the hotel, and I was the sole passenger on the elevator—that was, until it stopped at the next level—and Quentin stepped in.

"Hey, Jane!" said the man who'd just called me a thief in print, as if we'd never been anything but the best friends in the whole world. "Wow, you look great with blonde hair," he said. "Are you here with the movie?"

No, asshole, I'm here to buy Venetian glass. "Yeah," I said adjusting to the surreality of the moment. "Are you here with *Pulp Fiction?*"

"No, I'm here supporting my friend Alex Rockwell—I'm an actor in his film," he said. "I'm just here for a couple of days before I start traveling across Europe doing publicity for my movie."

"That should be fun," I said for lack of anything more clever springing to my lips.

"Well, a lot of work, too, you know," said Quentin. The elevator seemed to be taking an eternity to get to the lobby, but it finally stopped. "Good seeing you," he said as we got off. "Best of luck with the movie."

The doors opened, and I floated out on a cloud of disbelief. Did this guy even remember what he'd done to me over the past two years? In the lobby were three wide-open mouths, belonging to Don, Jefery, and Dale, who were there waiting for me and couldn't quite fathom the spectacle before their eyes.

The four of us went down to brunch with the Polygram Europe people, who were also there touting *SFW*. Next to our table was the Alexandre Rockwell table, and Quentin was in high form, waving his hands and holding court manically. Midway through the meal, Jefery extracted two midriff tops from his bag—his wife Pam is a clothing designer who has her own line called Juicy, and she had sent them along for me to enjoy on the trip. Sick of witnessing the exhibitionism at the next table, I went upstairs to put one of them on.

Having changed from pants into a short skirt and one of the tops, I came back down to rejoin the meal. The four of us decided to leave and ride the Ciga boats across the canals to the Lido, and then to take a walking tour of Venice. We got the check and left.

We spent several hours just walking along the canals, taking pictures, eating gelato, buying worthless junk, and drinking Campari-sodas at the Danieli. When Don and I got back to the hotel three hours later, we checked our message boxes. Each of us had a note.

Don's note was from Oliver, saying he wanted us to join him for dinner that night. My note was more mysterious, and it took a moment before its full impact actually took hold. It was on Excelsior stationery, written in red pen and a childish scrawl:

> *Dear Jane*
> *Hi, you look great with blonde hair. When we sat next to each other at lunch, you wore these great shorts and your leggs [sic] looked so sexy, I couldn't keep my eyes off of them. (Were you wearing them for me?) My number is 213 560 2147. Maybe we should talk.*
> XOXO
> QT

There was no doubt it was from Quentin—the bad spelling, the truly awful penmanship, it couldn't be from anyone else. Don was blown away.

This was either the first sign of the apocalypse, or we'd surely just entered the twilight zone.

I could barely contain my rage. We went up to Don's room, where I began jumping up and down on the bed in a fury, calling everyone I knew in Los Angeles to vent as I threw things around the room and almost destroyed his suite. Who did this sonofabitch think he was? And what did he think of me—that I was some bimbo who would just start fawning and forgive everything now that he was some sort of self-anointed superstar?

It was Don's turn to be the levelheaded one. He let me scream and rage until I was spent. When I'd finally worn myself out emotionally, he sent me back to my room to get dressed for the screening that night. We showed up for the film just long enough for the opening credits to run, before slipping off with Oliver for dinner.

We got to the restaurant, and after Oliver had had a few cocktails, Don said, "Show it to him."

"Show me what?" said Oliver.

"Quentin wrote me a letter," I said.

Oliver became instantly troubled. "No, no, I don't want to see it, I don't want to become upset."

"No, you'll get a kick out of this," said Don.

I pulled out the letter and handed it to Oliver, who was somber as he read it. Then suddenly, he broke out in peals of gap-toothed laughter.

"You mean we went through all this shit because Quentin has a thing for you?"

"Well, no," I said. "I think he's just so enamored of himself at this point that he believes nothing is outside of his reach."

We went back to the theater with Oliver that night in time for the closing credits, and the response from the crowd was extremely enthusiastic. It seemed to really gratify Oliver. Afterward, there was a party on the Lido for the movie, the first time that Warners had felt fit to celebrate *NBK*. Paparazzi cameras were flashing in our faces as we made our way down to the canal boats, reporters babbling in Italian as they pressed microphones into Oliver's face.

The party was elegant and wonderful. Warners had rented a splendid Italian restaurant, and it seemed like the food and the wine never stopped coming. At one point, Clayton pulled Don out in an alley and tried to pick a fight with him over the completely stupid and inconsequential matter of the final order in which our assistants' credits appear in the film, but Don was in much too good a mood to become embroiled in it.

Later that evening, Don and I found ourselves wandering away from the party, standing on a deserted canal bridge smoking dope with Woody Harrelson as he was doing yoga with his girlfriend.

"This is so weird, Murphy," I said, looking around us. The whole Lido was closed by that time, and we had the entire place to ourselves. "How did our lives get so strange so fast?"

"I can never quite believe it myself," he said. "It seems like only yesterday we were both trying to scam equipment out of the stockroom at USC and stopping traffic in the streets on student films, hoping one day we'd be able to make a living in this wacky business."

"And now here we are, looking like we live in some Fellini film."

We'd both had way too much wine and rich food as the warm canal late-summer breezes blew over us to think about anything clearly, but at that moment, all the bullshit we'd been through in this whole mad process seemed very much worthwhile.

By the time I got back to Los Angeles, I'd had time to calm down considerably on the Quentin front, enough to realize that both Quentin and we were going to be in this business for a long time; inevitably, our paths would cross over and over again. If this was his (admittedly bizarre) gesture of peace, it would be professionally wise to accept it; I would surely have more odious tasks to perform before my career in Hollywood was over. So I composed the following reply, and sent it to him via one of his agents, Lee "Circus Midget" Stollman (as Don aptly referred to him) at William Morris:

Dear Quentin,

I got your letter in Venice, and I must say I was confused. It seems hard to reconcile your friendly sentiments expressed in the letter with the things you say about me in the press. Was Italy a reflection of your true sentiments, or was it simply a momentary brain spasm?

If you would like to get together and talk, I would welcome the opportunity—I am tired of being in the center of a conflict I feel no connec-

tion to. This would just be me, Jane, not the partner of Don or the emissary of NBK *and Oliver. If you'd like to get together, please call me. If not, I understand, and I wish you luck with your films and congratulate you on the success of* Pulp Fiction.

Sincerely,
Jane Hamsher

I never heard from him again.

It was around the time we got back from Venice that the real killings began.

People often ask me if I feel "guilty" or "responsible" for what happened in the real world in the wake of NBK, and the answer is emphatically "no." But my feelings on that front have no bearing on the tragedy of the events that were going down.

It was late September in Paris that the first of the so-called "copycat" murders began, when two teenage lovers went on a killing spree, eventually shooting two policemen before they were apprehended. Because a search of their apartment turned up some sort of advertisement for NBK, the press went wild and decided that the movie had inspired the teens to do what they had, despite the fact that there was no evidence that they'd ever seen it. It was a lazy, easy headline, full of all the exploitive tabloid melodrama we'd been trying to expose in the film in the first place, but that irony seemed to be lost on everyone, as people started to wonder—could a film like NBK actually drive people to murder? And, if so, should such films be banned?

The British censors certainly decided to stop and pause on that thought, long enough to delay giving NBK the certificate it needed in order to be released in the UK. Contrary to reports, we were never "denied" a certificate; the censor simply waited to see what the potential political fallout would be before granting it. After a bit of political grandstanding in Parliament on the part of some savvy politicians who spotted an easy way to get their names into the headlines, the censor decided to grant us our certificate. The film was set for release in February 1995.

I think Oliver was tired at that point from standing up to all the controversy surrounding NBK on his own, so when I asked to go with him, he thought it was a good idea. The Warner Brothers Marketing Department, apparently still stinging from what they perceived as our "interference" with their marketing plans, denied Oliver's request to send me, this despite the fact that my UK journalism connections were strong. A whole world of controversy over the subject of censorship was brewing over there, and especially in light of the Paris killings, Oliver was going to have to answer to it. And being someone who's never been fond of being told what he can and cannot do, he told Rob Friedman he'd refuse to go on the trip unless I accompanied him. Besides, we were both looking forward to having the opportunity to view *NBK* through fresh eyes, outside of the American media culture it indicted so furiously. The UK seemed a good place to start.

A friend of mine from a British TV movie show was involved in doing a half-hour special on *NBK* at the time, parts of which would ultimately wind up being included on the director's cut video version of the film, and everything I'd scheduled required me to be there for a hell of a lot of work. The Warners people decided to spread the rumor that I'd somehow insulted their UK guy for being incompetent (completely untrue), that he was sore, and therefore Rob Friedman held his previous line regarding my trip. When Oliver stood his ground, they said they'd send me over, but only if I flew business class (something completely outside my contract, but okay) and they'd foot the bill only for as long as Oliver was in the UK, which was for two days. Now, I had a good ten days' worth of work scheduled, since by the time *NBK* was ready to be released, there was a 96 percent awareness rate on the part of the British public about the film due to all the controversy, and if Oliver wasn't going to be available, they wanted *someone* to assail. So off I flew, in anticipation of Oliver's arrival, with Warners' admonition that any expenses I incurred outside his two-day sojourn there would be on my own dime.

I didn't even have time to worry about it. Because from the time I got there, although the Warners' UK guy turned out to be a sweetheart, I became immediately embroiled in a battle with the U.S. people, trying to get clearances for film clips for the documentary that was being prepared. I don't think I slept a moment from the time I got off the plane until the time Oliver arrived. Then all havoc broke loose.

People who didn't have the guts to come out and attack Oliver personally had no problem jumping all over me, and I wound up on BBC–TV debating a critic who called *NBK* "the most evil film ever made." Every day, there was some radio station, some TV show, some magazine or newspaper that wanted someone to stand up to the allegations that had been flying furiously in parliamentary debates.

The high point of the trip was the address Oliver made to the Oxford Union. Following in the hallowed footsteps of Queen Elizabeth and Kermit the Frog, Oliver and I stood under paintings by Dante Gabriel Rossetti and William Morris, drinking champagne as we waited for him to be presented. When he walked out, the applause was thundering. What he wound up saying was mostly Oliverspeak, which I'm pretty good at interpreting after two years, but the idea that a student union full of England's best and brightest could make heads or tails of his weird concoction of Jungian psychobabble, Tibetan tantric-sexual mysticism, pharmacopoeia-induced prophetic visions, and paranoid grand-conspiracy theories was beyond credibility. However, he did manage to make one very good point, when asked if films like *NBK* should be made if people are going to go out and imitate the actions of the main characters. He noted that during a showing of *Schindler's List,* someone in the theater pulled out a gun during an execution scene and shot an audience member in the back of the head, killing him. If filmmakers are going to be held responsible for the ridiculous decisions that people make by extrapolating meaning that the filmmakers don't intend, then where do you draw the line?

The ovation he got at the end of his question-and-answer session was, I think, mostly out of respect for Oliver and what he accomplished during his career, rather than a response to any sort of brilliant oratory on his part. Nonetheless, it was great to see Oliver so gratified in the situation, considering how earnestly he'd put himself on the line in making *NBK,* and what he'd been through in order to defend that choice.

By the time I was ready to leave the UK, I was exhausted, drained, and at the end of my tether. I'd endured the daily mortar attacks from the press for ten days by myself, without anyone there to support me, winding up back at the hotel every evening in tears, and in the process indulged once again in my famous health-destroying trick of never sleeping.

And there was still the matter of my hotel bill to confront—Warners had booked me into a very pricey place, and eight days' worth of expenses were supposed to be forthcoming from me. Well, when I'd checked into the hotel in the first place, nobody had bothered to get a credit-card number from me. So on the last night of my stay, I invited one of my journalist friends over to thank him for all the work he'd done, we ordered up about $300 worth of food and expensive champagne, and spent the evening watching the famous Roger Corman B-picture *Death Race 2000* on video.

Then he shuttled my bags out of the hotel quietly, throwing them into a cab as I hastily deposited a polite note on the concierge desk with my room key enclosed, thanking them for their hospitality before jumping into the cab and fleeing to the airport.

It may have been an exhausting process, but it was worth it. We became the number-six-grossing film of all time with our rating in the UK. And I still love to indulge in the thought of the look on Rob Friedman's face when he got the bill for my entire hotel stay; an image of Rumpelstiltskin jumping up and down before he finally puts his foot through the floor in rage fills me with glee.

Sometimes it's the little things in life that make it all worthwhile.

While I had been involved in giving *NBK* its send-off up until the bitter end, Don had other things on his mind: namely, what do we do for an encore?

Before *NBK* came out, our biggest problem in setting up other projects came from the fact that nobody knew who we were—other than that we'd somehow fucked with Quentin Tarantino and lived to tell about it. Which did not obviate the necessity of the fact that we needed to keep moving, in order not to devolve into the scary prospect that Thom Mount had sketched out for us so long ago—two producers with one film in the theaters, and nothing to follow it up with.

Since Oliver was still exhorting us to bring him projects, and people certainly seemed to know who *he* was, it became easier for us to grab a studio's attention if he was somehow attached to the project. By the time *NBK* was released, we had a couple of projects simmering in development at various studios around town, with Oliver acting as executive producer and legitimizing us as producers in the process. But no project was nearer or dearer to Don Murphy's heart than one he'd sort of managed to blindside Oliver into involving himself with in the first place: *Planet of the Apes.*

Together with *The Poseidon Adventure*, *Planet of the Apes* had been the seminal film of Don's childhood, the one that made him want to get into the movie business in the first place. But the copyright to the project belonged to 20th Century Fox, the studio that had produced the original series of films. Don had investigated the situation when we'd first started our business, but at the time he discovered that the company's then-chairman, Joe Roth, despised the project and "didn't want to be making any ape movies," as Don described it to me.

Well, now Roth was out, and the former head of Fox Television, Peter Chernin, was head of the studio. Our friend Peter Rice was still in Acquisitions but was doing some work with the Production Department, and together with Chris Meledandri, another senior exec, he began looking through the studio's vaults to find projects in an era that successfully found studios reintroducing such '60s gems as *The Flintstones* and *The Brady Bunch* to a new audience, so the possibility of reinvigorating one of Fox's biggest franchises of all time no longer seemed a remote possibility.

"Um, Don, aren't you getting a little bit ahead of yourself?" I asked when he brought the subject up. "I mean, it's an awfully big franchise. We've made one movie. Does Fox have any reason to just turn this over to a couple of people who are as inexperienced as us?"

"That was Peter's question," Don said breathlessly. "He said we had to have an "A"-list director attached before they'd even consider letting us get our hands on it. And I had a great answer for him. You'll love this. Oliver Stone."

At first I thought I'd misheard him. "Oliver Stone? You mean *our* Oliver Stone? Political-conspiracy theorist, sixties-obsessed, axe-grinding Oliver Stone?"

"Yep, that's the one."

Now, *I* knew that Oliver Stone wasn't gonna direct any ape movie. But my only explanation for what followed is that Oliver probably didn't *hear* what Don was asking of him, since at the time he was embroiled in *NBK* bullshit, and the locus of his concentration was certainly elsewhere.

I imagine the conversation going down something like this:

"So, Oliver, *Planet of the Apes*," says Don.

"What about it?" says Oliver.

"Do you like it?" says Don.

"Um, sure," says Oliver as he looks at his collection of chicken-scratched notes that he obsessively carries around with him all the time, probably thinking about what he wants for dinner that night.

"So, if I could get us involved, you'd like that, huh?" says Don.

"Huh? Sure, Don, whatever," says Oliver.

Don came barreling back. "He loves the idea!" he said to Peter Rice.

Now, Rice had been on the receiving end of the Don bullshit line before, so he was somewhat dubious. "We only want him if he's going to write and direct," said Peter. "What we don't want is an expensive executive producer."

"Write, direct, produce, whatever," said Don. "We'll work it out between the lawyers."

Before I knew what hit me, Don had arranged for all the honchos from Fox—starting with then-President of Production Tom Jacobson, and going down through the ranks of vice presidents all the way to poor Peter Rice, upon whose shoulders this whole experience (and the future of his career in Hollywood) was resting—to come over to Oliver's offices for a meeting one afternoon.

"After all, Oliver Stone doesn't come to you, you come to Oliver Stone," Don said proudly.

Rarely do Don's high-flown, half-assed schemes bother me, but this one did. We were about to sit down with every bigwig from one of the major studios in town, which we were responsible for orchestrating, and there seemed to me one big problem. Like, what the hell did Don plan on saying in this meeting?

"Oh, I don't know, like, how enthusiastic I am, how I've always been a big fan, what great ape suits they can make now, all the marketing potential . . ."

"Well gee, Don, I bet they'll think your enthusiasm is really neat, and I'm sure they'll be happy that a true fan is going to be producing it—but the rest of it they already know, and call me crazy here, but I think they're expecting Oliver to sit there and talk about how much he wants to write and direct it."

"Oliver Stone doesn't have to audition!" said Don.

"I know he doesn't, Don, but he probably has no idea what you're getting him into."

The fated hour arrived. Van loads of Fox execs pulled up to the Ixtlan offices to meet the man, Oliver Stone—the kind of all-star director their studio would just love to land. Peter Rice was there, looking like a complete hero—he'd managed to pull off a real coup as a junior exec, snaring Oliver Stone into one of their prize projects.

We all sat down in the conference room, me in my usual spot next to Oliver. (I pass him notes if he forgets why he's there). Don was at the head of the table. Everyone conducted the obligatory introductions, and Tom Jacobson quite graciously expressed to Oliver just how enthusiastic they all were about his participation in the project.

"We think nobody could do the job you could," said Jacobson, voicing his admiration for Oliver's work, and his feeling that Oliver could invest the film with a level of sociopolitical subtext that Rod Serling had done when he wrote the original screenplay in the '60s, intending it as a thinly veiled commentary on race relations of the time.

Oliver looked like he just woke up and joined the conversation. "Huh?" he said. "Oh, I don't know, I watched the original movies again a couple of nights ago, and they were *awful*. I'm only here because of Don Murphy. You should talk to him."

It was the most dreadful silence I've ever heard in a room. Oliver had clearly gotten wind of all of Don's shenanigans in the process, and was now hanging him out to dry. I wanted to slide under the table; I probably would have spotted Peter Rice's career there, rapidly spiraling down the drain. The Fox guys all looked at each other, wondering what horrible series of circumstances had led them into this truly embarrassing and humiliating situation.

All eyes went to Don Murphy. Who, God bless him, just started talking.

"Well, you know, I've been a fan of the series since I was a kid. In fact, that's what got me into the business. And I think there would be terrific opportunities to use new technology to make really neat new ape suits, and—uh—there would be great marketing potential. Ape toys, Ape comic books, McDonald's Happy Meals—"

Peter Rice and I looked at each other in horror. HAPPY MEALS? THIS IS YOUR FUCKING PITCH? HAPPY MEALS!!

I looked over to Oliver, who was clearly enjoying the spectacle of watching Don flounder. The collective embarrassment level in the room was quantumly higher than anything I've ever registered before in my life. When suddenly, Oliver seemed to tune into something.

"You know," he said, interrupting Don, "I had an idea. And I haven't even shared it with you yet, Don. . . ."

You evil fucker.

". . . but what if . . ." said Oliver.

The Fox boys practically fell to their knees. "Yes, Oliver? What?"

". . . what if, time were not linear, but circular, and there was no difference between the past and the future . . ."

Don's mouth was hanging open in rapture at the thought of rescue on the horizon. The entire room was poised on Oliver's every word.

". . . and what if there were discovered cryogenically frozen Vedic Apes who held the secret numeric codes to the Bible that foretold the end of civilization. . . ."

Oh shit, he's having an acid flashback.

I looked over to the Fox guys, wondering what they were going to do. They were looking amongst themselves.

"It's brilliant," said Jacobson.

What?

"We think it's great," they all chimed in.

"Yes, I think it's quite good myself," said Oliver.

"So, Oliver, would you want to write this?"

"Well, I'm busy writing my next movie right now, but I'd like to work with a writer," said Oliver.

"Well, sure," they said. "And as for directing . . ."

"Of course, I'd want first shot at it," says Oliver.

"Oh, *of course!*"

"But mostly, I'd like to be executive producer, with Don and Jane producing."

"That would be great!" they said.

So Oliver Stone got Fox to take exactly what they didn't want on the project—an expensive executive producer. They called the next day and offered him a million dollars to do just that. To Oliver's credit, he really *was* enthusiastic about his idea—the only one who was less than enthusiastic was me, upon whom the task fell to try and make some sense out of that gibberish. I was fortunate to share that task with writer Terry Hayes, one of my screenwriting heroes, who had written *The Road Warrior, Beyond Thunderdome,* and *Dead Calm,* and who managed to craft a brilliant script.

What was ultimately to happen on the project, however, became one of the most canonical lessons Don and I ever learned in the movie business, namely—never work with an executive on a project you don't see eye to eye with. For even though Terry Hayes's script was terrific, and upon reading it Fox Chairman Peter Chernin vouched that it was "one of the best scripts he ever read," a political shakeup was in place at Fox that would finally doom our prospects for making the version of the movie we envisioned.

After the script was delivered, the senior executive on the project—Chris Meledandri, an extremely smart guy with terrific creative sensibilities, who had suggested Terry Hayes as screenwriter in the first place—was promoted and moved over to head Fox Family Films, a new division of the company. Although Meledandri tried to take the project with him to the new division, the studio chiefs would have none of it, so we inherited a new executive, one who had no previous involvement with the project, and hence no voice in shaping it in the first place.

Enter Dylan Sellers.

Now, I don't think I've described "development hell" yet, because up until *Apes* came along we hadn't been subject to it very much. But it goes something like this. The writer turns in a script. The producers and studio executives read it, give the writer their "development" notes, and he goes back and rewrites as best he can, trying to make everyone happy. If it comes back and it's great, the studio and the producers will try and attach a director and stars (if they haven't already), and hopefully the picture will get made.

This is the rosy picture of things, the way it's supposed to work, the way it *had* worked, while we were working with a smart guy like Meledandri. Then Dylan came along. We'd never met him before, and had no idea what he was like until we walked into a room with him and he started talking about his "ideas" for the script.

Uh-oh. Often executives will try to make you start changing stuff just to put their "stamp" on it, to feel like they've contributed something to the process and justify their exorbitant salaries to their bosses. Under the circumstances, the best you can hope for is that in these meetings some strong creative ideas will actually be tossed out by one party or another, and good producers will do their best to make the executive think it was his suggestion in the first place.

The story that Terry had written, using Oliver's original inspiration as a departure point, was an intelligent and thought-provoking script. It wasn't a "sequel" to the original *Planet of the Apes*, it was sort of a reinvention, since we didn't think we could better the first film, and none of its subsequent sequels seemed worth following up. Terry's script did, however, try to include the level of social commentary that Rod Serling's had, and as such was rather serious in tone. Dylan, however, had different ideas.

"What if our main guy finds himself in Ape land, and the Apes are trying to play a game like baseball, but they're missing one element, like the pitcher or something," said Dylan. "And when our guy comes along, he knows what they're missing, and he shows them, and they all start playing. Kind of like *The Flintstones*."

Nobody said a word. Terry, Don, and I just looked at each other. Then I think Don said something like "uh, great," and we went on discussing the story as if we hadn't heard him. But he kept bringing the same idea up, meeting after meeting. Since we were still working off notes we'd gotten from Chris Meledandri, and I knew Oliver would personally throw me out the office window if something like this ever appeared in a script that had his name on it, we decided to just ignore Dylan's baseball contribution.

Terry handed in his draft. There was no baseball scene. Dylan promptly had Terry fired. Which was not only really uncool as far as we were concerned, it was incredibly stupid. Because Arnold Schwarzenegger had gotten hold of Terry's script, decided he liked it, and wanted to be in it. We'd had a meeting with Arnold at his office, which looks like a Teutonic mead hall, with its hammer beamed ceilings and artifacts of *Conan* weaponry. Arnold had visions of a really bloody, violent, gory Ape movie that didn't include any lighthearted Flintstones gags. Arnold would work only with certain directors, however, especially on an action film this big. And one of the directors he wanted to work with was Philip Noyce, director of *Clear and Present Danger*, *Patriot Games*, and *Dead Calm*. Philip liked the script, he liked Arnold, and when Don called him, he said he was interested in directing it.

Dylan—or "Dildo," as Don had dubbed him by this point—had scheduled a meeting with Noyce to take place a few days after he fired Terry. He didn't include us in the meeting, or even tell us about it, so I guess he was really trying to assert his control over the project. What Dylan didn't know, but any pinhead should have realized, was that having done *Dead Calm* together many years ago, Terry Hayes and Philip Noyce were best friends; in fact, it was Terry who had given the script to Philip in the first place. There was no way Philip was going to betray his longtime friend, and come on board a project in the wake of such an absurd, incompetent series of events. He told Dylan he was passing.

Not long thereafter, I walked into Don's office to see him pacing back and forth with the phone in his ear, gripping it like the weapon he frequently mistook it for. He was in mid windup, red-faced with rage, stalking the room so the full force of his 6′2″ 200-pound frame was thrown into every word.

"When we were shooting *Natural Born Killers* in a maximum-security prison, there were three types of guys doing time," he screamed, his Long Island accent thick with rage. "There were the guys who realized they were stuck there together, and decided to make the best of it. Then there were the guys whom I called 'currently homosexual,' who decided to fuck each other because there was nobody else to fuck. Then there's the third category. The rapists. I thought we were in the first category," he said. "But I see we're in the third."

It occurred to me that he must be talking to Dylan, the idiot who had just completely dismantled our project. Nobody was more curious than I was to see how *this* particular conversation was going to wind up.

". . . and I just want you to know," said Don, without pausing to either breathe or think, "that I'm not like you. I'm not someone who will shake your hand in a meeting and then go out and attack you behind your back. I'm an up-front kind of guy. And I am telling you right now, to your face, that *I am going to fuck you.*"

Even though Don had done much to curb his penchant for explosive diatribes over the course of the years, he was exerting no control over that proclivity at that moment. When he got mad, he was still a runaway train that could jump his rails at any moment. And that moment had just occurred. I was certainly just as pissed off as Don was that this spoiled rich kid, who came from a family of Hollywood elite, felt like he could tear apart our project on his own say-so. It was difficult to say which of his salient qualities held sway—his stupidity, his arrogance, or his lack of imagination—but like so many of his ilk in Hollywood, he just continued to fail upward. But I knew that this present nonpolitic course of action that Don had embarked upon was going to mean we'd be in a heap of trouble real soon.

". . . Hello? Hello?" Don clicked the power button on the phone over and over, then looked up at me in amazement. "He hung up on me."

Now I could have done many things at this point. I could have called Dylan up myself and tried to make peace, although other Fox executives had warned me that Dylan was a dangerous viper who eventually would stab you in the back, no matter what. And although it would have been tough, I probably could have beaten Don into calling himself, apologizing, and trying to work things out. I could see the whole world of shit this was going to bring down on our heads as a result of Don's "forthrightness."

I knew all the things I should have done in this situation. I did none of them. I did the worst thing I could have possibly done under the circumstances.

I fell on the floor laughing.

Reports came flying back that Dylan walked into another executive's office, ashen-faced, and said, "Don Murphy just told me he was going to rape me." From there the story grew—Dylan was sitting at home with his darling two-year-old daughter on his lap, the picture of perfect domestic bliss, as Don went on his tirade. Dylan began a campaign at the studio, every day whispering into his boss's ears some bit of gossip he'd picked up about Don Murphy around town; if he couldn't find any, he made it up. But probably even more than Don's ranting and raving, the thing that pounded the final nail into our Apes coffin was Oliver's unwillingness to get involved in the situation.

There was a time, right after Terry was fired and Philip was still interested in the picture, when we'd gone to Oliver and begged him to use his clout and political muscle to undo what Dylan had done and pull everything back together. Even Dylan himself told Don later on, after the two had calmed down considerably, that if he'd known Terry was Philip's best friend, he never would have fired him. ("Why didn't you tell me?" asked Dylan. "Because I didn't know you were going to do anything that stupid," Don thought to himself.) But Fox was disdainful of the fact that they were paying Oliver a million bucks, and his absorption in the projects of his own he was trying to get off the ground at the time—*Noriega* and *Evita*, specifically—was so all-consuming that he had no energy left for *Apes*, or all the political bullshit it was mired in.

So Fox decided they needed to bring on another big producer, someone stronger than us, in order to get things back on track. For us, it was terrible—the erosion of Oliver's position meant the erosion of our own. Contractually, Fox couldn't put another producer on the project without Oliver's permission, but Oliver didn't seem disturbed by the prospect, despite our pleas that he not agree to their request. As Thom Mount said when we called him for advice, "Oliver clearly didn't realize that after all the work you guys had done, that for his million dollars his job was to protect you."

"You two should just take a check and be happy," said Oliver when we called him. "And don't alienate the producer. Your only chance of having any participation in this film is if you can get along. You know how difficult you two can be."

"Don't we have any say? We brought you to this project," said Don.

"Well, meet with the producer. Then we can talk about it," said Oliver.

"Promise me, then—promise me, Oliver—that you won't render a decision until after we've met the producer and you've spoken to us about it."

"Okay," said Oliver.

There was another event concurrent with all of this that was completely removed from any of the *Apes* happening; but it ultimately may have had an effect on the outcome of the whole affair.

Just prior to *NBK*'s release, Don had been investigating the rights to a project called *From Hell*, a graphic novel written by Alan Moore, who virtually invented the graphic novel. Alan had also written the canonical classics of the genre: *The Watchmen* and *V for Vendetta*, and was one of Don's big heroes. *From Hell* was a meticulously researched exploration of Victorian English society, woven against a backdrop of the Jack the Ripper murders. It was a tantalizing, lurid, dramatic, and scathing turn-of-the-century tale that had strong echoes of our own era, just the kind of stuff Don and I liked to do. We happened to show it to Terry Hayes, with whom we'd become good friends during the whole *Apes* affair. When the guys at Touchstone Pictures read Terry's *Apes* script and wanted to get into business with him, he showed them *From Hell*. They responded ecstatically and wanted to make a preemptive bid on it before we showed it to the rest of the town. We agreed. Disney had recently changed management, traveling from the hands of Jeffrey Katzenberg whose dictate was to put out a tremendous volume of cheap films to fill their distribution pipeline, and into the domain of former Fox head Joe Roth, who announced his intention to do fewer movies of a higher quality. So even though *From Hell* was an expensive project, Roth wanted to demonstrate that the *new* Disney would pay a premium for the things it wanted.

The deal was announced on the front page of the trade papers, along with our comment: "We're proud to be the people who brought Jack the Ripper to Disney." It was the first deal we ever did by ourselves, without Oliver attached. It was coming to a point where he was more of a hindrance to the projects we were trying to set up than he was a help. Word was buzzing around town that Fox couldn't get Oliver on the phone to do anything about *Apes*, and that neither we (nor they) could even get him to make key calls to help us secure a director who could handle such a challenging task. He was an awfully expensive piece of baggage for a project to carry, and we knew that having him involved would put us once again at his mercy, just like it had on *Apes*, something we simply didn't want anymore. It was time for us to graduate from the Oliver Stone film school.

If Oliver saw the announcement, he made no mention of it to us; Azita finally pointed it out to him, but he only grunted and made no comment. I wondered at the time what effect it would have on our relationship, whether he'd have more respect for us knowing that we could finally pull off a big deal on our own, or whether somehow he felt betrayed by not being included.

I could never be sure that what happened in the end on the *Apes* front was an act of retribution on Oliver's part against us in the wake of the *From Hell* deal, but he wasn't above doing something petulant and reproving just to show us who's boss. I also think he was coming to realize that our relationship to "the family," as he put it, would always be somewhat prodigal, and on our own terms.

On the day after our meeting with the bigwig producer Fox hoped to bring onto *Apes*, one of Oliver's executives called to tell us that Oliver had already gone and approved the person, without speaking to us, despite his promise to Don. Ultimately, the producer was never able to reach a deal with the studio, but that didn't make things any better. No matter how badly he'd treated us before, Oliver had always been as good as his word. It was total betrayal, especially in Don's eyes. Don sent him a fax:

> *So it turned out Quentin Tarantino was right. We never should have turned our backs. Thanks for the knife.*

On October 10, 1995, Dylan Sellers attended the premiere of the Fox film *Strange Days* at a theater in Westwood. Afterward, there was a party for the film at Hamlet Gardens, where all the Fox execs gathered to celebrate with the filmmakers. Dylan volunteered to drive one of his fellow Fox employees home, a guy named Lewis Cherot, who had worked his way up from the mailroom and was pretty much on the same level as Peter Rice. Dylan was drunk; he plowed through a stop sign at a three-way intersection in Beverly Hills and ran head-on into a tree. Dylan walked away from the accident just fine. But Lewis Cherot, who was just two days away from his twenty-seventh birthday, died instantly.

We had a lot of friends at Fox who were just shaking with anger and grief when Dylan turned up for work the next day. But his future as a Fox executive soon came to a halt. The Cherot family showed up personally to every hearing to ensure that Dylan couldn't cop a plea and would spend some time in jail. On December 4, 1996, Dylan was sentenced to a one-year prison term. (As we knew from experience with The Alien, that meant he'd serve about three months.)

Dylan was allowed to let his executive contract run out, and was then moved over into a producing deal at Fox. Tom Jacobson was fired, and Fox Searchlight head Tom Rothman was put in his place. The new regime had nothing but a bad taste in its mouth on the *Apes* front from every angle. They not only paid Don and me off of the film, they brought on Jim Cameron, another bigwig, to replace Oliver himself, someone they thought would exert more effort and muscle in the situation than he had.

If, in the end, what Oliver did to us was payback for branching off on our own with *From Hell*, the only person he sabotaged was himself. Around town, people now realized that if you were paying Oliver Stone a big salary to produce, you were buying the name and little else. As for Don and me, we were on our own once again. We didn't have Oliver Stone as godfather any more; we'd have to get by in big, bad Hollywood by ourselves.

We would do just fine.

Chapter 12

Whoever Dies with the
Most Projects Wins

And so, with the closing of the NBK production offices once and for all, Don and I were back where we started: my dining room. But not for long.

We got a call soon thereafter from Cary Granat, a friend and former Universal executive who had recently moved over to Miramax.

"What would you say if I wanted to offer you an overall deal here?" he said.

"I'd say you were full of shit," said Don. "Miramax is the house of Quentin Tarantino."

"I don't think that would be an obstacle," he said. "Listen, you're just the kind of people Bob and Harvey Weinstein want to be in business with. You're young, you're bright, you're aggressive. . . ."

". . . we work for cheap . . ."

"Well that too, but seriously. You have relationships with the kind of talent we want to be in business with. I think we could make it happen."

We thought Cary would sober up soon and forget all about the phone call, but he began to pursue us. The next thing we knew, we were meeting with Bob Weinstein. Bob liked us, he liked our projects, and he wanted us to be "part of the Miramax family."

Over and over, Don kept repeating like a mantra, "You know Quentin hates us, don't you? I don't mean mild dislike, I mean out-and-out hatred." Well, that didn't seem to bother anyone. We soon did a deal with them, set up shop over at their offices near the Disney lot, and they optioned two of the projects we'd been developing—*The Book of Skulls*, a science-fiction novel by Robert Silverberg which was being adapted by our USC classmate Scott Rosenberg and his brother Phil (Scott had written *Things to Do in Denver When You're Dead* and *Beautiful Girls* for Miramax), and a book called *I Shall Not Die,* a nonfiction piece about the Maori tribal wars in New Zealand in the 1860s, with Lee Tamahori (of *Once Were Warriors* and *Mulholland Falls* fame) set to direct.

However, two months into the deal, we got another call from Cary Granat. "We want out of the deal," he said.

Don was thunderstruck. "You've got to be kidding. Why?"

"It's just not working out."

"That's ridiculous," said Don. "We've been in a room with Bob Weinstein only that one time, and he loved us—that's why he did the deal and optioned our projects in the first place. And we barely even met Harvey—we only grazed him once when he was walking out of a room. How could it be 'not working out'?"

"Take my word for it," said Cary. "They're willing to pay you handsomely to get out of the deal. My advice is to take it."

Don wanted to get Bob Weinstein on the phone, to figure out what had gone wrong, but I told him not to bother.

"Something is really weird here—we clearly don't have all the information," I said. "If they simply didn't like us, they could just let our contract run out and not make any of our films. Yet Miramax, who are the cheapos of all time, are willing to pay us even more money to go away? Aside from the fact that I'm thrilled to finally be the Malcolm McLaren of the movie business, I don't want to be stuck not making pictures for a place that doesn't want us. I suggest you go to work on them and do your thing, Murphy."

And so he did. Once Don Murphy was done with them, they'd given us back all our projects free of charge, paid all our expenses for the next year (which they were contractually obliged to do anyway), and written us a big good-bye check on top of it.

Now, Miramax has an incredibly high turnover rate of employees (at one point, they set up a recovery group called "Miranon" for those attempting to get over the experience), so it wasn't too long before someone got fired and gave up the goods—Miramax had paid us off because Quentin found out about the deal. It wasn't hard to believe; Quentin had been running his mouth off for months, telling people that he made all the decisions at Miramax, and that when he snapped his fingers, Harvey Weinstein jumped.

"What a bunch of idiots," Don said when he heard. "Didn't we warn them at least fifty times?"

Well, if Quentin was trying to hurt us, he did us the biggest favor he possibly could have. Universal's Kevin Misher immediately snapped up *Book of Skulls*; we were developing a script on *I Shall Not Die* with Polygram; and the money Miramax had paid us off with had allowed us to acquire a lot more projects, which we were setting up around town at a furious pace. Working with a really smart executive named Jorge Saralegui, we'd set up two projects at 20th Century Fox; another friend, Michael Costigan, had pushed through one of our projects at Columbia. Proving that no matter how much they hate you at the time, they'll always take you back if your movie was a hit and you've got something they want, we set up two projects at Warner Brothers with our former director of development, Basil Iwanyk, who'd recently been hired as a creative executive over there. We still had *From Hell* at Touchstone, Keith Gordon was adapting *Savage Night* for us, and we'd acquired a book for Dave Veloz to adapt as his directing debut. We weren't just surviving, we were flourishing. Within a short period of time we had projects all over town at virtually every studio, and inadvertently Quentin had bankrolled it all.

But paybacks are a bitch, and Don still had one waiting for Quentin. One that he'd been nurturing ever since I'd gotten sick. Back in the early days of his career, when Quentin had gotten together with Craig Hamann, and written his first screenplay *My Best Friend's Birthday*, they had actually shot the film with the two of them starring in it, but they'd never finished it. Quentin still had the footage, and in interview after interview, he said how much he wanted to go back one day and complete the film.

Well, that left Craig Hamann in the lurch. Quentin was now a millionaire, and Craig was practically living out of the trunk of his car. Over and over, he'd begged Quentin to let him try to get the script made so he could establish his own career as a writer in Hollywood, but Quentin wouldn't let him. Don did a little research and found that although the legalities were cloudy, if the two of them had written the script with the intention of exploiting it theatrically, Quentin couldn't back out of the deal, and Craig still had the right to sell it, with or without Quentin's permission.

Craig is not only a good friend but also a truly nice guy, and for a long time he didn't want to go against Quentin's wishes—yet he was still struggling to make it. Quentin wasn't even offering to pay him for his portion of the rights to *My Best Friend's Birthday*—he just assumed Craig would always let him have them for free. Also, since Quentin was now rich and famous, Craig didn't have the resources to go up against him. Well, we now did. So Don began calling Craig, asking him to let us help him out in the situation. Craig finally began to realize that Quentin was no friend to him if he was only holding him back; still, he knew that if he tried to do anything with the script, and Quentin got him on the phone, he'd cave. So Don came up with a brainstorm, whereby Craig signed over his rights in the property to a corporation owned by Don, Cathryn Jaymes, Craig, and me. Don took great glee in giving the corporation the name "Expletive Entertainment." So if Quentin ever got Craig on the phone, all he had to say was "It's out of my hands now, Quentin." Which was true.

An article came out in *Daily Variety* announcing that a group of Quentin's "former associates," who had been "known to have differences with Tarantino in the past," now intended to attempt to exploit the rights to his first screenplay. We sent a letter to Quentin, inviting him to join us in the undertaking, in a spirit of harmony and collaboration. When he didn't respond, Cathryn Jaymes arranged for Marty Barab, a litigator friend of hers, to file suit to establish that Craig had the right to sell the property on his own, as long as he paid Quentin half of anything he got. Since Marty had always wanted to be a producer, he agreed to do the whole thing on contingency. It was deliciously ironic to Don and me that the thing Quentin had used to almost break us—a lawyer's willingness to sue on a contingency basis—was the tactic we were now using to help Craig out and get back at him at the same time.

I can't tell you what gave Don more glee—the fact that Quentin went purple with fury when he found out that his arch nemesis, Don Murphy, now controlled 50 percent of the copyright to his pet project, or that it was now coming out in the press that most of Quentin's screenplays had wound up in legal battles as he stabbed one friend in the back after another. We were certainly not an exception with *NBK*, just the most celebrated. It was great that Craig might finally get the break Quentin had denied him for so long. But most of all, I think the thing that made Don the happiest was that Quentin was now having to pay tons and tons of money to defend the suit.

"Every week, I like to call Carlos Goodman and keep him on the phone for at least forty-five minutes," said Don. "Because I know that the clock is ticking and every second is costing that cheap bastard Quentin truckloads of cash."

In the end, it would be really gratifying to help Craig. But no matter what the outcome of the suit, the lesson is the same.

Don't *ever* fuck with Don Murphy.

If we thought our break with Oliver was permanent, we were soon to learn that the Stone family is indeed like the Mafia—you can never really leave. Don had sent Oliver an early copy of one of Quentin's biographies for which he'd been interviewed, with a note suggesting we should all get together for drinks. Oliver's office called us up that day and scheduled the meet; evidently he was as anxious to pull us back into the "family" as Don was to be there.

There was good reason for all of us to get together besides a general love fest, for Warner Brothers had now decided to renege on their promise to release the director's cut of the film. Since its release, the press had tried to link *NBK* to more acts of killing than any other in history, and Warners wanted to distance themselves from responsibility as much as they could. In each and every incident, however, the individuals involved had deeply disturbed pasts that everyone seemed to be overlooking, and it became a chicken-and-egg kind of argument. Did *NBK* inspire a fourteen-year-old Texas boy to decapitate a thirteen-year-old girl, or did he simply find within it the echoes of a world he had always been living within, and action he'd already been moving toward, when he told the police he wanted to be "famous like the natural-born killers"? The desire to achieve one's fifteen minutes of fame by committing heinous acts of violence had a long tradition that inspired *NBK* at its inception; we could hardly be accused of inventing the phenomenon. Still, there were those who argued that our handling of the subject matter was so irresponsible that it some-how inspired a Georgia teenager to shoot an eighty-two-year-old man to death in Florida, especially after he shouted to an eager press, "I'm a natural-born killer!"

"The whole thing is absurd," Don told Oliver over cocktails. "It's the mental-retard defense."

"The what?" said Oliver.

"The mental-retard defense," Don reiterated. "If you're just minding your own business, getting minimum wage, stocking cigarettes at the fucking Swifty Mart, and suddenly someone comes in and pops you for no reason, that person's got to be a mental patient. I don't mean a literal drooling retard, I mean you have to be disturbed to go in and shoot someone in a quickie mart and then say it was because you saw a movie."

Oliver got that kind of glazed, unfocused look over his face he gets when he's not quite sure he's heard something correctly. But to the extent that he understood what Don was saying, I think he concurred. Still, it left us with the problem—not only was Warner Brothers refusing to release the director's cut, they were also denying our request to take it elsewhere. Now, they were perfectly within their rights not wanting to release the NC–17 version, but since they'd promised to do so in the first place, they should at least let us take it to another company that was willing to do so. Oliver asked us, if it came down to it, if we'd go to the press with him and battle it out. We said of course we would.

It never came to that; Oliver went in and met with Terry Semel, who agreed to give us back the rights (although I'm sure the specter of an angry and hostile Oliver Stone storming around in the media had quite a bit of bearing on their final decision). With the help of CAA's Manny Nunez, we finally reached an agreement with Trimark to release the version on video, along with some scenes that we'd shot for the movie but never included. At the same time, Pioneer put out a laser-disc version of the cut, orchestrated by Charles Kiselyak, the king of the deluxe laser disc producers. For the project, Charles compiled a great documentary that included behind-the-scenes footage Warner Brothers had shot for an electronic press kit at the time, in addition to new interviews he conducted with all of us. We were all two years away from the experience of shooting *NBK*, but there was no doubt as you saw the interviews of Woody, Juliette, Downey, Tommy Lee, Tom Sizemore, Oliver, Dave Veloz, Don, and me that we were all still traumatized when we looked back on what we'd been through in the making of the movie. It was an experience that none of us would ever be able to shake off.

Even if we wanted to put the experience behind us, it didn't look like anybody was going to let us. Most recently, someone John Grisham knew from his old days as a lawyer in Mississippi had been shot and killed by two teenage lovers on a killing spree after they'd done about twenty hits of acid and watched the movie. Grisham went on a press rampage; Oliver was not far behind. In the spring 1996 issue of the *Oxford American*, Grisham made the argument that films are "products," that are "something created and brought to the market, not too dissimilar from breast implants," and therefore filmmakers should be held legally accountable if their work inspired people to acts of violence. Oliver fired back in *Vanity Fair*, saying that Grisham "has become a very rich man off a body of work which utilizes violent crime as a foundation for mass entertainment." Thus, if you follow his line of reasoning, Grisham should be happy to assume liability the next time a "righteous revenge murder" or the "rape of a child" takes place, if it can be shown that the offender had read or seen *A Time to Kill*.

But for me, the most galling thing to come out of the whole discourse was the way that the *Vanity Fair* article seemed to conclude that although Grisham's breast implant argument was ludicrous, Oliver was ignoring the fact that he was a "mass-market filmmaker." "He communicates with a far larger, less-educated audience—one that may, for example, take his screen violence literally, and not see a 'moral order turned upside down,' " as Oliver described *NBK*.

Translated: People are stupid. Filmmakers should make only homogenized pap that will appeal to the limited intelligence quotients of the masses, preaching the value of virtuous, socially uplifting behavior. (And if anyone can get even two people to agree on exactly what that constitutes, I'd like to see it.) It's a cynical, bullshit, elitist attitude that denies filmmakers any possibility of artistic expression on a provocative level. And that, to me, is even more frightening, reprehensible, and hypocritical than Grisham's "breast-implant" theory.

Still, this is America. And anybody, as we knew all too well, can sue anybody else over anything they want to. So I shouldn't have been surprised, I suppose, when we were served in a lawsuit someone was mounting in which they asserted that *NBK* was responsible for the injuries caused to a convenience-store clerk when she was shot by the same two teenagers who had killed Grisham's friend. But nothing can quite prepare you for the shock of seeing yourself listed as a responsible party on a document which states that as a result of your movie, someone shot a woman "with no remorse and left her to die on the floor of the convenience store."

When we got that, I think we all knew that we'd be living this one down for the rest of our lives.

But for everything lousy that lands on our doorstep, something great always seems to come along and compensate for it. For reasons nobody can quite figure out, Michael Costigan and our agent Joe Rosenberg recently managed to convince the executives at Columbia that we would make a nice addition to the Sony family. They offered us an overall first-look producing deal, which of course we accepted.

It was a bizarre transition for us, of all people, to drop our independent status and be embraced by a studio. But if we hadn't known it before we embarked on this career path, we certainly knew by now—Hollywood is a place where nothing is too strange to happen.

It hasn't been an "ordinary" life by any means, and it doesn't look like it's ever going to be. During our twenties, both Don and I had foregone the financial stability, the marriages, and the children that our friends had. We were always starving, could never pay our rent, and went virtually undistinguishable (even to ourselves) from the legions of slackers and wannabes for whom the protraction of an impecunious, adolescent lifestyle was an end in itself. In the beginning, shoring ourselves up against overwhelming self-doubt as the years went by and any sort of tangible evidence that one day we'd succeed was nowhere in sight was the biggest job we did all day. How many times can you look your family and friends in the face, and say, "Um, I'm struggling to be a producer," and maintain any sort of self-respect in the midst of it all? It was easier to crawl in a hole, communicate with no one who might pose the painful question of "What is it, exactly, that you do?" and wait until a meaningful answer existed before you crawled out again.

Which is why it's so important to have a partner you trust, respect, and believe in, even when you don't believe in yourself. Pretty frequently I get asked what it's like to be a woman in the movie business, but I think the question people really want the answer to is what it's like to be a female *producer* in the movie business; it wasn't a question I was plagued with when I worked as a secretary or a P.A. And the answer, as far as I can tell, is that it's not that much different from trying to be a woman in a position of authority in any business. No matter how politically correct they may be, men are always going to have a negative reaction if you challenge them. They probably won't cop to it, because it doesn't make them feel very good about themselves. You get used to them becoming bitter over little things, stuff that wouldn't bug them if you were a guy. So in order to stay in the game, you find yourself hiding your true agendas, looking for openings, subtle ways to use your intuition to get inside someone's head and influence them in ways they aren't even aware of.

Is it manipulative? I guess so. But it puts off the inevitable—the all-out, wailing, screeching battle that will undoubtably erupt if you're not willing to fold your hand and give up on what you believe in. Many times, over the years, despite my best efforts, it's come down to that. I remember sitting around one evening, pounding a few cocktails with Antonia Bird (director of *Priest* and *Mad Love*), and we both agreed that the biggest thing you had to get over emotionally, when trying to be a successful woman in this business, was the need to be "liked." As women—at least women of our generation—we were raised to be pleasers. And if you want to get on with the business at hand, you just had to get used to the notion that a lot of people aren't going to like you, and it's not going to have anything to do with who you are or what you say or how you comport yourself. You'll never be "one of the guys," no matter what you do. And if I hadn't had Don Murphy there to back me up, I don't think I could have gotten through it.

It's not the life Don and I expected it was going to be when we started; we never envisioned the ways we'd both have to change in order to be able to function in this environment. The price that Hollywood exacts in exchange for its rewards is certainly high. It's hard, it's frustrating, and it never seems to get any easier. But it's also exhilarating. There's nothing that can compare with the feeling of looking up on the screen and seeing that against all the odds, you actually did it. But most of the satisfaction comes from having someone to share it with, someone who understands what it's cost to get here, someone who shares the same goals and visions.

Someone like—Don Murphy.

And so we began carting boxloads of our stuff over to our new offices on the Sony lot. We now had big, new spacious offices in the Sidney Poitier building, which we share with Jim Brooks and Cameron Crowe. At the same time, we began production on our next film, based on Steven King's novella *Apt Pupil*, which was being directed by our old USC pal Bryan Singer, the director of *The Usual Suspects*.

Don was elated. "Look out my office window," he said. "You can see the executive parking lot. Now I can watch everyone who's coming and going."

"Just what you always wanted," I said.

"No, 'just what I always wanted' is down the hall—there's a machine in the Xerox room that dispenses free diet Coke." (Since Don had done so much to calm himself down of late, I'd eased up on the caffeine ban.)

Our new assistant, Rick, carried one box after another into Don's office. Out came the action figures, the comic books, and the toys. In no time at all, they covered the place completely. Don was ensconced as lord and master of a kingdom of spooge.

Just then the phone rang.

"Who has our number over here yet?" I said. "We haven't even been here long enough to give it out."

"I left it on the answering machine as a forwarding number," said Don.

Rick stuck his head in the door. "Don, it's someone named Bernie on line one."

"Oooh! I have to take this," said Don.

I was puzzled. "Jesus, Don, you usually treat The Alien like shit. Since when did his calls become so important?"

"Since the hangin' judge finally locked him up for stealing insulin at a Thrifty's in the valley. He's doing thirty days, and he gets only one phone call a day."

I walked out of Don's office smiling, and began helping Rick unpack all of our crap.

"You're probably thinking all this is a little weird, huh?" I asked.

"No, not at all," replied Rick, trying to feign nonchalance.

"Well it is," I said.

But I wouldn't have it any other way.

Afterword

The story of *Killer Instinct* comes to a close, but its characters live on. Here is how they've fared:

Karl Austen changed law firms and pursued his dream of representing movie stars and filmmakers, signing people like Isabelle Adjani, Amy Brenneman, and Jude Law.

Roger Avary did, after a protracted struggle with Quentin, ascend the stage and receive his richly deserved Oscar for *Pulp Fiction*. Roger and his wife, Gretchen, gave birth last year to a beautiful baby girl, Gala. His television pilot, "Mr. Stitch," came out on video, and he has written or doctored numerous screenplays in development at the major studios. He is also executive-producing Craig Hamann's directing debut, *Boogie Boy*.

Lawrence Bender remains Tarantino's partner. On his own he produced *Fresh* and *White Man's Burden*, and the box office disappointment *Four Rooms*. He recently wrote an essay for a British collection about how hard it is to be successful.

Bernie, The Alien, was released from jail in early 1997. He's sworn to try to mingle with the people of Earth more efficiently, thus limiting future exposure to the prison system.

The Brave did eventually get produced, but with none of the original people involved. Johnny Depp and his brother co-wrote the screenplay, and Johnny directed and starred as the martyred hero. Marlon Brando played the role of the slimy snuff film producer. The film is scheduled for release in 1997.

Budd Carr worked again with Oliver Stone on *Nixon* as music supervisor. Budd was also hired by former Oliver associate Alex Ho to music-supervise the Steven Seagal–directed *On Deadly Ground*.

Robert Downey Jr. subsequently went on to star in *Only You* and *Restoration*. His quiet drug habit crept up on him, and he was arrested twice in 1996 for possession. He recently appeared with Diane Sawyer on "Primetime Live" stating that he had to get clean or he feared he would die. Currently on a court-supervised probation, Robert hopes to stay clean by working nonstop for the next three years.

Dale Dye, affectionately known to everyone on the set as "Captain Dye," continues to work with Oliver on all of his films as weapons advisor. He has also acted in *Forrest Gump, Crimson Tide,* and is prominently seen in *Outbreak* as the general who relieves Donald Sutherland of his command.

Paul Feldsher left Ciby and went to Touchstone Pictures. He then went on to produce the Winona Ryder film *Boys.* He currently works for Miramax in their London office.

Rob Friedman did not remain the head of the Warners Marketing Department for life after all, bolting before the end of his contract to become the head of marketing for the Paramount/Viacom empire.

Keith Gordon never did get to direct *The Brave* but finally realized his dream project, *Mother Night,* based on the Kurt Vonnegut classic. The film went on to win numerous festival awards. He is developing Scott Spencers' *Waking the Dead* with Jodie Foster's Egg Pictures and will direct Jim Thompson's *Savage Night* for JD Productions.

Woody Harrelson continues his movie star career, alternating between straight, light, comic roles like *Kingpin* and serious roles in the Oliver-produced *The People vs Larry Flynt.* He and his girlfriend recently gave birth to their second child, and he has started producing movies as well. Woody continues to lend his name to causes he believes in, appearing on the cover of *Hemp Times* calling for the legalization of marijuana and getting arrested on the Golden Gate Bridge to draw attention to the destruction of forests.

Terry Hayes entered the realm of million dollar writers after finishing his legendary *Planet of the Apes* script. He followed that up with another script for JD, *From Hell*. He is currently finishing an adaptation of the Ray Bradbury book *Fahrenheit 451* for Icon Productions which Mel Gibson will direct and star in. Terry moved to London with his girlfriend, Krista, and spends much of his time writing in Ireland.

Richard Hornung, the award-winning costume designer of *NBK*, died of AIDS-related illnesses in 1996.

Cathryn Jaymes survived the exit of Quentin Tarantino and remains a very successful manager in Hollywood. She is renowned for backing people who she believes in until they break, and is therefore genuinely loved by her clients, a rarity in the movie business. She is producing *Boogie Boy*, written and directed by her client and former Tarantino partner Craig Hamann.

Victor Kempster went on to work with Oliver on *Nixon*, getting to build and design his very own version of the White House. He is currently doing extensive research for Oliver's proposed version of *Alexander the Great*, content in the knowledge that there will be no boot trucks in the film.

Juliette Lewis went on from *NBK* to star in the Jim Cameron–produced *Strange Days*, the Nora Ephron–directed *Mixed Nuts*, costarred with Shirley McLaine in *Evening Star*, and appeared opposite Tarantino in *From Dusk till Dawn*.

David MacMillan won yet another Oscar for mixing *Braveheart* after being crammed on a bus for months during the filming of *Speed*. He remains a successful and sweet man living with his family in the Santa Clarita Valley.

Arnon Milchan and his New Regency enterprises continues to be Warner Brothers' biggest supplier of movies. He also recently produced Barbra Streisand's *The Mirror Has Two Faces* and tried to buy the MGM studio.

Thom Mount went on to produce the critically acclaimed *Death and the Maiden* which was directed by Roman Polanski with whom he had worked on *Frantic*. He is partners with Josh Kramer in the Mount/Kramer Company and is producing numerous pictures for Paramount. His production, the Sidney Lumet–directed *Night Falls on Manhattan*, opens in 1997.

Eddie Perez is still somewhere in Hollywood, on some film, working on stunts or guarding famous actresses, and making sure everyone has a great time in the process.

Chris Renna was savagely attacked in *Spy* magazine about being Oliver's "Dr. Feelgood" and responded with an odd, rambling letter that nobody quite understood. He can be seen as a prisoner with a swastika on his head in *NBK* and as the doctor who saves Anthony Hopkins's life in *Nixon*. He continues to work closely with Oliver both professionally and privately.

Peter Rice rode the *Planet of the Apes* train through till its crash, ending up a full-fledged executive at 20th Century Fox. He has become the studio's acknowledged specialist in young and exciting filmmakers around Hollywood. One of the first films he shepherded from beginning to end, Baz Luhrman's version of *Romeo and Juliet*, became the surprise hit of 1996.

Bob Richardson continued his revolutionary cinematography techniques in two films in the same year, Martin Scorcese's *Casino* and Oliver Stone's *Nixon*. He recently wrapped Oliver's *Unnamed* film (previously *Stray Dogs*) staring Sean Penn, marking a ten-year collaboration between the duo.

Joe Rosenberg moved from ICM to CAA, where he now represents Jane and Don and Roger Avary. He has become one of the most successful agents, writers, and directors in the business, representing both Tony and Ridley Scott, Michael Bay, and Luc Besson.

Richard Rutowski continues to write and produce for Oliver Stone. He played a Texan conspirator in *Nixon*, worked extensively on the *Unnamed* film, and still knows where to get the best pot in America.

Dylan Sellers pled guilty to manslaughter with extreme negligence and began a one-year jail sentence in December 1996.

Mike Simpson remains an agent at the William Morris Agency. Simpson's power was eroded when Morris merged with Tri-Ad, leaving Arnold Rifkin as the head of the motion picture division. Simpson still represents Tarantino, but Tarantino's continuing mantra is "If Morris doesn't do what I want, I have three letters for them: C-A-A."

Tom Sizemore followed up his role in *NBK* with great performances in *Wyatt Earp* and *Heat*. He married former tennis pro and actress Maeve Quinlan, who had been Juliette Lewis's stand-in on *NBK* during the Chicago sequences. His first leading role on a studio picture was in *The Relic*, which opened successfully from Paramount in 1997.

Raymond Sojack is still safely incarcerated in Stateville Prison.

Donita Sparks continues to tour and make great albums with her band L7.

Justin Stanley, aka Duncan, JD Productions' first assistant, survived, got married, and has developed a very successful career as a writer and producer of low budget films.

Elizabeth Stone finalized her divorce from Oliver soon after the completion of *NBK*. The parting was amicable and smooth; Oliver did not contest the divorce, and continues to provide for their children.

Quentin Tarantino won an Oscar for co-writing *Pulp Fiction*. He then embarked on a less-than-spectacular acting career, appearing in *Destiny Turns on the Radio*, *Desperado*, and *From Dusk till Dawn*. He recently bought a home in Beverly Hills for $3.4 million and is on his way to becoming the George Gobel of directors, famous for being famous.

Clayton Townsend moved on to work on Oliver's next project, *Noriega*. Oliver ultimately abandoned the project, but during that time Clayton began a relationship with the dictator's daughter, Sandra, and divorced his wife Jeannie, who had just given birth to their daughter, Charlotte. He did wind up line-producing again for Oliver on *Nixon*, and is currently working with him on his latest film *U-Turn*.

David Veloz used his break on *NBK* to turn into one of Hollywood's most sought-after screenwriters. He has written a film about Mexican Sub-commander Marcos for director Luis Mandoki, an action film that Ridley Scott will direct, and even an update of *The Treasure of the Sierra Madre* for Oliver Stone. He is working with JD Productions on *Permanent Midnight*, starring Ben Stiller, which will be his writing/directing debut.

Rand Vossler dismissed his lawsuit, accepted his payment, and had no further involvement in *NBK*. Quentin eventually stopped speaking with Rand, and Rand returned to his previous job as set technician while trying to produce other scripts. Rand vowed to use his settlement money to "show everyone and direct a short film." Instead he married his long-term girlfriend, Janice, with a lavish party and honeymoon. At last report, they were filing for divorce after two years of marriage.

Azita Zendel, Oliver Stone's assistant, passed the torch to a new person, and took six months off. She remembers the "Oliver" years as both stimulating and frightening, and is amazed at how well she held her own. She has begun graduate work at UCLA in film.

Michael Zoumas ended his partnership with longtime producer Michael Phillips and moved on to produce films for art-film powerhouse Avenue Pictures.

Oliver Stone won praise and achieved his best opening weekend ever for directing *NBK*. He then directed *Nixon*, starring Anthony Hopkins, for

Hollywood Pictures, one of the best films of 1995. He recently wrapped shooting his *Unnamed* thriller for Phoenix Pictures and Tri-Star. He is partnered as a producer with Dan Halsted in Illusion Entertainment, which has numerous products in development around town, and he recently became the father of a new baby daughter, Tara. His authorized biography *Stone*, published in 1996, only begins to tap into the madness. As he reaches fifty, he is looking forward to enjoying "a successful third act."

INDEX